CARRIER
- WARS -

CARRIER WARS

Naval Aviation from World War II to the Persian Gulf

BY EDWIN P. HOYT

McGRAW-HILL PUBLISHING COMPANY

New York   St. Louis   San Francisco   Auckland   Bogotá
Hamburg   London   Madrid   Mexico   Milan   Montreal
New Delhi   Paris   São Paulo   Singapore   Sydney
Tokyo   Toronto

1 2 3 4 5 6 7 8 9 DOC DOC 8 9 2 1 0 9

ISBN 0-07-030625-7

Library of Congress Cataloging-in-Publication Data
Hoyt, Edwin Palmer.
Carrier wars.
Bibliography
Includes index.
1. Naval aviation—History.   2. Aircraft carriers—
History.   3. World War, 1939–1945—Aerial operations.
4. World War, 1939–1945—Naval operations.   I. Title.
VG90.H69   1989   358.4'14   88-32645
ISBN 0-07-030625-7

Book design by Sheree L. Goodman

CONTENTS

INTRODUCTION

The aircraft carrier was an invention of the twentieth century, following very swiftly on the heels of the perfection of the airplane itself. Glenn Curtiss, one of the pioneers of aviation, was the first to take off in a primitive plane from the deck of a warship specially rigged with a wooden flight deck for the experiment. It was not a stunt, although many deep-water sailors disapproved of airplanes and saw in them no more than eyes for the fleet. They regarded the coming of aircraft as more or less a nuisance and thought more highly of the frameless rubber lighter-than-air dirigible or "blimp." This attitude persisted, even after the British built an aircraft carrier during World War I, although it was never really operational with the wartime fleet. The first true carrier was the former light battle cruiser *Furious*, which was not really much more than a warship with a flattened stern. In August 1916, however, the Admiralty began work on an Italian passenger liner, the *Conte Rosso*, and converted her to a flush-deck carrier of 14,000 tons. Rechristened HMS *Argus*, she persisted with the British navy until 1946, although she spent her last few years as a training ship. Actually HMS *Hermes* was the first vessel in the world to be designed and built from keel up as an aircraft carrier and the first to have an "island" superstructure. Shortly afterward, the British built HMS *Eagle*.

In the 1920s, several changes in naval thinking encouraged the building of aircraft carriers. One such was the experiment carried out off Norfolk by General Billy Mitchell, the early American air specialist, who contended that aircraft could bomb and sink battleships. He proved this by sinking several captured German warships. The admirals still scowled and said the experiment was a freak, but underneath the navy began to change. Out of the change came such carriers as *Langley* to the American fleet. Well before the beginning of World War II, the Americans and the British were building more carriers and improving them and their aircraft.

The Japanese, too, took up the aircraft carrier concept of the fleet and extended it further than did the western powers. Admiral Isoroku Yamamoto, a prime mover in Japanese naval aviation, had a good deal to do with the development of carrier planes, first the Nakajima 97, known to the Americans as "Kate," and later the Nakajima Tenzan, known as "Jill." In 1941 these were the most advanced torpedo bombers in the world. The Type 99 dive bomber ("Val") and the Suisei dive bomber ("Judy") were also very effective. The most common Japanese bombers, the twin-engined Mitsubishi Type 1 ("Betty") and the Mitsubishi Type 96 ("Nell") were primarily land-based aircraft, although they were so often seen in concert with the carrier bombers that there was some confusion. These were the workhorses of the Japanese fleet, and at least six versions of the "Betty" were produced during World War II. The navy fighter known as the Zero was, at the beginning of the Pacific War, the world's most effective fighter plane, rivaled only by the British Spitfire. These were all extremely advanced in the 1930s.

By the time the China Incident broke in 1937, the Japanese had perfected new carrier tactics. The bombing of four British gunboats (*Ladybird*, *Bee*, *Cricket*, and *Scarab*) and the sinking of the USS *Panay* on the Yangtze River just before the Japanese capture of Nanking indicated the power of Japanese aircraft. With their development, Japan became a leading naval power with a really superior strategic weapon: the concept of the carrier fleet. Half a dozen carriers operated together with screens of cruisers, battleships, and destroyers. Their combined striking power was enormous. In 1937 and 1938 the pilots practiced their skills on China's rivers and around her ports. The Japanese were very secretive about their naval operations, and the western powers did not learn of this highly effective strategic concept of a large strike force, so powerful against the infant Chinese aviation forces.

At the beginning of World War II the Americans and the British did not understand the optimum use of carriers as well as the Japanese did. Most of the American aircraft carrier commanders of the 1930s were converted "battleship" men whose wings indicated that they were observers and not pilots, whereas Yamamoto and most of his officers of higher rank were pilots.

The result of this advanced approach to naval aviation was a strong Japanese strike force that would be brought into play at Pearl Harbor for the first time. The reason was necessity. The Japanese had built 10 carriers in the years between the wars. They operated them in the same fashion as the Americans and British, each carrier functioning as an independent unit, the center of a task force. When the Japanese government decided to go to war with the western powers, Admiral Yamamoto, who opposed the war, realized that the only chance of a Japanese victory was to make a powerful strike at the outset and knock out the American Pacific Fleet. To do this he would have to employ a large number of carriers in a new sort of strike force. The Japanese Imperial Navy was reorganized to allow this change, and the whole concept of the carrier task force changed. It became an aerial armada, and the carrier replaced the battleship as the major unit of the fleet. Before that concept caught hold, the British and Americans, the other two principal world naval powers, used carriers in a much less spectacular manner. A carrier task force in the West consisted of a single carrier with escorting warships—usually a battleship or two, two or three cruisers, and a "screen" of destroyers whose principal duty was to protect the carrier and the other major warships from attack by submarine. This limited concept, in effect, created a greater danger for the carriers. The Japanese strike force system enabled the commander of the force to mount a circular defense of the carriers, which were surrounded by the other warships, with the destroyers on the outside. The ships all together could put up a fierce antiaircraft barrage against enemy planes, and the combat air patrol—the fighter planes assigned to rove the skies above the strike force—could concentrate in large number at any threatened point.

In the years after 1937 the Japanese carrier forces and carrier pilots gained combat experience operating off the China coast while the naval forces of the western powers were still playing war games. Thus as world war loomed in the late 1930s, the Japanese Imperial Navy was better prepared for it than any other, and the Japanese carrier forces were particularly experienced. There was only one unforeseen problem:

Because Japanese military superiority over the Chinese was so great, carrier pilot losses had been minimal. Therefore, the Japanese stuck to their system of carrier pilot training, which demanded about three years for proficiency. Those carrier pilots were superb, but the high command never stopped to think what might happen if general war came. That weakness was to come home to them in the first year of the Pacific war.

Opening Guns

On September 1, 1939, Adolf Hitler attacked Poland, and two days later Britain and France declared war on Germany. From the outset it was apparent that the key to Britain's defenses lay at sea, for it was from under the sea that the principal threat to survival came, from what had proved to be the most formidable German sea weapon of World War I, the *Unterseeboot*, the submarine.

The threat was underlined on that first day of war, when a German U-boat sank the passenger liner *Athenia*. The British immediately invoked the convoy system of sea passage that had proved so effective in World War I. But there were not enough destroyers or other escort craft to go around, and many vessels still traveled without protection. Winston Churchill, First Lord of the Admiralty, ordered the temporary use of Britain's seven aircraft carriers to protect the sea traffic approaching the British shore.

It was not a good use of carriers. On September 14, 1939, the *Ark Royal* was on patrol duty off the northwest coast of Scotland when she intercepted a distress call from the SS *Fanad Head*, which was under attack by a submarine (*U-30*) about 250 miles from *Ark Royal*. The carrier launched a flight of three Skua bombers led by Lieutenant Commander Dennis Cambell, commander of 803 Squadron. By the time they reached the ship, it was sinking from a torpedo, and the crew had taken to the lifeboats. The planes attacked, using bombs and depth bombs. One bomb blew the tail off one of the Skua planes, and it crashed. The same thing happened to a second Skua. The two planes crashed near the submarine. The pilots of the two Skuas, Lieutenants

Thurston and Griffiths, got out of their sinking aircraft, but neither gunner did. The pilots were rescued by the German U-boat crew and became the first naval aircrew prisoners of World War II. Lieutenant Commander Cambell returned to *Ark Royal*, and, on the basis of his report, a basic change was made in bombing techniques: No more small high-explosive bombs were to be carried by naval bombers; they were more dangerous to the planes than to the enemy.

That same day, the *Ark Royal* was sighted by the German *U-39*, which managed to get into attack position and fired three torpedoes. The skipper of *U-39* radioed exultantly that he had sunk a British carrier, and that report was trumpeted around the world by Dr. Josef Goebbels, the German propaganda minister. The fact was that the torpedoes had exploded harmlessly in the *Ark Royal*'s wake. Her escorting destroyers hunted down the U-boat and sank it.

————

Two carriers were operating in the western approaches to Britain: HMS *Courageous* and HMS *Hermes*. On September 14 their captains appeared at the naval headquarters in Liverpool to discuss the problems of antisubmarine warfare by carriers. It was a new idea, and from London the British Admiralty had dispatched a commander with instructions about procedures. Most important, the two carrier commanders were told, was the destruction—and not just warning away—of enemy submarines. The carrier pilots were to keep after the U-boats until they sank them.

Armed with these instructions, Captain W. T. Makeig-Jones of HMS *Courageous* went back to his ship. HMS *Courageous* left Plymouth on Saturday, September 16, sailing out to patrol the western approaches. Thus, in the second week of the war, one of Britain's oldest aircraft carriers was at sea in the Bristol Channel with four destroyers, looking out for trouble.

At 3:45 on the afternoon of September 17, the trouble began. The *Courageous* received a report of a submarine attack on the steamer *Kafiristan*. The *Kafiristan* was on her way into Liverpool with a cargo of sugar. Captain J. Busby was taking a nap in his cabin, having brought his ship safely so near to the British isles, and the second mate was on watch. Suddenly a submarine surfaced and put three quick shots from her deck gun across the bow of the *Kafiristan*. This was the international order to stop for search and was completely within the scope of the London Naval Agreement governing submarine warfare. In fact, Lieutenant Commander Ernst-Guenter Heinicke in the *U-53* took the position that by zigzagging, which the *Kafiristan* was doing, the captain of the merchant ship was violating the rules!

The second mate ordered the engine room to stop engines. Captain Busby, sensing the change in the ship, came on deck. He told the wireless officer to send a message in the clear. It was a distress message, SOS. But Captain Busby also told the officer to send the new SSS message, announcing that he was under attack by a submarine. This was definitely a violation of the London Submarine Agreement. By this time, after the sinking of *Athenia* without warning, the British were paying no further attention to that agreement. When the SSS message reached the wireless room of the *Courageous*, the captain was informed. Immediately he recalled the carrier's patrol aircraft, and a strike force of four aircraft was launched to hunt and try to sink the submarine.

Five minutes after the aircraft were sent off, the destroyers HMS *Inglefield* and HMS *Intrepid* were detached from *Courageous*'s four-ship destroyer screen, to proceed to the scene where the *Kafiristan* was being shelled and to attack the submarine. By 4:45 P.M. the carrier was moving on a course to intercept the *Kafiristan* to shorten the return flight of the air strike force and to be in position to deliver more aircraft to the scene if necessary. The speed of the ship was then 23 knots.

An hour and fifteen minutes later the captain rang for more speed, and the ship began traveling at 25 knots. The *Courageous* stopped zigzagging in order to shorten the distance traveled. Fourteen minutes later the first aircraft of the strike force reported in by radio: ''Bombed submarine. . . . ship in vicinity.'' This meant that the planes had arrived over the *Kafiristan*, found the submarine, and struck. But with what results no one knew. Twenty minutes later, Lieutenants Ellis and Barber reported that they were returning to the carrier and would make rendezvous at 7:15 P.M. The speed of the ship was increased to 26.5 knots.

The word came from two other aircraft: They were lost. The skipper ordered that bearings be given in code. At 7:00 P.M. one plane returned and began circling the ship. Captain Makeig-Jones reduced speed to 24 knots and made ready to take on aircraft. By 7:15 P.M. the speed was down to 18 knots, and the captain turned the *Courageous* into the wind to fly on the strike force. He ordered the zigzag pattern to begin again. The ship was protected by the destroyers *Impulsive* on the starboard bow and *Ivanhoe* on the port bow.

At 7:19 P.M. the carrier received messages from the two lost planes. The captain ordered direction finder bearings to be given out and also made smoke intermittently to guide the aircraft home. That combination worked very well; 10 minutes later the two aircraft appeared and were taken aboard the carrier safely.

The other two planes of the strike force were now short of fuel, and every minute counted. The skipper ordered the ship turned to port, again moving into the wind. At 7:42 P.M. the other two aircraft were in the landing pattern with a deck wind speed of 30 knots and were soon safely down. The ship resumed her zigzag pattern.

What Captain Makeig-Jones did not know was that his ship, the submarine hunter, was also being hunted by another submarine. That afternoon of September 17, the *U-29* was patrolling in the Bristol Channel, having been assigned this area by Commodore Karl Doenitz, chief of the German submarine service. Lieutenant Commander Otto Schuhart, the skipper of *U-29*, had sighted a 10,000-ton merchant ship that afternoon, but he had also seen a patrolling aircraft and had prudently given the order to dive. Later he brought the U-boat back up to periscope depth and resumed his patrol.

At 6:00 P.M. Skipper Schuhart was turning the periscope, when suddenly he stopped and moved it back. There before him was an aircraft carrier. He looked around some more for the destroyer screen. Counting only two destroyers, one on each bow of the carrier, he looked again. But there were no others. Fate had handed him a gift, a major enemy warship in his periscope, with virtually no protection from torpedo attack, particularly since the two destroyers were not ranging back and forth along the course but maintaining their positions on the bows. Thus Schuhart was able to work his way up very close to the big warship, only 500 yards from the nearest destroyer, which steamed on, oblivious to the danger. The men of *Courageous* were very busy just then, recovering aircraft.

At 7:50 P.M. just as the *Courageous* began her zigzag pattern after recovering the last two aircraft, Lieutenant Commander Schuhart fired three torpedoes. Five minutes went by, then came an explosion against the side of the aircraft carrier, immediately followed by another.

Lieutenant Commander Schuhart took his submarine down, deep —deeper than the German naval regulations prescribed—to 250 feet, for he knew the British destroyers would be after him, and he was right. They came charging up like bulldogs, and depth charges began dropping.

Immediately after the torpedoes hit, the *Ivanhoe* on the port bow turned and went after the submarine, whose periscope had then been sighted against the reflected glow from the western sky. The *Ivanhoe* started dropping depth charge patterns. HMS *Impulsive* then fell astern of the carrier and began picking men out of the water. The *Courageous* continued to make way for some time, leaving a string of men over- board behind her.

Below the surface, Lieutenant Commander Schuhart could hear the sounds of a ship breaking up. After the two torpedoes struck at 7:55 P.M., the *Courageous* began to heel to port. One torpedo had struck abreast of the petty officers' quarters. The second hit at the afterend of boiler room *B*. All the lights went out. The electric power system broke down completely, and the ship would not steer.

Down below, Engineering Lieutenant Shenton was on watch in the forward center engine room. Immediately after the two explosions, all lights down there went off too. The ship took a heavy list to port, and Lieutenant Shenton ordered the starboard engines stopped so they would not run away—the propellers had come clear of the water, and the intense vibration of the screws might destroy the shafts. He then ordered the engine room to be evacuated.

Steam pressure began to fall, and steam was leaking into the room from the port side. Lieutenant Shenton worked the emergency bulkhead valve closing lever and started out. He saw a stoker coming up from the boiler room with his overalls on fire. Someone ran to help him beat out the flames.

In the 'tween decks, orders were given to dog down the watertight doors. With the power gone and the lights out, and the heavy list of the ship, the doors still open could not be worked.

The captain had given the order to flood the starboard bilges and thus try to right the carrier. Lieutenant Sedgewick and a stoker petty officer went to Z seacock to try to flood the starboard bilge there. They were helped by a sublieutenant who had a flashlight, but they could not open the jammed valve. It was apparent to Captain Makeig-Jones that his ship was *in extremis*. He had their position sent out by the wireless office, and he ordered the code books and other secret papers collected and weighted. They were then taken down to the compass platform to be cast into the sea.

Some effort was made to lower lifeboats, but because of the heavy list the ship was taking, only the starboard cutter could be gotten over the side. Even that was of no use, for the boat banged its way down the plating, hit the water, and immediately filled with seawater. Soon it was completely waterlogged.

The fourth motor boat on the port side did also get put over, and this one was successfully put into the water. But that was all. A few Carley floats on the starboard side were gotten off, and some wooden gratings and loose woodwork were cast over to help men who were already going into the water.

Ten minutes after the torpedoes hit, the crew of the bridge of the *Courageous* could hear the interior bulkheads beginning to collapse from the weight of water coming in through the shattered hull. She was an old ship, actually the oldest in the fleet along with the *Hermes*, and her compartments were not built to withstand modern weapons. The cracking up, which Skipper Schuhart also heard deep down below, signaled the coming of the end. The list increased to 35 degrees. Captain Makeig-Jones ordered the signal bridge to hoist the signal flag "Stand by me." And he passed the word from the bridge that any man who wished to leave the ship was now at liberty to try to save himself.

Meanwhile, help was coming. The steamer *Veendam* was not far away. In fact, the people on the steamer's bridge saw the torpedoes strike and the listing of the carrier. At 7:30 P.M. they saw one of the destroyers blink out a signal by Morse lamp: "sinking." The carrier was about to go down. Captain A. Filippo of *Veendam* then ordered all the lifeboats and motorboats put over and headed for the carrier.

Impulsive had searched and searched for survivors behind the carrier until her captain was certain that every living man had been picked up. While the last drama was being played out on *Courageous*, some miles away the *Kafiristan*'s crew had taken to the boats. Then *U-53*

had fired two torpedoes and sunk the abandoned vessel. Skipper Heinicke had come alongside the boats and given the men their position.
He had radioed their position for help, he said.

And sure enough, a few minutes later the steamer *American Farmer*
appeared to pick up the survivors of the *Kafiristan*. While they were
doing so, a plane from an unknown source appeared overhead and
dropped down to machine gun the submarine on the water. The submarine immediately dived, leaving several men in the water. The plane
then dropped two depth bombs where the submarine had been, and
that put an end to any hope that the swimming submariners could be
rescued. The captain and crew of the *American Farmer* were aghast
at the "inhumanity" of the British aircraft crew in killing those German
sailors in the water.

Back near the *Courageous*, the officers and men of *Ivanhoe* continued to try to sink the submarine that had torpedoed their carrier.
After the first series of depth charges was fired, several witnesses swore
that they saw the submarine break water and then go down, followed
by a stream of black oil and bubbles coming up. It was wishful thinking.
Skipper Schuhart was safe, far below the surface.

The men of the two destroyers watched as the *Courageous* twisted
in her last throes. They hurried toward the sinking ship, but when they
arrived at the place, all that was left was an oil slick. She had turned,
listed to starboard, and then gone down stern first.

The *Veendam* lifeboats came into a heavy slick of fuel oil and
found all sorts of flotsam but not a single living soul. All around the
steamer's lifeboats, the crew saw lights and rafts but no people. Then
they saw a head in the water, and one boat pulled in a seaman from
the carrier. He was drowned. The ship's doctor worked over him, but
the man never revived.

The *Veendam* boats continued to search until 11:30 that night, but
they did not find a living person. At that time, an officer from one of
the warships came alongside the boats and asked if there were survivors. The *Veendam* men handed over the watch and keys of the dead
man they had found. The men took him back to their ship to prepare
the body for burial. On one of his socks they found a name, McLawry.
He was in fact Paymaster Commander Martin Lawrey, of the Royal
Navy.

And so the life of the *Courageous* came to an end, and so did the lives of more than 500 of the 1,200-man crew, including Captain Makeig-Jones, who went down with his ship.

The destroyers made one last hopeful sweep, but there were no more survivors. They headed then for Devonport, with 44 officers and 335 seamen from the *Courageous* and the bodies of three men who had been rescued but died before they reached port. The steamer *Dido* picked up 218 survivors.

Some other merchant ships rescued a few men who were later transferred to the destroyers *Kelly* and *Inglefield*, which had come back from the search for the submarine that had attacked the *Kafiristan*.

———

U-boat Skipper Schuhart had won himself a signal honor that day. He was the first U-boat man ever to sink an aircraft carrier, and the *Courageous* was the first aircraft carrier in history to be sunk by enemy action.

Out of this sinking came a new realization by Winston Churchill and the British Admiralty. Aircraft carriers were invaluable in antisubmarine warfare but not the sort of aircraft carriers that the *Courageous* represented—fleet carriers, designed to operate against other warships. They were too big and too vulnerable for this sort of work.

What was needed were small carriers. First Lord of the Admiralty Churchill foresaw the development of ''a new unit of search.'' He told the War Cabinet:

> Whereas a cruiser squadron of four ships could search on a front of, say eighty miles, a single cruiser accompanied by an aircraft carrier could cover at least three hundred miles. . . .
>
> Every unit of search must be able to find, catch, and to kill. For this purpose we require a number of cruisers superior to the 10,000-ton type or else pairs of our own 10,000-ton type. These must be accompanied by small aircraft carriers carrying perhaps a dozen or two dozen machines, and of the smallest possible displacement. The ideal unit of search would be one killer or two three-quarter killers, plus one aircraft carrier, plus four ocean-going destroyers, plus two or three specially constructed tankers of good speed.

That was the thinking in London in the opening days of the war. Britain's resources were then so strained that not much could be done to implement the idea, but it was not to be forgotten, nor was the lesson learned by the employment of a fleet carrier in a task that had put it at risk without a compensatory chance of achieving a major blow against the enemy.

So, although the *Courageous* was lost on September 17, 1939, the Royal Navy learned a lesson that was invaluable to the future conduct of the war. In that sense, the officers and men who went down with the *Courageous* had not died in vain.

Carriers at Risk

The nature of the war in Europe relegated the aircraft carrier to an adjunct role in the war at sea. Winston Churchill had learned that fleet carriers were too vulnerable to be used as convoy escorts. In the early months of the war, however, there was not much reason to employ carriers. Land-based aircraft had sufficient range to bomb enemy targets, and much greater bomb capacity than did carrier planes. The role of the carrier seemed so limited that Admiral Erich Raeder's German navy ignored it altogether and suspended work on the single German carrier under construction.

Then came the battle for Norway.

For several reasons, the British were vitally interested in Norway. One reason was its supply of iron ore, essential to the German war effort and very useful to the British. Another was the British sympathy for Finland, which then was at war with Russia, and Russia, which had not yet been attacked by Hitler, was theoretically allied with Germany. The only way to help Finland lay through northern Norway. Also, Narvik, an ice-free port, would give the Germans an excellent naval base, plus several submarine bases for attack on British shipping.

For these reasons the British and the Germans both moved to occupy Norway on April 8, 1940. The basic German attack was overland, supported by the German surface fleet and Admiral Doenitz's (he had been promoted) U-boats. The U-boats were not very effective at that time; Doenitz had discovered a fatal flaw in the firing mechanism of their torpedoes. The German surface fleet, however, included the new heavy cruiser *Hipper* and the heavy cruisers *Scharnhorst* and *Gneisenau*, and they were indeed formidable.

The British made two attacks on the German naval forces at Narvik and damaged and sank so many lesser ships of the German surface navy that never again would there be a major German naval action. Aircraft of the British fleet air arm were involved. The first carrier to get into action was *Furious* on April 10, 1940, whose planes bombed the German fleet and claimed hits but no sinkings on several ships.

Ark Royal and the carrier *Glorious* arrived two weeks later. By that time Swordfish Squadrons, 816 and 818 of the *Furious*, had suffered heavily from attrition, and *Furious* went back to England for service.

The British had been outmaneuvered and almost overwhelmed in Norway, and early in June they withdrew from Narvik. The alternative was to throw massive reinforcements into Norway, and these were needed on the western front. The *Glorious* covered the British withdrawal from Narvik early in June and evacuated a number of RAF planes and pilots as well. On June 8 *Glorious* was traveling in the North Sea toward home with a screen of only two destroyers, the *Acasta* and the *Ardent*. She was sighted by the German task force of Admiral Wilhelm Marschall. More particularly, she was found by the *Scharnhorst* and the *Gneisenau*.

It was a brilliant clear day with almost unlimited visibility, and the carrier was soon identified by the German lookouts. The two ships raced to attack. For some reason that will never be known, the skipper of the *Glorious* did not have any combat air patrol aloft. Perhaps he felt safe enough, heading for home waters, which were not so far away. But they were too far away as it turned out. The *Scharnhorst* opened fire when still 14 miles from the carrier, and her first shells tore up the wooden flight deck so that no planes could operate to help their carrier.

The destroyers turned toward the enemy, laying smoke and firing their 4.7-inch guns—which, considering the armor of the German ships, was like firing air rifles at automobiles. They also fired torpedoes, which was a different matter, but the range was very great.

Soon the *Glorious* was afire. Down in the hangar below the flight deck, the aviation fuel caught fire, and then bombs and torpedoes began to explode. Soon the *Glorious* was dead in the water, and the crew were abandoning ship.

The destroyer *Ardent* headed toward the *Scharnhorst* but was soon bracketed and then struck repeatedly by 11-inch shells until she sank. Then the *Glorious* capsized and sank.

The *Acasta* now was the focus of both German ships, but her skipper behaved with the bravery expected of British destroyer captains. He headed directly at his enemies, firing the ship's last torpedoes. Then in a few moments several shells from the *Gneisenau* and the *Scharnhorst* broke his destroyer's back, and she sank.

Meanwhile those last torpedoes were running toward the *Scharnhorst*. Her skipper had seen them fired and had turned on an evasive course for three minutes, but then he turned back to his base course and ran straight into one of the *Acasta*'s last blows. The *Scharnhorst* was hit near her afterturret and suffered heavy damage. Admiral Marschall turned around and headed toward Trondheim.

The *Acasta*'s last torpedo had saved a convoy carrying 14,000 British troops from Norway to Britain. The convoy was 100 miles north of the *Scharnhorst* and the *Gneisenau*, and in their path, and it was protected only by a handful of vessels. But that last torpedo had also cost the lives of hundreds of British sailors, because Admiral Marschall felt that the *Scharnhorst* was so vulnerable that he abandoned his plan of rescuing enemy survivors.

The survivors of the three British war ships were in the water, and virtually no one knew what had happened to their ships. The wireless operator of the cruiser *Devonshire* had picked up a message from the *Glorious* saying she was under attack by German surface vessels, but he dared not repeat the message because at that moment the *Devonshire* was only 100 miles away from the two big German ships, and any transmission would have been located. Aboard the *Devonshire* were the King and Queen of Norway, who were going to exile in England, and their protection was the paramount interest.

Thus the survivors of the *Glorious*, the *Ardent*, and the *Acasta* were in the water for 60 hours. Even in summer the waters of the North Sea are cold, and the attrition was frightful. By the time rescuers came up, only 46 members of the crews of those three ships were still alive.

A few days after the sinking of *Glorious*, Lieutenant Commander John Casson led an air strike from *Ark Royal* against the *Scharnhorst* in its Norwegian harbor. It was a brave attempt, but the British lost eight planes to the German fighters and antiaircraft guns and did relatively little damage to the big ship.

For the next few months Britain's war at sea was almost entirely defensive against the U-boats. The fall of France and the evacuation of British troops from the continent was another aspect of the war, not one in which aircraft carriers could play a major role. After that came the air battle of Britain, waged mostly by the Royal Air Force. The carrier was to have its day, though, many days indeed, as the war moved into the Mediterranean Sea.

The fall of France strengthened the naval position of Germany and her Italian ally. No longer did the British have the use of the French and French North African bases. Germany now controlled the French Atlantic ports and turned several of them into formidable submarine bases. In fact, Admiral Doenitz moved his center of operations from Wilhelmshaven to Lorient.

The Germans then developed their great Mediterranean Plan, which envisaged the capture of Gibraltar and Suez and the elimination of British naval power in the Mediterranean. The results could be far-reaching: Britain's oil supply from the Middle East could be cut off. The India trade could be almost stopped.

But the British moved swiftly. In June they sent Force H to the Mediterranean under Admiral James Fownes Somerville. It consisted of the major capital ships HMS *Hood*, HMS *Resolution*, and HMS *Valiant*, and the carrier *Ark Royal*, along with two cruisers and 11 destroyers.

The British were also moving as fast as possible to improve the quality of their carrier aircraft. The Hurricane and Spitfire, which had proved so valuable in the defense of Britain against the German air attack of 1940, were converted for carrier use. A fast carrier fighter called the Fulmar was also being built, and the carrier *Illustrious* came home to take on a load of these planes.

Winston Churchill quite properly saw the difficulties of using aircraft carriers in the waters around Britain, where they were extremely vulnerable to German air and submarine attack. And he saw as well the need for carriers in the Mediterranean, where British bases were far fewer. Although the necessities of war precluded many changes in existing carriers, the British had learned through the experience of the *Glorious* of the difficulty of the wooden flight deck. Churchill proposed that the *Illustrious* with its armored flight deck be taken down to the Mediterranean to replace the wooden-decked *Ark Royal*.

Italy had entered the war, and France had capitulated. What was to be done with the French fleet? Captain C. S. Holland of the *Ark Royal* was chosen to discover the attitude of the French Admiral Gensoul because Holland had once been naval attaché at Paris. But Gensoul would not talk, and so tough proposals were made to the French. They would either continue operations with their former allies, the British, or they would see their ships sunk. The French refused to cooperate, so on July 3 the struggle began. *Ark Royal*'s Swordfish were used as artillery spotters by the British fleet forces. Other Swordfish and some Skuas dropped mines at the entrance to Mers-el Kebir harbor. The battleship *Bretagne* and two destroyers were sunk, and the battleship *Dunkerque* was run aground.

The French battleship *Strasbourg* broke out of the harbor at dusk and ran off east. Six Swordfish from *Ark Royal* went in pursuit. They straddled the big ship with bombs but secured no hits. On the way home, two of the Swordfish crews had to ditch but were rescued by a destroyer.

At 8 A.M. on July 4 the second striking force from *Ark Royal* arrived over the *Strasbourg*, which was steaming at 28 knots off the African coast. The *Strasbourg* began firing at the planes with her antiaircraft guns. They then headed for the African shore and waited until sunset, then came back to attack the ship, keeping low against the land. The pilots, unfamiliar with modern torpedo tactics, dropped their torpedoes outside the destroyer screen and scored only one hit on the battleship. How they scored that is almost a miracle, given the technique they used. But that torpedo did not even slow down the *Strasbourg*. She disappeared in the darkness.

Next day British reconnaissance planes saw that in Oran Harbor the *Dunkerque* was being repaired for sea. So the *Ark Royal* sent two squadrons of Swordfish to attack. They took off before dawn on July 6 and arrived over the harbor at sunrise. They came in diving from 7,000 feet, flying over the breakwater in the path of the sun, and four of the six torpedoes fired hit the target. Then they retreated, passing two other waves of planes going in.

Carrier planes from the *Illustrious* also torpedoed a small ship that lay alongside the *Dunkerque*. All the planes got home safely, although one was hit. A shell took out the aftergun of this aircraft but fortunately did not explode.

So, the British had immobilized much of the French fleet at Alexandria and destroyed more of it at Oran.

June 1940 was a desperate time for Britain. France had fallen, and the Italians, sensing a quick German victory, joined in the war. That meant the British were deprived of the assistance of the French navy, and they now faced the strong modern Italian fleet, which was based at Taranto down at the Italian heel.

———

In August 1940, the Italian fleet reached the apogee of its wartime strength, with five operational battleships, including two of the newest in the world. The British were forced to move four battleships and two carriers down to Alexandria. They also reinforced Malta, sending a dozen Hurricane fighters from the carrier *Argus* to augment an air force that then numbered only three aircraft, known by the British affectionately as Faith, Hope, and Charity.

At that time the British had two carriers in the Mediterranean, the *Illustrious* and the *Eagle*. The very existence of that Italian fleet was a constant threat to every plan of the commander in chief of British naval forces in the Mediterranean, Admiral Andrew Browne Cunningham.

The British propensity for laughter in the face of disaster was tested later when 14 aircraft were launched from the *Argus*, 400 miles west of Malta. They ran into heavy headwinds, and nine of them crashed at sea; the nine pilots were lost. The problem here had been miscalculation: The margin for error had been too small, but that was occasioned by the risks involved, with German aircraft and Italian units still making the situation in the Mediterranean very difficult for the Royal Navy.

In the summer and early fall of 1940, Hitler was still preoccupied with his Operation Sea Lion, the projected invasion of Britain, but Admiral Raeder was much more interested in the Mediterranean. He was waiting for Hitler to make a diplomatic demarche with General-issimo Francisco Franco to bring Spain into the war on the Axis side.

Everything was in flux in that summer of 1940, and the carriers were playing a vital role in the Mediterranean, although not a celebrated one. They were delivering fighter planes and Blenheim bombers to land bases. The *Argus* made several such trips. By the end of August, the British government decided that this plan was too difficult and costly and set up a new system. The carriers and merchant ships delivered planes to Takoradi in West Africa, where the planes were prepared for service and then sent to Kano and then to Khartoum, overland, and eventually to Cairo. Thus a steady trickle of aircraft moved into British Africa.

The German Mediterranean Plan called for German use of bases in Spain, and when it came down to the decision, Franco decided not to give the Germans what they wanted until Hitler could demonstrate that the Germans were going to win the war against England.

That is how matters stood in October 1940. The carrier *Illustrious* arrived in the Mediterranean with her modern fighters and something else—the latest in radar equipment. Admiral Cunningham was glad to see her. Something had to be done about the success of the Italians in moving supplies and troops into North Africa. By mid-October, the Italians had dug themselves in at Sidi Barrani on the Egyptian coast. The big threat to the British was the Italian fleet of six battleships, nine cruisers, and 17 destroyers. The airmen of the British fleet were eager to attack that fleet and were sure they could destroy it.

And they were to be given a chance. The attack was first planned for late October, but problems arose. One was aboard the *Illustrious*. A fire in the hangar destroyed two of the old Swordfish aircraft, and the rest had to be stripped down and washed in fresh water and reassembled. These aircraft were indeed old, not made of aluminum as modern planes were, but of fabric stuck together with "dope." Salt water was anathema to them.

The second problem arose aboard the carrier *Eagle*, which had boiler troubles. It was decided that she was of no use at the moment, so five of her aircraft were transferred to the *Illustrious*, which sailed from Alexandria on November 8 for Malta, along with four battleships. On the way, the Fulmar fighters of the carrier shot down two shadowing aircraft, and Admiral Cunningham sent a force of cruisers and destroyers to search the waters around Sicily. The weather was very rough.

On the evening of November 11, the *Illustrious* was to be detached for a new operation. It was the twenty-second anniversary of the Armistice that had ended World War I. With four cruisers and four destroyers, she would make for the island of Cephalonia opposite the Gulf of Corinth, 70 miles south of Corfu. From that point the carrier's planes would take off to attack the Italian fleet lying at anchor in Taranto harbor in the heel of the Italian boot, 325 miles from the vital British base at Malta. There were to be two strikes, one at 8:30 P.M. and the other an hour later. The distance was about 170 miles. This was Operation Judgment.

At the final briefing in the wardroom, a large-scale map of Taranto was brought out, as well as aerial photographs taken less than 24 hours earlier. In the outer harbor of Taranto, called the Mar Grande, six battleships were moored in a semicircle. All were protected by anti-torpedo nets, but the British did not worry because their torpedoes were fitted with Duplex Pistols, a magnetic device that exploded the torpedo warhead when it passed underneath the target ship.

On the seaward side of the battleships were three cruisers. In the inner harbor, the Mar Piccolo, two other cruisers were moored, along with four smaller cruisers and 17 destroyers.

At 8:30 that night the first strike took off, led by the commander of Squadron 815. Twelve Swordfish straggled into the air. These extremely old-fashioned aircraft, biplanes of 1920s vintage, carried only 18-inch torpedoes. That is, six of the planes carried those torpedoes. The remainder carried bombs and flares.

The planes climbed through heavy cumulus cloud cover and emerged into the moonlight at 7,500 feet. One plane got lost and its pilot flew directly to Taranto, arriving a quarter of an hour before the others. He ambled to and fro, waiting for the main strike to show up. It was not very intelligent; all the harbor defenses were alerted, and the antiaircraft guns were firing as the other planes came in.

The flare droppers were at 5,000 feet, and they did their job. The harbor defenses then began firing at the flares, and soon the guns of the battleships and cruisers joined in. The combination of flare droppers, dive bombers, and torpedo planes, coming in from all angles, confused the defenses. As Commander Charles Lamb recalled it in his book, *War in a String Bag*:

> The guns at the entrance were throwing long streaks of flame across the harbour entrance, spitting venom out to sea, and the shells of these tracer bursts illuminated the first Swordfish so brightly that from above, instead of appearing bluey-grey, it seemed to be a gleaming white. I watched it wing its way through the harbour entrance, five thousand feet below and disappear under the flak, and imagined that it had been shot down at once. Then I saw the lines of fire switching around from both sides, firing so low that they must have hit each other. The gun-aimers must then have lifted their arc of fire to avoid shooting at each other, and I saw their shells exploding in the town of Taranto in the background.
>
> The Italians faced a terrible dilemma: were they to go on firing at the elusive aircraft right down on the water, thereby hitting their own ships and their own guns, and their own harbour and town, or were they to lift the angle of fire still more? Eventually they did the latter, because all the other five attacking Swordfish managed to weave their way under that umbrella to find their targets. Had the arc of fire been maintained at water level all six would have been shot to pieces instead of two, but the guns would have done even more extensive damage to the ships and the harbour itself. . . .
>
> . . . . Somebody was bound to be hit of course, and poor Lieutenant Bayley and Lieutenant Slaughter from HMS *Eagle* disappeared in flames to their deaths, on their run in. "Hooch" Williams and Scarlett managed to put a fish into one of the *Cavour*-class battleships before they were struck, and then plummetted down into the sea on their way to a prisoner of war camp for the next four and a half years.

After the event, the pilots agreed that the low level of the attack accounted mostly for its success. They came in low—two pilots later swore that their wheels touched the water as they attacked—then they dropped their "fish" and their bombs and sped away, and the next wave started.

Altogether the British dropped 11 torpedoes and 48 250-pound armor-piercing bombs. The hail of antiaircraft fire was intense. Later it was learned that the Italians fired 123,500 rounds of 4-inch ammunition and 7,000 rounds of 3-inch ammunition.

The British air flotilla adopted a new tactic, diving in to attack from several directions, thus intending to confuse the enemy antiaircraft guns. The tactic worked. One torpedo sank the old battleship *Cavour* in the shallow water of the harbor. The old battleship *Duilio* was also hit by one torpedo and damaged so badly that her repairs took six months. The new battleship *Littorio* was hit by three torpedoes but was able to move away for repairs that would take three months.

In this one stroke, the naval ratio in the Mediterranean was changed. Earlier the Italians had outpowered the British, but this was no longer the case. Half the Italian battle fleet was disabled for the next six months. All this was accomplished by the British with the loss of two aircraft; two airmen were killed and two were captured. After this disaster, the Italian fleet hurried out of harbor to Naples, and the east central Mediterranean was again left to the British.

Taranto thus paved the way for a major British military operation under General Archibald P. Wavell. Major General Richard O'Connor led a force of 36,000 men into battle against the Italians. The object was to capture Libya and strengthen the British position in Egypt.

3

The Sinking of the *Ark Royal*

The *Ark Royal*, one of Britain's modern carriers, was launched in the spring of 1937. She had an iron flight deck 800 feet long and eight other decks. She carried 1,575 officers and men and five squadrons (60 aircraft) of Blackburn Skua fighters and Fairey Swordfish bombers. The Skuas were really two-seater fighter dive bombers, with a speed of 200 knots and armed with four front-firing machine guns and one rear gun. The Swordfish, as noted, was an awkward-looking biplane, with an open cockpit for a crew of two. It could carry an 18-inch torpedo or a 1,500-pound bomb load.

The Germans thought they had sunk the *Ark Royal* in the very early days of the war when she was attacked by *U-39* on September 14. But after the sinking of the *Courageous* and the decision of the Admiralty to withdraw carriers from convoy protection, the *Ark Royal* was sent to the South Atlantic to search for a German raider that was destroying commerce there. This ship was actually the *Graf Spee*, although the men of the *Ark Royal* did not know it. The carrier did not participate in the action against the *Graf Spee* on December 13; three British cruisers bottled her up in the Rio de la Plata, where ultimately she was scuttled by her captain.

The *Ark Royal* returned to England in mid-February, 1940, for a refit and then in March sailed for the Mediterranean. Then came the Norway operations, and she and the carrier *Glorious* were called back to home waters. The *Ark Royal*'s aircraft participated in most of the naval operations in the Norway campaign. The pilots had some strange adventures. According to the *Ark Royal* action reports:

20

A Skua on fighter patrol over the Andalsnes area, having shot down a Heinkel 111, was forced to land owing to lack of petrol, and came down within a mile of the crashed German aircraft. Both crews sought refuge in a house near by. An armed Norwegian then appeared. Knowing neither English nor German, he had some difficulty in distinguishing between friend and foe. At last the Skua crew succeeded in establishing their identity, and one of the Germans, who produced an automatic pistol, was promptly shot. Eventually, after borrowing skis, which neither of them had ever used before, the British pilot and observer reached safety on the coast, fifty miles away.

Another Skua pilot (a midshipman) flying alone, found himself separated from his section after air combat. Shortage of petrol compelled him to land on a frozen lake alongside a damaged RAF Gladiator, but he was advised to leave at once owing to the presence of German aircraft and the anticipation of a fresh attack. He filled up with petrol from the wrecked Gladiator, borrowed a Norwegian school atlas, and after flying unaided across 350 miles of sea, made a good landfall in the Shetlands, where he refuelled and then joined a naval air station.

The *Ark Royal* fought the Norwegian campaign to the end and then provided fighter protection for the escaping British troopships during the evacuation. The *Glorious*, as noted, was sunk in this operation, but the *Ark Royal* fought on. On June 13 she sent 15 Skuas to attack the damaged battleship *Scharnhorst* in Trondheim harbor. They scored some near misses on the big ship, but eight of the Skuas were lost, including their crews. The early activities of the *Ark Royal* produced nothing definitive in the way of victories. That was the sort of war that was being fought just then.

But when the war ''hotted up'' in the Mediterranean, as noted, the *Ark Royal* saw some real action. After the fighting of the summer of 1940, the *Ark Royal* went home to England for a refit, and then early in 1941 she was sent back to the Med as a part of Force H. The object of the Germans and Italians then was to control the Mediterranean, and the object of the British was to protect Malta and Gibraltar bases, and to help the land forces fighting in Africa to be sure that the Germans did not succeed. Carrier fighters and bombers were essential in the actions of the fleet against the German *Luftwaffe*, the Italian navy, and the German submarines that Hitler was pouring into the Mediterranean.

The *Ark Royal* remained in the Med as part of Force H for months, then went home for a refit. And that is how she managed to take part in one of the great sea battles of World War II and, in fact, to direct the outcome of that battle: the pursuit and sinking of the mighty German battleship *Bismarck*.

In the Atlantic, the spring of 1941 saw several attempts by the Germans to use their big capital ships—the pocket battleships and battleships—to turn the tide of the sea war. The aircraft carriers available to the British had to be employed mostly in the Mediterranean where British bases were few and the need for air support was great. So carriers did not play a great role in the Atlantic actions for another year. The cruiser *Hipper*, the battleships *Gneisenau* and *Scharnhorst*, and the cruiser *Admiral Scheer* were all out sinking ships in convoy in the Atlantic. On March 15, German Admiral Guenther Lütjens, with his battleships, *Scharnhorst* and *Gneisenau*, sank 13 tankers and freighters and captured three more and sent them to German ports with prize crews. The *Ark Royal* was now employed to try to find these raiders, but her aircraft could not fly at night. Although the ships were spotted late in the day, the raiders got clean away.

And then it was May 1941, and Germany's greatest ship was getting ready to sail. She was the *Bismarck*, a ship listed at 35,000 tons but actually displacing 50,000 tons. She had four gun turrets, eight 15-inch guns, and a very strong escort: the cruiser *Prinz Eugen*, which carried eight 8-inch guns and made a speed of 32 knots.

The Germans were about to launch *Rheinabung* (the Rhine Exercise), which was really a campaign to use surface ships to destroy British shipping in the Atlantic, and thus speed along the U-boat campaign to starve Britain out of the war. In this plan the *Bismarck*, the great battleship, was to tie up major British ships on the convoy routes in the Atlantic and allow the lighter German vessels to work as raiders and decimate the sea lanes.

On the morning of May 18, 1941, all was ready. That morning Admiral Lütjens met with his two captains, Lindemann of *Bismarck* and Brinkmann of the *Prinz Eugen*. He discussed with them his plan of attack.

The *Bismarck* and the *Prinz Eugen* would sail that day directly into

Arctic waters, fuel from tankers near Jan Mayen island, and then speed through the Denmark Strait into the Atlantic. The tankers would be with them all the way. The German admiralty had sent eight tankers out ahead, some to the area south of Greenland and some to the Azores. Admiral Lütjens expected to be out for three months and wanted plenty of elbow room.

That afternoon the ships took on their new crews, including many extra men who would be expected to man the prizes they captured. The *Prinz Eugen* sailed. Then the *Bismarck* weighed anchor and sailed. The band assembled on her quarter deck playing "*Muss i' denn*," a sentimental song the German navy adored. And so did the hundreds of people assembled at the port to watch her go.

Darkness fell, and still the ships were far apart. It was part of the plan, to avoid detection by the British air reconnaissance planes. That night, when the vessels reached the area of Arkona off the Prussian coast, they made rendezvous and also met a fleet of destroyers and minesweepers that would escort them for a while. Admiral Lütjens made a speech to the men of the *Bismarck*: They were going hunting, he said, and he wished them a good bag.

Then it was off into the night, heading for the north through the Baltic Sea. They had no idea where the British Home Fleet might be; the weather had been too bad for German aircraft to fly over Scapa Flow, the Home Fleet anchorage. Admiral Lütjens was particularly conscious of two major ships, the brand-new British battleship *Prince of Wales* and the old, redoubtable battle cruiser *Hood*, for many years the pride of the British fleet.

Admiral Lütjens had hoped that no ships would be seen on this initial day of the voyage, but he was not that lucky. The Swedish vessel *Gotland* came along and steered a course parallel with their own for several hours. There was nothing suspicious about that. The *Gotland* was off the Swedish coast where she had every right to be, but when she turned away her wireless operator sent a message. Although Lütjens's own operators could not read it, he was convinced that the *Gotland* had betrayed his presence to the enemy.

The admiral was right in a sense: His presence had been betrayed to the enemy but not by the *Gotland* only. The first inkling that something unusual was happening in the Baltic came from Gdynia in German home waters. An ordinary dockworker had walked away from the port to send a message to a "relative" in Switzerland. The "relative" sent another message to a friend in Portugal, and the Lisbon friend sent a message to his office in London. Thus the word that the *Bismarck* had sailed reached an inconspicuous desk in the British Admiralty. And that message was soon joined by others.

The *Bismarck* and her entourage sailed through the Great Belt between the Danish islands, then north through the Kattegat, through the Skagerrak north of Jutland Peninsula and up along the Norwegian coast to a little fjord near Bergen, where they refueled, beginning on May 21. The sea was calm, the air quiet, the only fliers were birds. That morning German reconnaissance pilots had flown over Scapa Flow and reported that the British Home Fleet was quietly at anchor there.

The British were not asleep, however. On May 21 the Admiralty asked the Air Ministry to search for two battleships and three destroyers heading north. And within a matter of hours British reconnaissance planes were over the fjord. Almost before the photographs reached London the ships were gone, heading north once more.

From Stockholm came *Gotland*'s word that the *Bismarck*, the *Prinz Eugen*, and a whole flock of smaller ships were heading north through the Baltic. From a secret wireless station in Norway came the word that a resistance agent in Kristiansund had seen the bow wave of an enormous ship speeding by. Yes, Admiral Lütjens was quite right to be concerned.

The weather favored Admiral Lütjens. It was stormy, and the clouds were low and dark. The admiral was in a hurry. Until he could break through into the Atlantic he was in a box and would be at a great disadvantage if discovered. Once in the broad waters of the Atlantic, the *Bismarck* would be in her element.

The destroyer escorts were sent back, and speed was increased. On May 23 the *Bismarck* and *Prinz Eugen* plowed on through rain squalls and heavy clouds, nearing the ice line that ran close to the Arctic Circle. They moved toward the northwest coast of Iceland.

On the morning of May 23 Admiral Sir John Tovey, commander of the British Home Fleet, had the word that the *Bismarck* was out of the North Sea and into the Atlantic. He was aboard his flagship, the new battleship *King George V*.

The German ships forged on through the ice-free passage. This was the land of the midnight sun, but the weather was so bad it did not matter. All around them was heavy fog. Concealed in that fog was the British cruiser *Suffolk*, and that morning Admiral Tovey had ordered her skipper to keep a sharp eye out on her patrol area in the Denmark Strait. He had also sent her sister ship, the *Norfolk*, up to give her a hand. And the admiral had given the order to the entire Home Fleet at Scapa Flow to get up steam and prepare to sail on short notice. The Admiralty now had planes out from Coastal Command bases flying searches. The cruisers *Manchester* and *Birmingham* were sent to the Faeroes, just in case the Germans tried that route.

Admiral Tovey laid his battle plans: He would take the *King George V* and the *Repulse* out, and Admiral Holland, commander of the battle cruiser squadron, would take the *Hood* and the *Prince of Wales* out to search for the enemy ships. Soon he knew where to search. In the fog off Iceland the *Suffolk* suddenly came out in the clear, and there, just seven miles away, her captain saw the *Bismarck*! Swiftly he turned the ship back into the fog and swept around at flank speed to get behind the German ship. Then he began to shadow her using the ship's new tracking radar.

The radio crew of the *Bismarck* intercepted the British messages, and so Admiral Lütjens knew that he was discovered and the hunt was on.

The cruiser *Norfolk* was coming up fast—too fast it turned out, for she appeared suddenly out of the fog just six miles from the *Bismarck*. Captain Lindemann lost no time. The 15-inch guns began to fire, and *Norfolk* was straddled by three rounds that sprayed the cruiser with steel splinters. But she got away in the fog and then took position on the *Bismarck*'s port quarter, using her radar to track the German warship.

The day wore on. As night approached, Admiral Lütjens ordered speed cut to 28 knots for the run through the Denmark Strait. From time to time the men of the vessels saw one another but not long enough for the *Bismarck* to do anything about the shadowers. The important matter to Admiral Lütjens was to run the strait and get into the open sea. Then he could turn and deal with his pursuers.

Already Admiral Tovey had acted, sailing on May 22 and taking the *Repulse* and the carrier *Victorious* with him. He had sent the battle cruiser *Hood* on ahead toward Iceland, accompanied by six destroyers. The *Hood* was to refuel off Iceland and then move southwest and cover the Iceland-Greenland exit into the Atlantic and the Iceland-Faeroes exit.

Admiral Lütjens was in even more of a hurry now. His meteorologists warned that the weather was clearing. But although he wanted to raise speed, he actually had to lower it to 24 knots because they were traveling through mushy ice.

Dawn came and the fog persisted for Admiral Lütjens. By the middle of the morning the two German ships reached the narrowest part of the passage, about 40 miles wide, that separated the Greenland icefloes from the edge of the minefield the British had laid north from Iceland. They were nearly free, but then the weather did change. Off to starboard the men on the bridge of the *Bismarck* could see the snow-capped mountains of Greenland above the ice.

To port there was nothing to be seen but fog. And behind the bank of fog were the British cruisers, still tracking, still sending their messages about the position of the German warships. The *Suffolk* was opposite Vesfirdir. The *Norfolk* was south of the *Suffolk*, watching the edge of the minefield. *Hood* and her destroyers were coming up as fast as possible from the south.

At 6:00 P.M., Admiral Lütjens was feeling more at ease. They were nearly clear. A few more hours, and the convoys of the Atlantic would be waiting for them.

Aboard the *Suffolk* the watch changed, and Able Seaman Newell took over the starboard aft lookout station on the bridge of the cruiser. For these waters it was a dream job; the bridge was heated and the biggest problem was to keep from being lulled to sleep by the motion of the ship. Newell picked up his glasses and began to sweep the horizon of his sector, back and forth, back and forth. It was tedious work. Suddenly he stopped and moved the glasses back. There, framed in the lenses, was a huge black shape, a warship that had just slipped out of the mist. She was not seven miles away. And behind her came another. "Ship bearing green one four. . . . Two ships. . . ."

Captain Robert Ellis moved swiftly. His first task was to make sure his ship survived this meeting with the 15-inch guns. He ordered her turned hard to port into the fog bank. The change was so quick that in the wardroom the crockery went crashing from the dining tables.

Captain Ellis sent a signal to the Admiralty. As the *Suffolk*'s wake led into the fog, the message was on its way. Before the fog closed in, the men on the bridge of the *Suffolk* had one more look at the *Bismarck*, her bow wave high as she traveled at top speed past them. Then the only man who could "see" the *Bismarck* was the radar operator, watching the blips move along on his scope.

Soon the blips disappeared. The *Bismarck* had run out of the radar's range. So Captain Ellis had to come out of the fog to shadow the German ships. He took a position about 13 miles behind the *Prinz Eugen*, at the edge of his radar range, and hoped *Bismarck* would not double back on him.

The *Bismarck* was then otherwise occupied, however. The *Norfolk* had received the message about the *Bismarck*, and Captain Alfred Phillips had steered for the edge of the fog to the open water north of him. He emerged from the fog, and there, less than six miles away was the *Bismarck*, coming straight at the *Norfolk*.

Admiral Lütjens did not hesitate. The moment the *Norfolk* was seen, the German guns trained on her and within seconds began firing. Captain Phillips ran back for the fog, but before he could get out of sight the *Bismarck* fired five salvos. The shooting was excellent. The first salvo hit just 50 yards off the *Norfolk*'s bridge, and one shell actually ricocheted over the ship. The other shells were all close, and fountains of water 150 feet high rose all around the ship. Shell splinters fell all over the *Norfolk*; miraculously, not a man was hurt. Then the fog closed around the *Norfolk* and she was safe. All she had to do was wait for the heavy ships to come up and deal with the *Bismarck*.

The heavy ships had no information, however. The message sent by the *Suffolk* had not reached London. The ship's wireless aerials had iced up, and the signals had not carried farther than the *Norfolk*. So the *Hood* and Admiral Tovey's ships steamed on blind. It was a long time before the wireless messages got through.

When the wireless operators aboard the *Hood* finally were able to pick up the message, the *Hood* and the *Prince of Wales* had joined up and were just 300 miles away from the German ships. They were steering a course that would converge on the Germans in less than half a day. That was no good, Admiral Holland decided. It would mean a night action, and the *Prince of Wales* was so new that she had not even been worked up properly. Night action was too difficult for her.

So Holland ordered a change of course to make an interception an hour before sunrise, and the two British warships moved along at 27 knots through the heavy sea.

It was 8:00 P.M. on May 23. Admiral Holland was confident; he had a great ship under him and a crew of great experience. The *Hood*'s eight 15-inch guns were a match for the *Bismarck*. She also had the radar advantage. There was one problem, but it did not seriously disturb Admiral Holland. The deck and even turret tops of the guns were not armored. That weight would have been a serious problem for a ship not designed to bear it; the *Hood* had been built in a day when weapons were simpler. The big threat now was aerial bombs, but the war moved so fast that no time was found to put the *Hood* in for the sort of refit that would have armed her decks. So far the *Hood* had been lucky. She had taken a few German bombs but had suffered no serious damage.

By 9:00 P.M. the destroyers were suffering in the heavy weather, pitching and tossing. Admiral Holland informed them that if they could not keep up he would have to go on without them. Speed was all-important. The destroyers could follow at their best speed and catch up later.

After the *Bismarck* had fired those five salvos at the British cruiser *Norfolk*, Admiral Lütjens could no longer see his enemy. Or his enemies. Who knew what lay out there in the fog? So he ordered the *Prinz Eugen* to pass and lead the way, to be the eyes of the *Bismarck*. The *Bismarck* slowed for a moment, the *Prinz Eugen* went streaking by at 30 knots, and then the *Bismarck* sped up. Behind them the *Suffolk* was having a hard time keeping the ships in radar range, but Captain Ellis somehow managed to get the power to keep going.

All night long the chase continued, with Admiral Lütjens bent on getting away into the open sea and the British ships bent on stopping him. The German crews stood at action stations all that night, until Captain Brinkmann let his men of *Prinz Eugen* go to Condition 2 late in the night.

Steadily, Admiral Holland's leading force drew up on the Germans. The *Hood* was leading, and her officers and men were preparing for battle. Admiral Holland turned the force northward so that when he met the Germans, they would be silhouetted against the northern sun. The *Suffolk* lost contact with the Germans, but regained it several hours later and reported that the *Bismarck* was just about to break out into the Atlantic. She was then about 35 miles away from the *Hood* and the *Prince of Wales*.

They drew together at about 5:00 P.M. At 5:52 P.M. the *Hood* opened fire on the *Prinz Eugen*, but the shells were not close. The *Prince of Wales* fired on the *Bismarck*. Both the German ships returned fire. The first *Bismarck* salvo fell ahead of the *Hood* and the second astern.

The Germans had all the best of it. The wind was in their favor. The *Bismarck* was firing eight guns against the *Hood*. Because of the angle of approach, the *Hood* and the *Prince of Wales* were firing only nine guns.

Soon the *Prinz Eugen* secured a hit on the boat deck of the *Hood* and started a fire in the 4-inch shells stored there. The ammunition began exploding. Then the *Bismarck* secured a hit amidships. A column of flame four times the height of the mainmast shot up above the *Hood*. This meant real trouble. One armor-piercing high-explosive shell had done it all: It had penetrated the unarmored deck of the *Hood* and exploded in the 4-inch ammunition magazine. The 4-inch magazine had caused an explosion in the 8-inch magazine, and the bowels were blown out of the ship, which suddenly listed to port, then shook, and started going down by the stern. In a very few moments the ship was over at 25 degrees. And then the bows were vertical to the sea. Men were struggling on the decks and in the water. Aboard the *Bismarck* the Germans saw the *Hood* blow up and break into two pieces. The guns of *A* and *B* turrets fired one more time. And then the *Hood* sank. The battle had lasted less than 22 minutes. And suddenly the *Hood* was gone, carrying down to their deaths 1,400 men.

Now the battle was unequal, largely because the officers and men of the *Prince of Wales* were unready and untried and their guns were not firing properly. So the *Prince of Wales* turned away and ran for cover to save herself. The *Bismarck* had won a signal victory. She had been hit three times, once in the oil storage tanks so that she leaked fuel. The *Prinz Eugen* had not been hit at all. Still, that oil leak was serious because it meant the *Bismarck* was leaving a trail as she went. So Admiral Lütjens decided to head for the French coast to make repairs.

The destroyers sped to the scene of the *Hood*'s sinking to rescue survivors. They searched for many hours, but all they found were three Carley rafts and bits of wood floating in the water. Aboard one Carley raft was a single midshipman. Aboard a second raft was a single seaman, and aboard the third raft was another seaman. That is all. Of the total crew of HMS *Hood*, only three men survived. It was the greatest single naval loss of the war.

The news shocked all England. It also moved the Royal Navy to a consuming desire for revenge against the German battleship.

And now into the battle came the carriers. HMS *Victorious* had sailed with the *King George V*, although the *Victorious* was being loaded with fighter planes for Malta and had only nine Swordfish torpedo planes aboard. She was rushed forward, and late in the afternoon launched the torpedo planes. They found the *Bismarck* on her way to France and managed to get close enough, despite the battleship's fierce antiaircraft fire, to put a torpedo into her. The torpedo struck the 15-inch belt of armor and did little damage, but Admiral Lütjens was impressed and knew that come morning he could expect more planes, many more planes, so he hastened toward the French coast. Morning came, and with it the sighting of the *Bismarck* by a Catalina flying boat of Coastal Command. Then two carrier planes showed up to shadow the German ships.

Later in the day, the cruiser *Renown* and the carrier *Ark Royal* came up. The *Renown* was too ancient a ship to take on the *Bismarck*, but the *Ark Royal*'s Swordfish were another matter.

The seas were frightening. The flight deck was pitching through a 56-foot arc. Somehow 15 Swordfish got off that deck, and 14 of them moved slowly (their cruising speed was 85 knots without any headwinds) toward the enemy. They found the *Bismarck*, formed into small groups, and attacked from different angles, launching 11 torpedoes and missing with all of them. Soon they were back with more torpedoes. Eleven of the 15 pilots missed, two failed to launch torpedoes at all, and the fourteenth torpedo struck amidships but caused no damage. The fifteenth torpedo, however, smashed the steering engine room. The rudders had been hard over when the torpedo hit, and now they were stuck. The *Bismarck* went into a circle, making headway only by alternating her propellers against the push of the rudder. At that moment, Admiral Lütjens knew that his ship was doomed. Aboard the *Bismarck*, he signaled "We fight to the last shell. Long live the Führer." It was hardly the message of a winner.

Hours passed. Night fell. The men of the *Bismarck* struggled desperately to free up their rudder, but it would not budge. Morning came and so did the British fleet swooping down on the *Bismarck* like a pack of dogs on a solitary injured wolf. The battleships *Rodney* and *King George V* began firing their big guns. Soon shells were smashing the great warship and she was set afire. Finally only two of her 15-inch guns were still firing. Altogether 75 torpedoes were fired at the *Bismarck*, and scores of them hit home. Still she did not sink. The British battleships grew low on fuel and had to turn away from the crippled enemy ship. The cruisers kept working on her. Finally at 10:40 A.M. on May 27, 1941, the great battleship capsized and sank. More than 2,200 men went down with her, including Admiral Lütjens and Captain Lindemann.

So the *Hood* was avenged, and the German battleship was sunk, and that came about because one slow old Swordfish torpedo plane delivered one torpedo that crippled the mighty ship and made it impossible for her to escape. It was a strange sort of victory but still an extremely important one, and without the carrier *Ark Royal* it would never have been accomplished. After the fight, as though it had all been routine, the *Ark Royal* went on back to Gibraltar and about her business in the Mediterranean. No great tales were told and no great claims made about the mighty effort her Swordfish pilots had made against the *Bismarck*. It was all in a day's work of the job—the job of sinking Adolf Hitler.

—————

On November 13, 1941, Force H was returning from operations to Gibraltar. The sea was smooth, with a little ripple from a 10-knot southwest wind stirring the surface. Visibility was good with low cloud cover and occasional rain squalls. The water was deep here, about 1,100 fathoms.

At 8:17 that morning a signal was sent through the fleet: enemy submarines had been reported in this vicinity and great vigilance was to be exercised. As the day went on, the destroyers had no asdic contacts until 3:17 P.M. Then a destroyer reported that it had a submarine contact to port, and the fleet altered course to avoid the area. At 3:35 P.M. another destroyer observed something on the starboard bow, but on checking it appeared to be an illusion. So the fleet sailed on, without a care.

Meanwhile, down below, submarines were trailing the carrier *Ark Royal*. Lieutenant Franz Georg Reschke's *U-205* had been tracking the carrier for nearly a whole day. At about 5:00 A.M., when the destroyer *Legion* thought it had discovered something, Reschke was firing three torpedoes. He fired, dropped the periscope, and ran. He thought he had secured at least two hits. In fact, he had secured no hits at all, and the men of the *Ark Royal* did not even know that Reschke had been shooting at them. The destroyer on the starboard wing of the carrier reported an underwater explosion in the ship's wake. No one knew what it was, and since no harm had been done, no one much cared.

At 6:15 A.M. six Swordfish aircraft were flown off the carrier to carry out a dawn antisubmarine patrol. Nothing was sighted, and the search ended just before 9:00 A.M. Several other antisubmarine patrols were flown that day with no result.

Also stalking the carrier was Lieutenant Friedrich Guggenberger's *U-81*. He watched with great interest as the *Ark Royal* slowed and sped up and turned into the wind to take on returning aircraft. At 3:40 P.M. Guggenberger fired a spread of three electric torpedoes. At 3:41 one of them struck the carrier on the starboard side, abreast of the island. A column of water rose to the level of the flight deck, 55 feet above the water, and splashed onto the starboard sea boat, wrecking it. The force of the explosion also blew open the bomb lift doors under the bridge, and brown smoke came up from the side. Five aircraft at the forward end of the flying deck were thrown into the air, and an armored plate below the bridge was blown upward.

At first many aboard the ship felt that the *Ark Royal* had suffered an internal explosion. No wake or periscope had been seen. Something had happened; there was no doubt about that. The ship immediately began to list, and the list soon reached 12 degrees. After half an hour the list had increased to 18 degrees.

From the bridge, the captain tried to order the engines reversed, but the telegraphs were jammed, and the bridge was knocked out of communication with the ship. The main switchboard room telephone exchange and lower conning tower had been damaged and flooded with oil. The two watchkeepers were waist deep in oil, but they managed to escape. Action stations was ordered by bugle and by word of mouth. The first lieutenant left the bridge and went down to the engine room to give the order to cut to half speed astern, and to stop the ship.

By this time the lower conning tower, switchboard, and stoker petty officers' bath flat were all flooded. So were the starboard boiler room and several passageways. The starboard engines were soon out of action.

When the lieutenant returned to the flight deck, he set up a human chain of communications between the engine room and the flying deck.

The destroyer *Hermione* supplied portable pumps, hoses, and cable, but the list was increasing. The captain then decided it was time to get ready to abandon ship if the list got worse. He ordered hands to leave action stations, and everyone to move to the port side of the struggling ship.

At 4:00 P.M. a signal was sent to HMS *Legion* to come alongside, aft on the port side. In a short time 1,487 officers and men were moved off the carrier onto the destroyer. Some jumped on hammocks off the forecastle. Others used lines rigged from the ship. The captain had to order several officers off the ship because they wanted try to save her, but there was nothing they could do. The *Legion* cast off at 4:48 that afternoon.

The port cutter and the whaler and one skiff were lowered, and so were a number of Carley floats, aircraft dinghies, and cork mats. Some 30 sailors jumped into these.

At 4:30 P.M. the engine room crew was ordered below to raise steam. The captain moved around the ship inspecting the damage. The ship seemed to be holding well enough, he decided. There was no need for panic.

In the engine room, however, the situation was growing desperate. The starboard boiler room filled with water, which overflowed into the center boiler room. The machinery control room then flooded, and water also seeped into the starboard engine room. By pumping the men reduced the list to 14 degrees.

At 5:00 P.M. the engineers reported they could not keep steam up in the port boiler room. That meant no electric power for pumps, lighting, or ventilation.

A destroyer, the *Laforey*, was brought alongside, and cables were run to her electrical system so that pumps could be operated. It was getting dark. The list was 17 degrees, and the lower hangar deck was quite dark. Six pumps were gotten into operation. The first lieutenant roamed around the ship, seeing that hatches and scuttles were screwed down, and the valves dogged down.

On the flight deck the navigator and others established a communications system, using a field telephone connected by battery hookup with the engine room, and transmitting other signals by light and by hand. The navigator stayed on the flight deck until the list was 25 degrees and it was no longer possible to stand on the deck.

The struggle to save the ship continued. At 7:45 P.M. the engineering officer said he needed more men aboard. The *Legion* and *Laforey* were brought back again, carrying engine room, electrical, and shipwright parties. Volunteers were called for; nearly everyone volunteered so they had to pick out 80 men to go aboard *Ark Royal*. A few extra men slipped aboard unnoticed while the transfers were being made. By 9:30 they had raised steam in one boiler and soon afterward in a second boiler.

Two tugs arrived. One of them, the *St. Day*, put on a terrible exhibition of bad seamanship and disappeared for two hours. The other, the *Thames*, came along and took the ship under tow. At 8:35 P.M. the *Ark Royal* was moving ahead at two knots.

By 10:45 the engineers were able to shift over to the ship's own power, and the destroyers were let go away. Some lights came on. The pumps continued to work. The list was now 16 degrees, and the ship had steam in the port boiler. The captain now talked brightly of the hope of bringing the ship home safely to Gibraltar. Within an hour, he had been told, they would have steam in the port drive shaft, and the ship speed could be increased to six knots. At 2:15 in the morning, however, the list of the carrier had increased again, to 17 degrees. They had flooded everything floodable on the port side of the ship. Finally, the tug *St. Day* showed up again and was put on the port side to help with the tow.

Then came more trouble. A fire started in the boiler room, and the engineering officer had to give the gloomy report that his hopes had been too high. It would be another two hours before steam could be gotten into the shaft.

Also, the men below were beginning to collapse. The chief engineer came up, exhausted. Two stokers had to have artificial respiration. The engineers then discovered that the funnel uptake was flooded and the furnace gases had no way of escaping. So the salvage work had to stop and the dynamos had to be shut down. The lights went out and the steering engine quit.

The *Laforey* was brought back alongside, but now the list was 20 degrees and it was too dangerous to come alongside aft because of the propellers. So the *Laforey* had to secure outside the tug *St. Day*, and the electric cables had to be passed across the tug to the carrier. It was very difficult going.

By 3:40 A.M. the destroyer's pumps were again working for the carrier, and yet for some reason they did not seem to affect the list now. A party went around the ship to try to find the problem, but it was elusive, or rather it was a whole series of problems.

The *Ark Royal* was now only 30 miles from Gibraltar, and speed was up to five knots.

The sloop *Penstemon* came alongside with a huge pump and everyone cheered, but the pump could not be hoisted aboard on account of the strong list. Then the negative reports came in. The navigator announced that his party would have to evacuate the flight deck because of the list, and they went down to the lower hangar deck.

The commander of engineering reported at 4:00 A.M. that there was nothing more to be done. The pumps were no longer making any headway, and the list was increasing. In fact, he said, it was now up to 27 degrees. Preparations had to be made once again to get all the 250 men who had come back aboard off the vessel. Lines were rigged, and the men were moved back aboard the *St. Day*.

The list at this point was so severe, having reached 28 degrees, that no one could move about the deck without using his hands. The order was given for the men on deck to slip down onto the tug, and everyone was ordered up from below. At 4:30 A.M. the last man left the ship. The list was 35 degrees.

She hung on there for one hour and 40 minutes. She hung again at 45 degrees, and then she slipped a little more. Then, when the flight deck was at 90 degrees to the sea, she hung again, and the island lay atop the sea like a raft. It was 14½ hours after the torpedoing.

Then explosions began, and finally the ship stopped hanging on the surface and slid below. It was 6:13 in the morning. One—only one—man was lost of the whole crew of 1,749. The saving of the crew of the *Ark Royal*, under conditions where hundreds of men volunteered for the most daring and deadly tasks, was one of the great sea rescue stories of all time, made possible only by the superb discipline of the ship and its officers.

Admiral Yamamoto's Strike

Admiral Isoroku Yamamoto was one of the foremost opponents of war against America, so it is ironic that he was the man who carried out the primary attack that opened the Pacific War.

For 15 years in the 1920s and 1930s, Yamamoto had worked without success to achieve a peaceful settlement to Japan's differences with the United States and Britain over naval parity. One reason was the unwillingness of the western powers to accept Japan's conception that she was to be to Asia what Britain was to Europe, the primary sea power. This made it impossible for any settlement to be reached and played into the hands of the Japanese army, which was controlled by expansionists. By 1937 these militarists had seized control of the Japanese government, and after that war became inevitable. It was just a question of time.

Yamamoto continued to be a thorn in the side of the expansionists, so much so that in 1938 he was sent to command the combined fleet —Japan's fighting navy—so that he would not be assassinated, as had been a number of leaders who were known to favor peace and settlement of international problems without war.

Observing the war in Europe from his vantage point aboard the combined fleet flagship, Admiral Yamamoto was very much impressed by the success of the British at Taranto, particularly the tactics of the torpedo plane pilots who came across the major Italian fleet elements from all angles, and despite the slowness (85 mph) of their old biplane Swordfish bombers, managed to do enormous damage to the Italians while losing only a handful of men.

This performance at Taranto gave Yamamoto a hope he had not before held: that it might be possible to strike such a blow at the American fleet in the beginning of operations that the United States would be willing to make peace and allow Japan the freedom of action she wanted in China and on the Asian mainland. *If* the American battle fleet could be destroyed—that was the question. Taranto showed Yamamoto that it could be destroyed, given enough carriers and enough planes concentrated in one place. The place, of course, was the American anchorage at Pearl Harbor, where the entire Pacific Fleet tied up when it was not conducting operations. The method would have to be a preemptive strike in the very opening hours of war. And that is how Admiral Yamamoto made his plans in 1941 when General Hideki Tojo set the stage for a general Pacific War.

The idea was anything but new to the Japanese. For a thousand years the samurai had been fighting one another in the service of various emperors, shoguns, and daimyos. They had evolved their own ethical code of warfare, and it included the preemptive strike, which was deemed unfair by the western powers. "Win first, fight later" was the samurai slogan.

That strategy had been followed by Admiral Heihachiro Togo at Port Arthur in 1904 and had been so successful that it crippled the Russian Pacific Fleet at the outset of the war and made possible the swift victory of the Japanese, who did not have the resources then to fight a long war. The idea of repeating the preemptive strike was approved by the naval authorities in Tokyo and became fleet doctrine in 1941.

To carry out such a strike, the naval air arm would have to be reorganized, so that a large number of carriers could be employed under a single command. This was done in April 1941 with the establishment of the First Air Fleet, which included three of Japan's carrier divisions. This change was not made without opposition within the navy. Japan had its "battleship" men, just as America did, and they believed that the big capital ship with big guns was the vital element of the fleet. They feared that the massing of a carrier attack force, with relatively few battleships and cruisers involved, would diminish the battle force. Admiral Yamamoto was convinced, however, and ultimately that made the difference.

Once the method of attack was decided, a number of serious technical problems had to be solved. Most important of these was the perfection of an aerial torpedo that would work properly in very shallow water, for the fleet anchorage of the American navy was shallow indeed, not more than 25 feet around Ford Island, where the battleships moored. The torpedoes could not run more than 12 meters deep, and that was quite an order. The Japanese torpedo experts were the best in the world at that time and they solved the problem.

Next came the program of training for this unusual attack. Down near Kagoshima, the Japanese fleet anchorage on Kyushu Island, the navy chose Ariake Bay, which resembled the topography of Pearl Harbor. There the ships' crews and pilots trained in the summer of 1941.

In September, the Japanese navy held its annual war games, moving them up two months to rehearse the Pearl Harbor strike should the political negotiations then being held with the United States fail. The militarists expected them to fail, so stringent were their demands. The games presupposed that the whole scheme of Japanese attack would be carried out against the Philippines, Malaya, and the Dutch East Indies as well as Pearl Harbor. Admiral Yamamoto's interest centered on the Pearl Harbor operation, however. He spent September 16 in a secret room. Here it was decided that the task force would approach from the north. A mock attack was staged, with the Blue forces representing the attacking Japanese and the Red forces representing the defending Americans. The alert Red forces defended very well and drove the Blues away with relatively little damage to their own installations. It was a good lesson about what might happen if the Americans were sufficiently alert, and Admiral Chuichi Nagumo, the man who would head the real Pearl Harbor strike force, staged another attack from a more northerly position, arriving off "Oahu" at sunset, surprising "the enemy" and sinking two carriers and damaging a third. During these war games, one factor was repeatedly stressed: the need to strike swiftly and bring the precious carriers home again. Several of the more junior officers discussed the question of repeated strikes against the American installations, but the matter was not mentioned at the highest levels.

Ultimately six carriers were assigned to the Pearl Harbor operation. They continued to train at various places around Japan, some of them in the sheltered waters of Ariake Bay. By mid-October an increasingly large number of officers had been taken into the secret of the mission; it was essential if they were to train their pilots and the ship crews for this attack in restricted waters on the American fleet. The pilots practiced maneuvers that would be like those they would undertake on attack day: They climbed to 6,000 feet over the eastern tip of Sakurajima (the volcano), then circled down the valley of the Kotsuki River at 500-yard intervals, going down the valley toward Kagoshima and flying over the city at treetop level.

To the left of the Yamagataya department store was a water tank near the shore. As the pilots passed over the department store, they were to come down to an altitude of 60 feet and "release a torpedo." It was when these instructions were given that the pilots realized just what a dangerous task they were going to have. This was very much as it would be when they came in north of Oahu, passed over the cane fields and down the valley into Pearl Harbor. Why, a man could get killed just in the training!

And so in the fall of 1941 the people of Kagoshima had to get used to "wild pilots" buzzing their city streets at very low levels and naval authorities who would do nothing to stop them. The citizens never did get used to it, or know why it was being done.

The training was rigorous, sometimes as much as 12 hours a day. The dive bomber pilots learned to drop down to 1,500 feet before releasing their bombs, thus increasing the chances of a direct hit. They used an old battleship, the *Settsu*, as their target. The torpedo bombers practiced against a rock off Akune in southwest Kyushu, making so much racket that local farmers complained that their chickens stopped laying that summer and fall.

The least satisfactory of all the operations was the training of the level bombers, which were scheduled to attack the battleships with armor-piercing bombs. Their job, it seemed, would be the easiest, but their performance was a matter of deep concern to the training officers.

In November 1941, the Pearl Harbor operation became a reality. That day the Tojo cabinet decided irrevocably on war with the United States and Britain, and the cabinet members learned of the coming attack on Pearl Harbor to open the war. A message was sent to Admiral Yamamoto, who was then aboard the flagship *Nagato* off the coast of Shikoku, and the next day he went to Tokyo.

It was early November before the Mitsubishi factory in Nagasaki completed the order for the special torpedoes that would be used. When they were tested, most of them ran very well in 12 meters (40 feet) of water.

In the fleet, where little was known about the coming operation except by a handful of men, speculation was common. Some thought the Japanese navy was going to attack Vladivostok. Some settled on Singapore. Some thought it would be Manila. Admiral Nagumo held a meeting aboard his flagship, the carrier *Akagi*, with all the unit commanders who would take part in the Pearl Harbor attack, and for the first time some of them learned where they were really going and what they were going to do. The next day Nagumo took the fleet out to sea for a dress rehearsal, using the Japanese fleet units anchored in Saeki Bay as their "targets." The results were most gratifying.

On November 4, Admiral Yamamoto returned to the *Akagi* from Tokyo and told his chief of staff, Vice Admiral Matome Ugaki, that it appeared the Pearl Harbor attack was on, although the final decision would not be made until December 1.

The next day, November 5, the task force staged its second dress rehearsal. It was even more successful than the first. On November 6, Admiral Yamamoto went up to Tokyo again. That day the various carriers sailed, each to its individual home port, for last minute maintenance and supply. Shore leave was granted, and the vast majority of the sailors thought they were preparing for another training cruise.

On November 11, the submarines that would participate in the Pearl Harbor attack sailed from Saeki Bay for the Marshall Islands, where they would refuel and then proceed to Hawaii. They sailed at the eleventh minute of the eleventh hour of the eleventh day of the eleventh month, a sign regarded as most reassuring for the future of this important operation.

Also on November 11, Armistice Day of World War I, Admiral Yamamoto wrote to his friend Rear Admiral Takeichi Hori about the coming action, and said how much he detested the whole concept of war against the United States. "What a strange position I find myself in—having to pursue with full determination a course of action which is diametrically opposed to my best judgment and firmest conviction."

That morning, Yamamoto left Tokyo for the Yokosuka naval base and then flew down to where the *Nagato* was waiting for him. On November 13, he and his staff attended a series of meetings devoted to various aspects of the naval operations that were to begin against the Americans, the British, and the Dutch. On November 15, they met with representatives of the army to try to coordinate the various attacks on the Philippines, the Dutch East Indies, and Malaya. It was also decided that if anything changed, Yamamoto could call back the forces at any time—even after the planes had taken off from the carriers for the Pearl Harbor attack.

When one officer said that this would be impossible, Yamamoto grew furious. For 50 years, he said, the Japanese navy had been dedicated to complete discipline to keep world peace. If any officer believed he could not obey orders at the last minute to turn back from a course of war, then let him say so and resign his commission. There was no more complaint. Yamamoto cooled down quickly, as he always did.

Yamamoto also spent some time talking to Admiral Shimizu, the commander of submarines, about the I-boats (a type of Japanese sub) and midget submarines that would be used in the Pearl Harbor attack.

The *Akagi* had gone to Kagoshima to pick up her planes. She moved into Saeki Bay, and there Admiral Nagumo and his staff boarded.

The new carriers *Zuikaku* and *Shokaku* sailed from Kure on November 16. And the *Soryu* and the *Hiryu* also picked up their planes, as did the *Kaga*.

Security was very tight, so tight that the security men, knowing that the departure of so many planes and pilots from the various air bases would create talk, masked the operation by bringing in many planes from training bases to the bases near the big cities. Thus the amount of air activity seemed not to change at all around Japan.

The Americans were not altogether fooled, however. Their radio intelligence unit at Pearl Harbor was aware of a reorganization of the Japanese carrier fleet, though not quite sure of the reason. The movements of the carriers were monitored through their various radio broadcasts, but so careful had the Japanese been that there was no indication of a coming operation of any importance. Thus, as the Japanese strike force headed northward to the Kuril Island jumpoff point, its security was complete.

On November 17 the Combined Fleet flagship *Nagato* sailed into Saeki Bay and Admiral Yamamoto and Chief of Staff Ugaki boarded the *Akagi* so that the commander could speak to the members of the First Air Fleet and urge them on to glory. A hundred officers assembled on the flight deck. Yamamoto's speech was off the cuff, and it was designed to prevent the navy people from becoming overconfident. He told the officers that the Americans were going to be formidable opponents, not the "paper tigers" the Japanese propaganda machine had been making of them for months. "Although we hope to achieve surprise, everyone should be prepared for terrific American resistance in this operation," he said. "Japan has faced many worthy opponents in her glorious history—Mongols, Chinese, Russians—but in this operation we will meet the strongest and most resourceful opponent of all."

Yamamoto also praised his opponent, Admiral Husband E. Kimmel of the U.S. Navy, who was entrusted with so much responsibility. Yamamoto regarded him as gallant and brave and expected him to put up a stiff fight. Kimmel's reputation for carefulness indicated that the operation might not after all be a surprise to the Americans. The Japanese had to be ready for this, said Admiral Yamamoto.

"It is the custom of Bushido to select an equal or stronger opponent," Yamamoto added. "On this score you have nothing to complain about; the American navy is a good match for the Japanese navy."

There was a little party and some toasts, and Admiral Yamamoto expressed his confidence in the victory to come. Then the admiral went back to the flagship, and Admiral Nagumo paid a return visit. There were more toasts and an air of comradeship that masked Nagumo's many doubts about the whole operation. For, as noted, Nagumo was a battleship man, not an aviation man, and he had a basic distrust of carriers that sprang from his knowledge of their vulnerability. But he lacked knowledge of their major strengths, and particularly of the strength of numbers, which gave the carriers an excellent air cover at all times if they were properly employed.

Nagumo would never have been Yamamoto's choice for commander of the carrier strike force, but in this matter, following Japanese naval tradition, Yamamoto was not consulted. Nagumo was chosen because of his seniority in the Japanese naval service, and that was all there was to it. Not even the feisty Yamamoto considered complaining about that process.

So the fleet prepared to sail in an atmosphere of calm and confidence.

Finally, at about 4:00 P.M., the *Soryu* and *Hiryu* carriers left the bay with four destroyers, bound for the rendezvous point in the Kuril Islands, from which the operation would soon get under weigh. And after them came the other ships, one by one. The die was now cast. Unless they were called back, these ships would sail on to Pearl Harbor and attack.

The Japanese strike force rendezvous was at Hitokappu Bay on the island of Etorofu, about six miles wide and six miles long. It was the ideal place: shrouded in mist and with very little population in the two fishing villages of the island. The ships began arriving in the third week of November, and by November 22 the last of them, the *Kaga*, had come in.

On November 22, Admiral Nagumo held a briefing aboard the *Akagi*, using the scale models of Oahu Island and Pearl Harbor that had been constructed for the purpose. The briefing officer, who had just recently returned from Hawaii where he had acted as an intelligence agent, also had the most up-to-date information from Japanese naval intelligence about the disposition of ships and aircraft around the islands.

When the briefing was over, one nagging question remained: What about the American aircraft carriers? The Japanese knew that at that moment there were three carriers in the Pacific, but they did not know where they were or where they were likely to be when the attack materialized. The trouble was that the carriers operated by themselves, each with its own task force, and quite independent of the battleship fleet.

On November 23, Admiral Nagumo held a meeting to which the key personnel from every ship of the task force were invited. There he announced the coming attack on Pearl Harbor. Then staff officers outlined the plan: Two waves of aircraft would attack and "deal the U.S. Pacific Fleet an all out fatal blow." No one said anything about a follow-up attack. Admiral Nagumo had no such plan. He was already extremely nervous about the operation, and he intended to hit and run. No matter that the staff had provided for fifty-four fighter planes to scout and protect the fleet at all times. One group of 18 planes would be flying over the force all day long, while two other groups, each of 18 planes, would be on the decks of their carriers, ready to take off immediately in case of trouble. But that margin of safety was not enough to satisfy Admiral Nagumo. He still wanted to hit hard and get out immediately.

Staff officer Minoru Genda then explained that the real purpose of the attack was to destroy the American aircraft carriers and at least four of the battleships so that the American Pacific Fleet would be immobilized for at least six months.

The signal that surprise had been achieved and that the attack was to proceed according to plan was to be the words "Tora, Tora, Tora" (Tiger, Tiger, Tiger!) broadcast by the flight leader to his aircraft. Once that signal was made there would be no turning back.

The plan in its detail was explained to the 26 groups of pilots who would carry it out. The first attack would be launched 230 miles north of Oahu. The group would assemble and pass over the *Akagi*, then begin the flight to Pearl Harbor. First would be the leader. Then would come the horizontal bombers, each carrying a 2,000-pound bomb designed to penetrate the deck armor of the American battleships. On their right would be the torpedo bombers and on their left the dive bombers. The fighters would be 3,000 feet above the bombers for protection. The second wave would follow the same procedure but would launch when the carriers were 200 miles north of Oahu.

At dawn on November 26, the Japanese attack force sailed from Hitokappu Bay into the cold, foggy North Pacific. They were on their way, and there would be no turning back unless a miracle occurred in Washington, where the American and Japanese diplomats were sparring.

The next day, November 27, Admiral Kimmel at Pearl Harbor held a meeting with army and navy officers to discuss plans for defense. The question of a possible attack on Pearl Harbor came up.

"What do you think about the possibility of a Japanese air attack?" Admiral Kimmel asked Captain Charles E. McMorris, his fleet war plans officer.

"None. Absolutely none," said Captain McMorris.

Admiral Nagumo's strike force moved ever eastward, always on the alert for American aircraft and American submarines but seeing none. The ships sailed in close formation, training all the while, but relaxed nonetheless. The pilots played *go* and *shogi* every night, they laughed and joked, and they also prepared to die.

"They did not fear death," said Commander Fuchida, the leader of the flight to come. "Their only fear was that the attack might not be successful and that they would have to return to Japan with their mission unfulfilled."

The gloomiest man in the task force was easily Admiral Nagumo, who still did not like the operation and did not really seem to believe that it would succeed. He went around his ship with such a long face that staff officers asked his chief of staff to calm him down.

On November 30 the task force was traveling through heavy fog. They refueled in the afternoon and had a good deal of trouble. The task force moved forward at 14 knots, refueling every day to keep the ships topped off.

On December 1, back in Japan, Admiral Yamamoto prepared for an audience with Emperor Hirohito. At the palace, the war council met, and Prime Minister Tojo announced that the empire stood at the threshhold: It would be either glory or oblivion. The forces were in motion: Ships and men were heading for Pearl Harbor, Guam, the Philippines, Malaya, the Dutch East Indies, Thailand, Burma, and Timor. Pearl Harbor would be the first, but the other attacks would follow in order.

On December 3, Tokyo time, Admiral Yamamoto went to the Imperial Palace for his ritualistic audience. The emperor granted audience to the commander in chief of the navy on the eve of war, and this was it.

Aboard the admiral's flagship, Chief of Staff Ugaki had already opened the formal orders and sent the fatal message "Climb Mount Niitaka," which meant that the Pearl Harbor raid was on and that it could be stopped now only by a direct order from Admiral Yamamoto.

On December 4 the Japanese task force ran into heavy weather, so heavy that the usual daily refueling was canceled. On December 5 all the tankers but one left the force and moved toward the rendezvous point where they would wait for Nagumo's safe return.

"Goodby," signaled the *Toho Maru.* "We hope your brave mission will be honored with success."

The tension in the Japanese fleet had reached a critical point, and most tense of all was Admiral Nagumo.

On Saturday, December 6, the Japanese force fueled for the last time, and the last of the tankers left the fleet. The fleet forged on toward Oahu, the destroyers in the lead behind the light cruiser *Abukuma*, two battleships behind them, and behind this force the carriers, with destroyers covering their flanks. At 3:30 A.M., Hawaii time, the Japanese pilots began to stir restlessly. Some of them had not slept at all. Commander Fuchida, the leader of the air mission, dressed in red underwear and a red shirt—so that if he were wounded in the coming battle the blood would not show and demoralize his other pilots. They went to breakfast. The wardroom radio was tuned to a Honolulu radio station that was playing soft, pleasant music. The pilots assembled in their ready rooms aboard the carriers. Admiral Nagumo came down to talk to Commander Fuchida.

At 5:50 that morning the six carriers turned into the wind and headed east at 24 knots. The pilots walked to their planes, tying around their heads the special *hachimaki* (headbands) bearing the word *Hissho* (certain victory). Weather delayed the takeoff for a little while, but then the first Zero fighter moved off the deck of the *Ikaga*, and the others began to follow. Fifteen minutes later 185 planes of the first wave of attack were in the air. Only two fighters failed in the takeoff. One ditched (the pilot was rescued by a destroyer), and the other had to turn back with engine trouble. At 6:20 the group set course for Oahu.

Just before 7:00 A.M. on that Sunday of December 7, 1941, the American destroyer *Ward* shelled and destroyed one of the Japanese midget submarines that were trying to penetrate into Pearl Harbor. The sinking report was made to Pearl Harbor, but the Americans were psychologically so totally unprepared for war that the report was disbelieved; it did not trigger the immediate call to defense that it should have. Even Admiral Kimmel, who had the report, decided to "wait for verification."

Because of that caution, no one informed the army. At 7:00 A.M. the army's Opana Mobile Radar Station at Kahuku Point picked up a set of blips coming in from 132 miles to the northeast. The enlisted men manning the station reported to their information center, but the lieutenant on duty there was brand new, and he did not for a moment believe the planes could be anything but American. So he did nothing. The army did not notify the navy of the event.

At 7:03 A.M. the destroyer *Ward*'s Captain William W. Outerbridge supervised another attack on a submarine, a big one this time, and saw black oil rise to the surface after he had dropped depth charges. Once again his radio report brought no excitement.

Meanwhile the Japanese planes droned steadily on toward Pearl Harbor, detected but undisclosed.

At 7:50 Commander Fuchida was over Oahu; below and ahead down the valley he could see the American Pacific Fleet at anchor in Pearl Harbor. He gave the signal: "Tora Tora Tora" (Tiger, Tiger Tiger!).

The first American to *know* that Pearl Harbor was under attack was Rear Admiral William R. Furlong, commander of the service forces of the Pacific Fleet, who was up early and taking a walk on the quarterdeck of his flagship, the minelayer *Oglala*. He saw several planes overhead and saw one of them drop a bomb. His first reaction was anger at the carelessness of some American pilot, but then he saw the Rising Sun—"Red Meatball"—insignia as the plane turned, and he knew. He was the first man to react instantly:

"Japanese. Man your stations."

So the battle began.

The Japanese aviators had planned very well, with one minor error: The torpedo planes were supposed to strike first, but the leader of the dive bombers misunderstood a signal and went first.

Bombs began to rain on Pearl Harbor. One struck a hangar on Ford Island, and it began to burn. A torpedo struck the old battleship *Utah*, which immediately began to sink. Another hit the cruiser *Raleigh*, knocking out the electricity and causing her to list hard to port, with danger of capsizing.

Still another torpedo sped underneath the *Oglala* and struck the *Helena*, next to her, doing heavy damage to both ships. Another hit the battleship *Arizona*, and she began to sink. A bomb hit on the quarterdeck. Another blew up her magazines. Six torpedoes hit the battleship *West Virginia*, and then a bomb hit her.

Two bombs hit the repair ship *Vestal*. Three torpedoes slammed into the battleship *Oklahoma*, and then bombs, and she capsized. Two torpedoes struck the battleship *California*. Two Japanese bombs hit the battleship *Tennessee*. Bombs rained on the battleship *Nevada*.

Soon Zero fighters and dive bombers attacked the naval air station at Kaneohe, on the north shore of Oahu Island, and destroyed most of the PBY patrol planes kept there. Other planes smashed Hickham Field next to Pearl Harbor. Still others hit Wheeler Field, the army air base in the middle of the island.

The Americans fought back. Five torpedo planes from the carrier *Kaga* were shot down in the attack on battleship row, and other planes were lost in the attacks on Kaneohe and Hickham Fields. The only air field that was not attacked was the one at Haleiwa on the north shore.

The second wave of high-level horizontal bombers, many from *Shokaku* and *Zuikaku*, increased the damage, hitting hangars and ships. The battleship *Nevada* had managed to get underway, but in the second wave many bombs hit her. She grounded in the mud off Hospital Point. Had she not, she would have sunk. The second wave also sank the minelayer *Oglala* and grounded the repair ship *Vestal*. This second attack also went against the battleship *Pennsylvania*, which was in dry dock. She was damaged by two bombs. Other bombers destroyed the destroyers *Shaw, Cassin*, and *Downes*.

So the Pearl Harbor attack came to an end. The Japanese had lost 29 aircraft, one I-boat, and five midget submarines. Their air strike had made a shambles of Pearl Harbor, sinking or heavily damaging eight battleships, three light cruisers, three destroyers, and four auxiliary ships, and destroying nearly 200 aircraft and damaging another 150.

On the surface, the Japanese attack was a complete success, and the pilots went back to their ships congratulating one another. But there was one flaw: They had not found the U.S. aircraft carriers.

Some of the staff officers aboard the Japanese flagship wanted to complete the job, to destroy the dockyards, fuel supplies, the submarine base, and whatever ships remained, but Admiral Nagumo was too nervous to listen to them. He had done his job. He had struck Pearl Harbor, and no one could say that he had not won a victory. Those

American carriers, out there somewhere, worried him enormously. He had forgotten what he had been told by Admiral Yamamoto, that his task was to inflict maximum damage to the enemy and that he might be expected to lose a third of his force. Now, having lost none of his ships, he was thinking defensively.

Back in Japan, the Combined Fleet staff nearly all agreed that Nagumo should be ordered to make another attack. Admiral Yamamoto refused to overrule the man in the field, however, no matter how he felt about it personally. The problem, as the younger officers said openly, was sending a mouse to do the job of a lion, and that responsibility lay with Tokyo, not with the Combined Fleet.

Therefore, no search was made for the American carriers, although the *Enterprise* was at that moment within striking distance. And the submarine base and the oil storage facilities were not attacked. When Admiral Chester W. Nimitz arrived at Pearl Harbor at Christmas to take over, he was astounded to see that the Japanese had left so much undestroyed. "The fact that the Japanese did not return to Pearl Harbor and complete the job . . . left their principal enemy with time to catch his breath, restore his morale, and rebuild his forces," Nimitz said.

Above all, the precious American carriers remained unhurt.

The Lonely Ship

The first American aircraft carrier was the USS *Langley*, built in 1912 as a collier and converted to a carrier in 1918. By 1941, when the Pacific War began, she was so old and so outmoded that she was no longer used as a carrier but a seaplane tender. At that time she was stationed with other elements of the U.S. Asiatic Fleet in the Philippines, but not for long.

After Japanese carrier planes bombed Manila and wrecked the Cavite naval base, Admiral Thomas C. Hart, commander of the Asiatic Fleet, began sending his ships south to the Dutch East Indies, where they might have a better chance of survival and certainly could be of more use. The *Langley* was one of the first to go. In February she was sent down to Australia to pick up a load of P-40 fighter planes and deliver them to Burma to help with the defense. Thus the *Langley*, with only two-thirds of her old flight deck left and unable to launch aircraft any more, was again an ''aircraft carrier'' as she headed out of Fremantle on February 22, 1942, bound initially for Tjilatjap, Java, as part of a convoy protected by the cruiser USS *Phoenix.*

The *Langley* carried 30 P-40 fighter planes and 45 U.S. Army pilots and ground crewmen. But almost immediately she was detached from the convoy by orders of Vice Admiral Conrad Helfrich, the Dutch officer who had assumed command of defense operations in Java after the departure of Field Marshal Wavell, who was being moved to Africa, where he might have a chance of winning a fight instead of losing one.

The diversion was made because Admiral Helfrich was desperate for aircraft. The *Langley*'s skipper, Commander Robert P. McConnell, knew what a chance she was now taking. The old ship could make only 13 knots, and with only a handful of 3- and 5-inch guns she could hardly protect herself against enemy bombers. There was really very little alternative, though. The Allied forces in the Dutch East Indies were very much in disarray and totally overpowered by the Japanese.

The bombers were around, too, as Commander McConnell knew. The aircraft of Admiral Nagumo's four carriers of the air strike force had been sent south by Admiral Yamamoto to help in the conquest of the South Pacific. They had appeared on the morning of February 19 over Darwin, 188 carrier-based bombers, working with 54 land-based bombers. That day there were dozens of ships in Darwin Harbor. By the end of the day, the airfield was in ruins, the town was reeling from disaster, and 13 ships were sunk and nine damaged. The Darwin raid was of a piece with everything else the Japanese did these days, completely successful, even beyond the Japanese hopes.

Allied intelligence did not know where the Japanese carrier force was, but the report that McConnell had indicated it was operating somewhere around the waters through which he would have to pass. In fact, Nagumo and his carriers were on the move toward Ceylon to attack Colombo and the British naval base at Trincomalee, trying to repeat the Pearl Harbor performance and knock out the British East Asia Fleet.

At about 7:00 A.M. on February 27, the *Langley* was nearing Tjilatjap; she met the destroyers *Edsall* and *Whipple*, which were to escort her in. Overhead circled a pair of Dutch PBY patrol bombers, giving the officers and men of the *Langley* a comfortable feeling of being protected. At 9:00 A.M. an unidentified plane was sighted at high altitude. Commander McConnell knew that the plane had to be Japanese and that he could expect an air attack from land-based bombers within an hour or so.

Sure enough, at 11:40 the bombers came. The *Langley* crew went to general quarters, and the ship began zigzagging to try to confuse the enemy bombardiers. Nine planes came in. The 3-inch antiaircraft guns were manned, but their shells could not reach the bombers, which were flying at 30,000 feet. At least the popping of the 3-inch shells kept the bombers up there, and the *Langley*'s zigzagging kept them from dropping their bombs on the first two passes. On their third pass the Japanese scored five direct hits and three near misses on the old carrier. Fires seemed to break out everywhere. The P-40s on the flight deck began to burn. Men rushed to put out the flames, but the bombs had ruptured many of the water mains. The telephone system went out, and Commander McConnell had difficulty maintaining contact with the crew. The bilge pumps had been damaged, and water began flooding the engine room. Now a wave of six Japanese fighter planes came over to strafe the decks of the *Langley*. They destroyed more of the P-40 fighters but then turned away, apparently low on fuel.

Half an hour after the attack, the *Langley* was in serious trouble. She was listing 10 degrees to port, and water was 4 feet deep in the engine room. The ship had dropped in the water, and Commander McConnell could no longer negotiate the harbor at Tjilatjap because the *Langley* was lying too deep in the water for the shallow entrance. He decided to take the ship up the Java coast. The water in the engine room made it impossible. The engines quit, the propellers quit turning, and the ship coasted to a dead stop. Her list increased to 17 degrees. The ship was top-heavy with the weight of the fighter planes that were dogged down on the deck. Commander McConnell knew that she might capsize at any moment, so at 1:45 P.M. he ordered the men to abandon ship. Life rafts were lowered, and boats from the two destroyers came alongside to pick up swimmers. Soon almost all the men were off the ship. Commander McConnell had decided that he would follow the tradition of the sea and go down with his ship, so he stayed aboard. But his men in the boats below began to shout at him, and finally persuaded him to leave the sinking vessel.

Or *was* she sinking? Stubbornly, the *Langley* continued to float. Commander McConnell asked the skipper of the destroyer *Whipple* to sink her with a torpedo. The first torpedo hit aft of the crane in the magazine area of the starboard side, but the magazine did not explode. Instead the flooding caused by the hole in the side brought the ship back to an even keel. A second torpedo was fired into the port side amidships, and it caused a fire on the poop deck.

Torpedoes were in short supply in the American navy, so the skipper of the *Whipple* did not want to use more. Instead, the crew fired their 5-inch guns until they had put nine 5-inch shells into the *Langley* at the water line. Still she floated. The *Whipple* moved away then, leaving the *Langley* still afloat, burning, and very low in the water. It was obvious that she would soon sink. That evening a Dutch PBY pilot reported that he saw the ship sink.

The destroyers were ordered to rendezvous with other ships and put the *Langley* survivors aboard them, then return to duty at sea. Most of the survivors of the *Langley* and the army fliers were soon transferred to the tanker *Pecos*, which then headed for southern Australia, but the *Pecos* was attacked by Japanese bombers. Many of the *Langley* survivors were killed aboard this ship or thrown into the water when she sank. Once again the destroyer *Whipple* came up and picked as many men as possible out of the water. Then came the threat of a Japanese submarine, and rescue operations were suspended when 220 of the 666 men who had been aboard the *Pecos* were saved.

In the end, only 146 of the *Langley* crew of 439 officers and men survived. When Commander McConnell reached Fremantle, he wrote up a report of the events and sent it to Vice Admiral William Glassford, who had been second in command of the Asiatic Fleet and was now commander of U.S. naval forces in the Southwest Pacific. Admiral Glassford did not like what he read, and he sent the report on to Admiral King in Washington, with an endorsement that suggested that Commander McConnell had been derelict in his duty and that the *Langley* might have been saved. Admiral King could not see how it might have been done, however. The ship was obviously sinking when she was abandoned. To have remained aboard her or to have remained in the vicinity would have been to endanger the survivors aboard the destroyers *Whipple* and *Edsall*, as well as the crews of those two warships. Admiral King wrote that he quite disagreed with Admiral Glassford, and the case of the *Langley* was closed.

The Japanese Score
Once More

As Admiral Nagumo's strike force attacked Pearl Harbor, Vice Admiral William F. Halsey's U.S. Naval Task Force 8 was returning there from a mission of landing aircraft at Wake Island for defense against possible attack. As soon as Halsey was informed of events, his planes began searching for the enemy, but the decision of the Japanese to attack from the north had been prescient. As Nagumo retired at high speed to the north, the American planes were searching as far as 700 miles to the south, as were the planes of the *Lexington* task force. Rear Admiral Wilson Brown thought the Japanese "carrier" (only one!) had launched from a point 200 miles south of Oahu. The *Saratoga* task force was out of it, having just arrived at San Diego. The *Saratoga* loaded planes all night and sailed for Oahu on Monday morning.

Admiral Kimmel recalled Admiral Halsey's task force to Pearl Harbor for antisubmarine warfare. Admiral Brown headed toward Midway Island. Had he continued in that direction, and had Admiral Nagumo followed the suggestions—not outright orders—of Admiral Yamamoto, there would have been a carrier fight. The Combined Fleet Command had told Nagumo, once he headed home, to stop by Midway, which had just repelled a Japanese destroyer attack, and help in the assault on that island. Admiral Nagumo had begged off, however. Then he had been ordered to send planes to strike Wake Island. He dispatched the carriers *Soryu* and *Hiryu* for that purpose but took most of his ships resolutely home to Japan, bound to remain out of trouble and risk his strike force no further.

The American carrier task forces failed to get into action in this critical period just after Pearl Harbor for almost purely political reasons. Almost immediately after the Pearl Harbor attack and the failure to find the enemy carriers, Admiral Kimmel ordered the *Lexington* task force to raid Jaluit Island and then to defend Wake. He also ordered the *Saratoga* to Wake and was prepared to order Admiral Halsey's *Enterprise* to defend Wake as well when Halsey came into port. In fact, Kimmel's plan was for Halsey and Brown to find the enemy and fight him while the *Saratoga* force defended Wake.

Before this could be done, the American politicians intervened, Admiral Kimmel was relieved of command, and Vice Admiral W. S. Pye, who was given interim command, hesitated to risk the carriers (and his career) and so he did not. The defense of Wake Island was abandoned. The Japanese, who had been fought off by the defenders in the beginning, then managed to overwhelm the island garrison.

Thus through timidity at Pearl Harbor the Americans missed their first chance to strike the Japanese at Wake Island. They might not have found the carriers there, for the *Soryu* and the *Hiryu* had made a passing strike at Wake Island as ordered and then gone home. The Americans could have driven off the surface force of cruisers, destroyers, and transports that was attacking Wake, however. They could have sunk much of the force, saving Wake Island as an American base and, much more important, winning a victory badly needed for American home morale. Admiral Pye missed his single chance to achieve greatness.

That winter, the Americans fumbled in trying to learn how to make the best use of their carrier task forces. From Washington, Admiral Ernest King, commander in chief of the combined fleet, was demanding action, but he got precious little of it. To stop the Japanese drive in the South Pacific and to protect Australia, he wanted carrier raids on the islands of the South Pacific. All he effectively got from his task forces was a single raid on the Wotje, Maloelap, and Kwajalein atolls of the Japanese Marshall Islands bases, conducted by Halsey on January 31. Similar raids by Admirals Brown and Fletcher did not come off; they were just too timid. Halsey raided Wake Island again on February 24, and Marcus Island on March 4. These raids did little but irritate the victorious Japanese and did absolutely nothing to slow down their carrier activities.

In support of the Japanese army movements south in February and March, Admiral Nagumo was ordered out with the carriers once more, this time to raid Australia. He swooped down and, in a series of raids beginning March 8, hit Port Moresby on New Guinea, a prime target for Japanese invasion, and following the raid on Darwin also struck Derby, Broome, and Tulagi in the Southern Solomon islands. All this was a portent of things to come, for the Japanese had designs on all these places.

By April 1942, the Japanese army was moving like a juggernaut across southeast Asia and the Pacific much faster than anyone in Tokyo had dared hope. The British army in Malaya had been conquered and Singapore was Japanese. In the Philippines the Americans were reduced to the Bataan Peninsula and Corregidor, and a few guerillas were fighting in Mindanao. The Dutch East Indies were under Japanese siege. Only one Allied force in Asian waters continued to be a thorn in the Japanese side. This force was the British fleet in the Indian Ocean, now based, after the fall of Singapore, in Trincomalee on Ceylon Island. The force consisted of several battleships, cruisers, destroyers, and the light carrier HMS *Hermes*. Admiral Yamamoto decided that they ought to be eliminated as a major nuisance and so ordered Admiral Nagumo. Once he finished the strikes in the south in support of the Japanese army forces moving against the Bismarcks and New Guinea, Nagumo was to head into the Indian Ocean and destroy the British fleet and bases on Ceylon.

———

The aircraft carrier HMS *Hermes* had returned to the Indian Ocean early in 1941. She was engaged in convoy protection in those early days and was joined by the *Indomitable* in December, although the latter was mostly used to ferry aircraft.

Early in 1942 Admiral Sir James Somerville had three carriers and five battleships, plus cruisers and destroyers, in the Indian Ocean. The strength of the force is exaggerated by the figures; most of the ships were antiquated and no match for the new Japanese navy. Only the carrier *Indomitable* was large enough and well enough equipped to stand up to such ships as the *Kaga*. The third carrier was the *Formidable*. The *Indomitable* was by far the best of these ships, and its aircrews could manage night operations. It had nine Sea Hurricanes, 12 Fulmar fighters, and 25 Albacore torpedo bombers. The *Hermes* had only a dozen Swordfish aboard.

Admiral Somerville had one advantage in this matter: The Royal Navy maintained a secret base at Addu Atoll in the Maldive Islands, 500 miles southwest of Ceylon. Admiral Somerville was of the opinion that if he could avoid the superior Japanese carrier forces by day, he could beat them at night. When the crunch came, unfortunately, his two best carriers, the *Indomitable* and the *Formidable*, were at the secret base in Addu Atoll, and only the *Hermes* was near the official fleet base at Trincomalee.

On March 5 Admiral Nagumo's planes bombed Colombo. They sank the destroyer *Tenedos* and the auxiliary warship *Hector* and did some damage to the port facilities, although not nearly so much as they claimed. Then, cautiously as usual, Admiral Nagumo moved around to the other side of Ceylon for a strike on Trincomalee, the British naval base.

The British knew he was coming. At 5:00 P.M. on April 8, the *Hermes* and other elements of the British Eastern Fleet were lying in Trincomalee when they received orders from Admiral Somerville to get up steam, recall all libertymen, and head out to sea. They were to be 40 miles south of Trincomalee by dawn.

The other elements involved included the heavy cruisers *Cornwall* and *Dorsetshire* and several destroyers.

This order was going to take a little time to carry out. Captain R. Onslow of the *Hermes* announced that the ship would sail at 1:00 A.M. It would take that long to round up the men ashore and get ready for a fight.

The *Hermes* finally sailed out, guarded by a group of Fulmar fighters from the Ceylon air bases. At 5:30 A.M. she turned inshore to the 100-fathom line, then moved south in shallow (20-fathom) water at eight knots. That was good protection against surprise by enemy submarines, which hated anything inshore of the 100-fathom line. Next morning the fleet was in position by dawn. So was Admiral Nagumo's strike force, with five carriers not far away.

Admiral Somerville had also put to sea from Addu Atoll with the heavy elements of the fleet and the two newer carriers, looking for the Japanese fleet. Several of his scout planes made contact with the enemy fleet, but they were shot down before they could put out a fix on it, so Somerville was still groping that day. At 7:20 A.M. the men of the *Hermes* went to their action stations. A report had just been received of an air raid heading for Trincomalee. The Japanese struck the base, but again Admiral Nagumo was very nervous. They did not do much of a job of destruction, far less than they had managed at Pearl Harbor.

One of the Japanese float planes, scouting for the fleet, passed over the *Hermes* quite by accident. The pilot reported back that here was a single carrier alone except for two destroyer escorts, ripe for the picking. Indeed she was. Her aircraft had been flown off, and she had no combat air patrol.

On the bridge of the *Hermes* that morning, Captain Onslow consulted with his officers and decided to turn north at 9:00 A.M. and adjust speed to arrive back at Trincomalee at about 4:00 P.M. At 9:30 came the word from the flagship that the *Hermes* had been spotted by search planes from Admiral Nagumo's force and that the Japanese radio broadcasts indicated an attack was imminent. Fighter protection was being sent from Ratamalana, and Fulmars were coming from China Bay to help the carrier defend herself. In the lower conning tower Lieutenant D. G. Glen was getting ready for action as damage control officer. At 9:45 he had a message that they had been sighted by enemy planes and must expect attack.

At 10:25 A.M. the radiomen of the *Hermes* reported to the bridge that they could now hear the Japanese pilots conferring on their radios, fairly close. Lieutenant Commander E. W. Cholerton, the gunnery officer, told his men to load their guns with high explosive barrage shells and put on their antiflash gear and steel helmets. They waited, then, watching the sky for incoming aircraft. The weather was fine, the sky clear with a slight cloud cover and a light breeze scarcely disturbing the sea. It was a fine day for an air attack.

Lieutenant Commander E. K. A. Block, the navigator, on the bridge of the carrier, was taking a bearing on the Batticola Lighthouse, when he looked up and saw the red meatball insignia of Japanese aircraft turning out of the sun. It was 10:35 when the bridge reported:

"Enemy aircraft in sight bearing Green 140 degrees."

Commander P. H. F. Mitchell, the engineering officer, went down to the engine room when he heard the captain order full speed ahead. Lieutenant Commander Martin was down there. Everything was going very smoothly. Mitchell returned to his office to see if someone had sent down the antiflash helmet he had ordered. As he neared the door to the central stores flat, the first bomb hit. In a few seconds more bombs hit, the passage filled with smoke, and the lights went out. Seeing the dull glow of a fire ahead, Mitchell turned back. Even his flashlight did not help; he could see objects no farther than 3 inches from the bulb.

Commander Mitchell moved around and finally made his way out on the port battery deck. There he was trapped. The ship was down by the bows, and he could not go aft because steam was gushing out from the forward dynamo room. He stayed where he was until the order came to abandon ship, and then he went over the side. Another five bombs were dropped after he left the ship, the last one appearing to drop on the ready ammunition for the aft 4-inch gun.

As the Japanese planes came within range, the ship's antiaircraft guns—the 4-inch guns and the Oerlikons—began firing steadily. The ship was attacked by about 50 Japanese dive bombers. The first bomb was a hit on the flight deck. Then came another and another.

An hour later Mitchell heard the antiaircraft guns firing. Then came the explosion of bombs. The lights went out, came on, and went out again as the bombs continued to rain down. The telephone went out. The ship was turning violently as the captain tried to avoid the bombs.

"Half those bombs are near misses," Glen said to Commander Henstock.

Glen had a report that oil was leaking in the main telephone exchange. He went to investigate. Water was pouring in. Meanwhile more bombs were dropping. The bathrooms of the petty officers were flooded, so Glen had rooms on the other side of the ship also flooded to balance. More bombs came, and Glen's attempts to counterflood became impossible. The ship had a 20 degree list to port by this time.

Paymaster Lieutenant Peter Stent was in the cipher office on the second deck above the flight deck on the starboard side of the island. Three minutes after the first bomb hit, the lights went out and there was no more power. In the boiler room, Lieutenant F. W. Y. Batley saw the lights go out. The boiler room filled with smoke that made it impossible to observe the water level of the boilers, even after the Oldham lamps were rigged up. The ship listed to port but seemed to move all right until the two forward boilers began to lose pressure. Batley shut down those two boilers, leaving the two aft boilers working, and he tried unsuccessfully to get the main stop valves shut. He turned the work in the boiler room over to Chief Stoker Grant and went up over the grating and down into the boiler room *B*. On the way he had to turn back because a fire broke out, and the stokers were forced to evacuate. An explosion had fractured the oil and the steam pipes. Lieutenant Batley started back for boiler room *A* but discovered that the crew had been forced to evacuate here too when the steam went out of the other two boilers. With the boiler rooms out of action, it was inevitable that the ship was going to sink. Batley and the others went on deck. Commander Cholerton saw three planes diving toward the ship from high on the port bow. They were single-engine planes with fixed landing gear, coming down at an angle of about 65 degrees. The ship's Action Report continues:

"I saw them release one bomb each—simultaneously, it seemed," said Commander Cholerton, "and it hardly seemed possible for them to miss hitting us."

By now the ship seemed very slow and sluggish as the result of the first attack. More attacks were made at regular intervals, from all angles, and I noticed that some of the planes were twin-engined monoplanes with retractable undergear. And they were firing machine guns or cannon from each wing tip. After about three minutes the Vickers machine gun situated on the platform of the forward side of the top, and manned by Marines Youdall and Loxton, was rendered useless by a violent explosion from the forward lift well, and I ordered the crew to leave their post and take shelter inside the top. Looking over the flight deck I saw that the forward lift had been blown completely out and was lying upside down on the deck.

The shocks to the ship were steady and dreadful. Commander Cholerton expected the whole top to come tumbling down, especially the homing beacon on the very top. The bombs continued to fall, until the ship was struck by at least 40 bombs, with perhaps an equal number or more near misses that did their own damage. The bombing was very accurate. "There was nothing in the nature of a wide miss," said Lieutenant Commander Block.

Commander Cholerton saw his ship listing 40 degrees, and he knew she could not stay afloat much longer. He tried to get in touch with the bridge, but the telephones were dead. He saw many men swimming away from the ship, so he leaned out of the top and saw Lieutenant Creed on the bridge and shouted to him, asking if "abandon ship" had been ordered.

"Yes, bring your chaps down," said Lieutenant Creed. So Lieutenant Commander Cholerton urged his men down the mast ladder.

When Lieutenant Stent was sure the ship was sinking, he made sure all the ciphers and secret messages were locked in the steel chest in the cabin and the key was removed. With the key in his pocket, he abandoned ship, just five minutes before she sank.

Lieutenant Batley and the other men of the black gang got out. Everyone in the boiler rooms was saved except two men in boiler room A: a water tender who was killed by the explosion that wrecked the boiler, and a stoker who tried to escape through the port passage instead of using the escape ladder.

Captain Onslow moved into the armored shelter on the bridge and conned the ship by voice pipe. He stayed until the ship's engines stopped, and she was dead in the water. Captain Onslow hoped that the damage control parties below (with whom he had lost contact) could somehow right the ship and that the engineers could restore power, but it was a forlorn hope. The *Hermes* was listing heavily to port, with her flight deck awash. Lieutenant Commander Block then suggested that it was time to abandon ship, and the captain came out of his command post and agreed. The word was passed just in time. The ship was going fast even though the 4-inch guns were still firing on the side opposite the water. Lieutenant Commander Block moved down to the chart house level below the compass platform, and then stepped off into the water.

When the order came to abandon ship, Lieutenant Glen went down to the flight deck through the escape hatch. The port side of the flight deck was already in the water and had a great patch of oil on it. He realized that if the port battery was under water, the engine rooms, boiler rooms, port passages and flats and wardroom must be flooded, so he ran down the flight deck and swam off, away from the ship.

Glen turned and looked back just as five more bombs hit the ship on the port side and she turned up with the flight deck almost vertical. She was still moving ahead and the stern was swinging toward him, so he swam away. Then he heard an enormous explosion in the stern, and the ship sank.

Commander Cholerton heard two more explosions on the starboard side, and he could feel the mast moving to port as he climbed down.

"Move quickly, lads," he shouted, "or you won't get out of this."

So the ladder was cleared and the commander had time to swing across to the starboard side as the ship went down at 10:55 A.M. with a roar. As she went down he could hear one 4-inch gun still firing, a gun manned by A. B. Page, who was never seen again.

When Commander Cholerton next remembered, he was in the sea alone. He swam to a piece of wood and clung to that, and then swam to a Carley float. Others reached it, too. They paddled around, picking up other survivors, and sticking close to other rafts. Surgeon Lieutenant J. A. Smart swam from raft to raft, administering morphia to wounded men and treating others when he could, until they were picked up by the hospital ship *Vita* at 1:15 P.M. The *Vita* also picked up Lieutenant Commander Block at this time. He was in the water for about three hours before he was rescued.

One of the other people picked up was Lieutenant Stent. He stood on the deck of the *Vita* and threw into the sea his key to the cipher box of the *Hermes*, to join that once proud ship down below, and also her captain. In the old tradition of the sea, Captain Onslow went down with his ship that sad day.

7

The Japanese Tide Slackens

Until May 1942, there seemed to be no stopping the Japanese anywhere. The war went so rapidly in the Dutch East Indies that the Japanese had difficulty putting together prison and internment camps and finding men to man them. They moved into New Guinea, and had plans to capture Port Moresby, to move on to Samoa and other islands in the south, and ultimately to attack Australia. Why not? Who was to stop them? The British had not in Malaya. The Americans had not in the Philippines. The Dutch had not in the East Indies. Imperial General Headquarters, first incredulous at the ease of the military victories, began to believe its own propaganda: The Japanese army and navy were invincible. The westerners were totally inferior to them.

One of the few level heads was that of Admiral Yamamoto. Like others, he listened to the broadcasts from Tokyo, but he shook his head at the exaggerations of the propagandists. Every time any sort of victory was won at sea, Radio Tokyo played the ''Battleship March.'' Yamamoto grew sick of hearing it and predicted that this sort of behavior would hasten the downfall of Japan. But of course he did not say this openly. By this time no one could, not even Yamamoto.

Meanwhile, Admiral King in Washington was urging action to slow down the Japanese juggernaut. All he had gotten so far were the Halsey raids on the Marshalls and a little-publicized but very successful raid by Admiral Wilson Brown on Lae and Salamaua in New Guinea after the Japanese landed there. The American planes came in over the

Owen Stanley Mountains and caught the Japanese by surprise, sinking a minesweeper, a transport, and a converted light cruiser.

The next thing King got was a grandstand play suggested by one of his staff and some army officers. Thus was born the Doolittle raid, in which 25 B-25 medium army bombers would be rigged to take off from a carrier and bomb Japan. It was to be an act of retaliation for Pearl Harbor and a morale builder for the American people, who so far had seen nothing but defeat.

On April 8, as Admiral Nagumo was moving around the Indian Ocean, Admiral Halsey departed from Pearl Harbor with Task Force 16, which included the carriers *Enterprise* and *Hornet*. The B-25s were aboard the *Hornet*. The planes took off on April 18 and made their raid. They did virtually no damage, except to surprise the Japanese and warn them that their islands could be bombed no matter what promises General Tojo made. But every single plane was lost, as Admiral Nimitz's chief of staff, Admiral Draemel, had predicted at Pearl Harbor, and several crews were captured and either executed by the Japanese or imprisoned. There was an even greater disaster, unknown to the Americans at large. When Chiang Kai-shek had been told, not consulted, about the coming raid, he had objected. It would only force the Japanese to terrible excesses against the Chinese people for harboring the Americans who would land there, he said. And he was absolutely right. After the Doolittle raid, the Japanese launched a suppression campaign in Chekiang Province and farther west. In the occupied territory every village where the Japanese believed the Chinese had harbored the Americans was razed. A number of airfields in Free China were attacked and destroyed. Because of this grandstand raid, 250,000 Chinese lost their lives. In the end, even Admirals Nimitz and Halsey, who had favored the Doolittle raid in the beginning, recognized that it had accomplished virtually nothing in a military sense and had tied up for weeks two carriers, four cruisers, eight destroyers, and two oilers and had put the two carriers quite needlessly at risk. They did not even know how near the danger had come, either, because as the Halsey fleet was moving toward Japan, so was Admiral Nagumo, on his way back from the Trincomalee raid. It was fortunate for Halsey that their paths did not cross. The decks of one of his carriers crammed with B-25s, wingtip to wingtip, would have made a prime target.

That spring of 1942, Admirals King and Nimitz, meeting in San Francisco, agreed that there was something to be learned from the Japanese method of using carriers and that in the future the American carriers would operate in pairs whenever possible. It was a difficult decision because the Japanese had more carriers than did the Americans, and the Americans were now engaged in a two-front war, with the emphasis on the campaign against Hitler in Europe. Fortunately, the British navy did not feel the need for American assistance in the Mediterranean, so American carriers were not required there, and fleet carriers, as had been proved already, were not right for convoy work.

That spring Admiral King was counseling aggression to the Pacific Fleet. He made quite certain that the carrier task force commanders understood they were supposed to put their ships at risk. Admiral Wilson Brown, who was very conservative, was removed from command of a task force and sent to command the amphibious training program at San Diego. He was replaced by Rear Admiral Aubrey W. Fitch, who was a pilot. Fitch was given command of the *Lexington* carrier task force, and was told to operate in conjunction with Vice Admiral Frank Jack Fletcher, in the *Yorktown* task force, in the South Pacific.

They were hurried south because the Americans had become aware of a new Japanese drive, this one against Port Moresby, New Guinea, and Tulagi, a little island in the southern Solomons, across the strait from Guadalcanal. If the Japanese succeeded, they would hold all of New Guinea, and they would be able to move against Australia, Samoa, and New Caledonia. Admiral Nimitz had been ordered by Admiral King to do everything possible to break up this occupation.

Admiral Fletcher had been down in the South Pacific since early March, accomplishing virtually nothing because he was so afraid of risking his carrier. King was not very high on this performance, but Admiral Nimitz, who knew that he had no one in the command with the necessary experience to replace Fletcher, argued for Fletcher's retention, and glumly Admiral King agreed for the moment. That agreement meant that Admiral Fletcher would be in command of any action in the South Pacific as senior officer present.

King would very much have liked to have Fletcher attack the Japanese main base at Rabaul, from which the operations at Lae and Salamaua were supplied, but Fletcher was not ready. He did not want to lose the element of surprise, which he felt was everything in carrier warfare. His timidity was the result of a basic distrust of the carrier as a weapon.

Admiral Fletcher received a report that the Japanese were moving south from Rabaul, and he said he would attack the Shortland Islands. As he came up he found the Japanese ships that had been reported there were gone, so he did nothing. The fact was that the Japanese had come and established a seaplane base in the Shortlands and then gone. This was true all over the area; the Japanese were establishing bases to augment their big center at Rabaul and to prepare for the drive south. The American carrier force was in the area, but it did nothing to stop the Japanese.

April passed, and still Admiral Fletcher had not moved in the South Pacific. The Japanese were moving, though. They were deeply involved in Operation Mo, the plan for the capture of Port Moresby and the establishment of the seaplane base at Tulagi. Vice Admiral Shigeyoshi Inouye was in charge of this operation, which involved a force of transports carrying troops and supplies to Port Moresby, another force carrying the same to Tulagi, and a protective fleet of carriers and cruisers. Admiral Aritomo Goto commanded one force, built around the light carrier *Shoho*. It consisted of four heavy cruisers and one destroyer. Vice Admiral Takeo Takagi commanded another carrier division consisting of the fleet carriers *Shokaku* and *Zuikaku*, two heavy cruisers, and six destroyers.

As the forces assembled, then, the Japanese had three carriers in the South Pacific and the Americans had two.

On April 30, the Japanese naval units set out, some from Rabaul and some from Truk, the major Japanese naval base in the area, sometimes called the Gibraltar of the Pacific. The invasion of Tulagi would come first, and then the capture of Port Moresby.

With the information that the Japanese were on the move, the Australians withdrew their small garrison from Tulagi, which was the headquarters of the Australian protectorate over the Solomons. On May 3 the Japanese landed there, the transports protected by a handful of warships. There was not the slightest opposition. It was the sort of capture the Japanese were now becoming used to. Six seaplanes were brought in and moored in the protected harbor. Construction troops unloaded their equipment and prepared to build barracks and a base.

Seeing that there was no opposition of any sort, the Japanese ships unloaded and then headed away from the shore and sought the comfort of deep water. There remained the cruiser *Okinoshima*, Admiral Shima's flagship, and two destroyers, five transports, and a number of gunboats and small craft. The admiral would supervise the construction of the seaplane base.

Word of the successful landings was sent to Rabaul and to Truk. The carriers *Zuikaku* and *Shokaku* had ferried deckloads of aircraft down from Truk to the Rabaul vicinity. They flew off these planes and got their own aircraft ready for operations.

Up north at Rabaul on New Britain Island, the invasion force for Port Moresby sailed that day, 11 transports full of men and supplies, protected by six destroyers. Also, showing that the Japanese meant business about establishing a base there, along came a number of minesweepers, two oilers, a repair ship, and a minelayer. A seaplane carrier brought up seaplanes for the base that would be established, thus giving the Japanese "eyes" to watch over Australia.

Offshore lay the protective force for the Port Moresby operation, the light carrier *Shoho*, and four cruisers. Admiral Inouye expected to have a naval fight before the Port Moresby operation was completed. He expected also to catch the Allied forces in a pincers between planes of his light carrier *Shoho* and the two fleet carriers *Zuikaku* and *Shokaku*. Furthermore, the 11th Air Fleet at Rabaul would support the admiral's forces with land-based fighters and bombers.

Had the Americans not sent Admiral Halsey off on the spectacular Doolittle Tokyo raid in April, the carriers *Hornet* and *Enterprise* would also have been available for the interdiction of the new Japanese attack. That would have given the Americans four carriers to the Japanese three. By the time Halsey reported in at Pearl Harbor late in April, however, it was too late. Halsey was ordered to sail on April 30 for the South Pacific to take over command and stop the Japanese, but Admiral Nimitz was sure Halsey could not arrive there in time. The battle would have to be fought with the forces at hand: the *Lexington* and the *Yorktown*, plus whatever surface forces the Australians could raise. These included several cruisers. The Americans also had the destroyer *Perkins* and the cruiser *Chicago* in the area.

On May 1, under Admiral Nimitz's orders, Admiral Frank Jack Fletcher's task force was to meet Admiral Fitch's force, and they were to operate together in the Coral Sea. They did meet and, as usual, Admiral Fletcher's first thought was to fuel. He began what he thought would be a four-day process. On May 2 General MacArthur's intelligence officers learned from the Australians that the Japanese were moving on Tulagi, and Fletcher broke off and headed to sea. On May 3, as the Japanese walked ashore on the sandy beach at Tulagi and set up camp, Admiral Fletcher was in the middle of the Coral Sea, fueling again. After he had finished he sent the tanker *Neosho* to a rendezvous point, where he planned to meet Admiral Fitch. It was at sea, 300 miles south of Guadalcanal Island, and Admiral Fitch was headed that way. Fletcher, meanwhile, had a report from Australia that the Japanese had landed at Tulagi. He set course for Guadalcanal at a speed of 23 knots. Soon the weather began to rough up. At 10 minutes before sunrise on May 4, 1942, the *Yorktown* began to launch the six fighter planes of the combat air patrol that would protect the carrier and its accompanying ships from air attack for the next few hours.

After that came the scouting force, 28 dive bombers, in two sections. The bombers were armed with 1,000-pound bombs. Behind them came 12 torpedo bombers, each carrying a torpedo. There were no fighters to accompany them. Recently a directive had been issued about the deficiencies of the fighter gas tanks in combat conditions. They were supposed to seal themselves against damage, but they were not working properly. So Admiral Fletcher kept the fighters back to be near the carriers, alternate as combat air patrol, and stay out of trouble at long distance.

As the sun came up, the planes were heading toward the Solomon Islands to attack Tulagi and any enemy ships they found there. They moved along at 17,000 feet through a succession of squalls.

Lieutenant Commander W. O. Burch was leading the first element of 13 dive bombers as they approached Tulagi. Down below in the sunlight, he could see the Japanese flotilla. The dive bombers were now at 19,000 feet. They nosed over and at 10,000 feet went into their steep bombing run of 70 degrees. At 2,500 feet the pilots pulled back their joysticks and bombed. Below, the Japanese antiaircraft gunners on the destroyers and other ships began firing. None of the American planes was hit. All the dive bombers dropped their bombs. Commander Burch circled and then headed back for the *Yorktown* to report four bomb hits on ships and one probable hit.

The second wave of attacking American planes was the 12 torpedo bombers led by Lieutenant Commander Joseph Taylor. He was an experienced pilot even though the war was new; he had led the torpedo planes in the successful attack on Lae a few weeks earlier. The torpedo bombers came down to within 50 feet of the water, waiting until they were 500 yards from the enemy ships before releasing their torpedoes.

Two of the torpedoes missed and blew up on the beach. Two planes attacked a transport. One pilot attacked a ship but forgot to turn on the release switch and thus did not drop his torpedo. Six torpedoes struck the minesweepers *Toshi Maru* and *Tama Maru* and the destroyer *Kikuzuki*. The minesweepers sank, and the *Kikuzuki* was damaged so badly that her captain beached her. The American torpedo bombers then headed back to their ship.

Then down came Lieutenant W. C. Short and the other 15 *Yorktown* dive bombers. They bombed though not very effectively. After bombing they strafed the Japanese float planes in the water. One pilot had swum out to his seaplane, bent on getting into the air and challenging the invaders. He started the engine, revved up, and was speeding across the water for takeoff when the strafers came in. They caught the seaplane just as she lifted off the water, hitting the pilot; the plane crashed into the bay.

An hour later the planes of the strike force landed aboard *Yorktown*; they were gassed, rearmed, and ready to take off again. On this second strike, Lieutenant Commander Burch found that the Japanese were now moving around like hornets whose nest had been attacked. The transport was steaming out of the harbor, bound for Rabaul. One destroyer was in motion, as were several of the smaller ships. Several of the seaplanes were in the air, and one of them challenged the Americans. He was soon shot down. Another seaplane was chased to Makambo Island where it landed safely, as the American planes were driven off by antiaircraft fire. This second attack did little damage. The Japanese gunners had recovered from their shock, and their fire was much more accurate. Several bombers were damaged, and one torpedo bomber pilot got lost on the way back to the *Yorktown*. His radio receiver was not working. The carrier could hear him transmitting, asking for information, but he could not hear the answers. So he ran out of gas and ditched the plane somewhere in the Coral Sea. Pilot and gunner were lost.

Another scouting mission, northeast of Florida Island, found some of the gunboats that were fleeing Tulagi, and attacked them, sinking three.

Admiral Fletcher launched four fighters this time to accompany the bombers and attack the seaplanes. They found three planes in the air over Tulagi and shot down all of them. On the way back two of the fighter planes got lost and landed on the south coast of Guadalcanal Island. The planes were not recoverable, but the pilots waved from the beach, and that night the destroyer *Hammann* was sent to pick up the downed aviators.

Another strike was made on Tulagi later in the afternoon. The American planes sank a few barges, but they did not damage the cruiser or the remaining destroyer. Still the pilots thought they had sunk a large number of ships, and that night in the wardroom of the *Yorktown* they were very jolly. It was a pleasant change to be talking about victory after the series of humiliating defeats the western forces had suffered at the hands of the Japanese.

That night Admiral Fletcher headed for the rendezvous point 300 miles south of Guadalcanal. The destroyer *Hammann* showed up in the morning with the two planeless pilots. The destroyer *Perkins* showed up, too, having searched all night for the downed torpedo plane but having found nothing at all.

Vice Admiral Takeo Takagi, in command of the Japanese carrier strike force of 11 ships, steamed toward the area where he thought the American planes had originated. In the morning he reached a point 100 miles south of Santa Isabel Island but found no American carriers. He took a look at Tulagi but saw only the beached destroyer and wreckage of smaller vessels. The Tulagi force had been disbanded, and all the surviving ships had left. There would be no seaplane base at Tulagi just now.

Admiral Takagi's search planes from the *Zuikaku* and the *Shokaku* then spent the rest of the day combing the sea around the Solomons, trying to find the American joint task force, but they were too far to the south for him. One search plane, a four-engine Kawanishi flying boat, did actually spot the American carriers. Undoubtedly the pilot and crew radioed the carriers' position to the Japanese, but they were then attacked by the combat air patrol and shot down. The message went back to the 25th Air Flotilla at Rabaul, but it did not reach Admiral Takagi that day.

Admiral Inouye's 28-ship Port Moresby invasion force was at sea, heading for New Guinea. The planes of the light carrier *Shoho* made several attacks on Port Moresby that day to soften it up. In response, land-based bombers from Australia twice attacked the convoy but were driven away by the combat air patrol. That night of May 5, the invasion force anchored at the Shortlands and fueled.

South of Guadalcanal, the American ships were also fueling. That night, figuring that the Japanese would head south from Rabaul, Admiral Fletcher headed north, but Admiral Takagi's ships, after searching all day, headed south around the Solomons, so that American and Japanese forces traveled on converging courses.

At 8:00 A.M. on May 6 a Japanese Kawanishi flying boat spotted the American carrier force about 400 miles south of Tulagi. Admiral Takagi then changed course and headed south. It was his intention to get on the far side of the Americans with the carriers *Shokaku* and *Zuikaku*, and then to catch the Americans in a pincers between those ships and the light carrier *Shoho* up north with the Port Moresby invasion force.

Now came a change in the Japanese plan. The Port Moresby invasion force was ordered to stay out of the way while the two Japanese carrier forces defeated the American enemy. The carrier *Shoho* and the seaplane carrier *Kamikawa Maru* sailed for DeBoyne Island near New Guinea.

On the night of May 6 the Americans and the Japanese were both itching for action. Admiral Fletcher sent the tanker *Neosho* to a new rendezvous point down south, out of the way of the coming action. It was accompanied by the destroyer *Sims*.

At 7:30 A.M. on May 7, Japanese search planes from one of the carriers radioed back that they had found the American task force. Below them were a carrier and a cruiser, they reported. Pilots were not always good at identifying the ships they saw below them; the American pilots had misidentified most of the ships at Tulagi. Beside the difficulties of seeing the surface clearly from altitude, the fliers of both sides suffered from their own eagerness to find something big. Thus the Japanese pilots from the carriers identified the two ships below—the tanker *Neosho* and the destroyer *Sims*—as "an aircraft carrier and a cruiser." Admiral Hara, commander of the carrier division, sent his strike force to hit the two warships. After repeated attacks, they sank the *Sims* and left the *Neosho* dead in the water, her radio gone, unable to communicate her plight and the condition of her crew. (She was not discovered until May 11, when the 109 survivors of the *Neosho* and the 14 survivors of the destroyer *Sims* were finally rescued.)

As usual, at dawn the combat air patrol of the light carrier *Shoho* had gone aloft to move out over the ships of the Port Moresby invasion force and provide an air umbrella for them. But at 6:30 that morning the cruiser *Aoba* reported that the American carrier task force was only 140 miles away from the *Shoho*, so her planes were called back from the Port Moresby convoy. They refueled and reloaded and prepared to take off and strike the enemy. Three fighter planes were launched over the carrier to provide its own combat air patrol.

Just before 7:00 A.M. the *Yorktown* launched its own search planes, and soon they were reporting ships. But the trouble was that the carriers and destroyers and cruisers they reported just did not exist at the spots they were supposed to occupy. The search failed, though not entirely. The locations were wrong, but the airmen had seen something: Admiral Marumo's little force of two old light cruisers, a seaplane carrier, and three converted gunboats that were a part of the Port Moresby invasion force. At 9:25 A.M. the *Lexington* launched an air strike. Ten fighter planes, 28 dive bombers, and 12 torpedo bombers went out to find and destroy the enemy.

Commander W. B. Ault was leading the *Lexington* planes. After he passed Tagula Island in the Louisiades, he began looking down ever more carefully. Then one of his pilots spotted a carrier, two cruisers, and several destroyers off to starboard. That was an accurate report. The force was the *Shoho* unit.

The Americans attacked coming down from 15,000 feet. As they nosed over, their planes were spotted by Captain Izawa of the *Shoho*, and he moved to take evasive action. Now, for the first time, the American pilots also met the Japanese Zero, that incredibly fast, slippery fighter plane. One Zero shot down the plane of the executive officer of the scouting squadron, one of Ault's wingmates. Ault and his other wingmate came hurtling down and dropped two bombs. One struck so close to the *Shoho* that it knocked five planes off the flight deck.

Captain Izawa turned the carrier into the wind and prepared to launch three fighter planes. The Americans attacked from the starboard side. One American plane was damaged by antiaircraft fire and had to pull out of the fight and head for Rossel Island in the Louisiades, where, it was hoped, the pilot could land or bail out and be rescued. The others—the fighters, torpedo planes, and dive bombers—all rushed in to attack. Soon they were joined by the planes of the *Yorktown*: 24 bombers, 10 torpedo bombers, and 8 fighter planes.

Captain Izawa held his ship steady as his three fighter planes were launched. Then, when they had cleared the decks, he prepared to turn and continue his evasive action. By then, however, the torpedo planes of the *Lexington* were attacking, and two torpedo wakes appeared off to starboard. The captain ordered the helm pushed hard to starboard: The ship turned, and the torpedoes missed. Izawa had not counted on the extra forces from *Yorktown*, however, and they were now on him. Two bombs struck the rear elevator of the *Shoho*'s flight deck and smashed it. Fires started on the hangar deck where the gasoline was stored and began moving toward the torpedo storage room. Then at least three torpedos struck the stern on the starboard side of the *Shoho*, knocking out the ship's electrical system and wrecking the steering. More bombs, more torpedoes.

Up above, the American and Japanese pilots were discovering one another and the performances of their aircraft. The Japanese Zero and its floatplane counterpart were remarkably agile and fast. The pilots were very skillful. The American planes were much slower, and the fighter planes had a hard time trying to turn with the Zeros. The Americans discovered one important fact that day: The Japanese Zero was very vulnerable. There was no armor for the back of the pilot's seat; a burst in the back would kill the pilot. There was no armor or self-sealing factor for the Japanese gasoline tanks; a few shots in the tanks and they would blaze. The Japanese discovered that they could outmaneuver the enemy but that the Americans were hard to shoot down because their planes were armored and their gas tanks did not burn easily. The battle went round and round and round.

———

Down below, the *Shoho* was dying. Bombs and torpedoes had turned her into a mess of smoking and burning wreckage. She was dead in the water, her communications were out, and the water mains were burst so that the damage control teams could not fight the fires effectively. Ten minutes after the attack began, the American planes photographed the scene. The photos showed only the bow of the vessel; behind, the rest of the ship was a mass of smoke and flame.

Thirty minutes after the attack began, water had risen to the gun deck, and the *Shoho* was sinking. She was so obviously destroyed that *Yorktown* pilots began looking for other targets to attack.

When the *Yorktown* torpedo pilots came in and dropped their torpedoes, and these slammed into the side of the *Shoho*, Captain Izawa ordered the ship abandoned. She went down very quickly, carrying 631 members of her crew. Only 132 men lived to fight again, and many of the dead were valuable air crew members. The destroyer *Sazanami* came along into the debris and began picking up survivors.

———

The Americans had lost several fighters and bombers, at least one bomber through the pilot's lack of common sense. He had tried to engage a Zero fighter in single combat with his heavy dive bomber, and the result was what had to be expected.

The Americans headed home, jubilant at having sunk a carrier. They thought it was one of the big ones, of course.

"Scratch one flattop," shouted one pilot into his radio, as he turned toward the *Lexington*.

Back in the carrier fleet, Admiral Fletcher and Admiral Fitch were too concerned to be much amused. They knew that the battle had not really begun yet: Somewhere out there were two of the newest

Japanese fleet carriers and their planes, and the Americans did not know where.

Not so far away, Admiral Takagi now had a very good picture of the American position, particularly following the reports from the *Shoho* as she came under attack. He decided to launch planes in mid-afternoon so they would reach the American ships at sundown when they would be least watchful and most vulnerable. The planes headed for the area about 150 miles southeast of the Louisiades. Although the Japanese intelligence was accurate, the weather intervened. The day had become heavily overcast, and then it was 90 percent overcast, and consequently, the Japanese planes flew right by the American carrier force and missed it in the clouds. The American radar picked up the Japanese planes when they were just 18 miles away. They launched more planes, attacked a group of nine Japanese fighters, and shot down all nine of them, with a loss of two planes of their own. They had discovered an effective tactic against the Zero: hit and run. That way their superior diving capacity and armor came into full play.

That was almost the end of the battle for the day but not quite. As darkness was falling, the ships around the American carriers suddenly began firing their antiaircraft guns. Up above were a number of Japanese aircraft of the strike force—trying to land on the American carriers in the mistaken notion that these were their own ships. The whole fleet began firing, and the Japanese planes turned and ran. Later that night the American radar picked up little blips surrounding a big blip. Admiral Fitch concluded that this was the Japanese force, and he passed the word to Admiral Fletcher. Here Admiral Fletcher missed a chance to win the battle. He could have ordered a night attack. Although the Japanese were within range, they did not know it, for they did not have radar. The surprise might have been complete. In assessing Fletcher's failure, the critic must remember that at this stage of the war the night battle was a relatively new concept in the American fleet. On the other hand, the Japanese, particularly the destroyermen, were very skillful at night fighting. Admiral Fletcher dismissed the idea almost immediately. To be sure a night attack would have been very risky, but all war is risk—a fact that several of the American admirals of the early war months seemed to be unable to cope with.

Admiral Fletcher should not be criticized any more than Admiral

Inouye, who also knew the Americans were close, but who decided against ordering a night battle. His reason was partly that he was not quite sure where the Americans were, and Admiral Koso Abe, commander of the Port Moresby attack transports, asked that the carriers move in and protect his ships. Admiral Inouye considered the matter. The mission was to take Port Moresby, he decided, not to destroy the American carrier force. (Here he would have had an argument from Admiral Yamamoto, who held that until the American carrier force was destroyed, the whole Japanese war effort was at risk.) Inouye was the man in the field, however, and he made the decision. So, because of the conservatism of one American admiral and one Japanese admiral a night battle was avoided. The Japanese moved off to the north, not to the west, and Admiral Fletcher headed to the southeast to wait for morning.

———

On the morning of May 8 the planes of the U.S. carrier *Lexington* were ordered to search for the Japanese force. Admiral Fletcher, who was most unsure of himself as to carrier strategy and tactics, had already decided to give tactical command of operations to Admiral Fitch, the airman.

Four hours of the night had gone by without radar contact. The Japanese could be anywhere. Admiral Fitch launched a 360-degree search, each plane taking a pie-shaped wedge of the circle and covering it at the outer edge. They were in the air by dawn, and for two hours nothing happened. Then Lieutenant Joseph Smith saw something below him, took another look, and reported excitedly to the *Lexington* that he was flying over a Japanese force that included two carriers, four cruisers, and three destroyers. The force was about 120 miles northeast of the American carriers.

At just about the same time, a Japanese search plane sent out by Admiral Takagi discovered the American carrier force. So much for Admiral Fletcher's theory that surprise was everything in carrier warfare. There was no surprise this day. The forces were evenly matched, two fleet carriers against two fleet carriers. Now the battle would be decided by skill and nature. Yes, nature would take a hand, and it favored the Japanese. They had the luck of weather this day: Their ships were in the cover of a cold front, which meant plenty of clouds.

The Americans were in an area of a meteorological high, steaming along in bright sunshine.

Still, daring would have as much to do with this battle as the luck of the weather. Admiral Hara got the jump by taking the risk of launching a strike force at the same time he sent out the search planes. It was an enormous risk: If the search planes did not find the American carriers, then the Japanese strike force effort would have been wasted; some, even many, of the planes might be lost; and when they returned to the carrier without fuel they would have to be serviced before they could fly again. That might mean a deck immobilized with parked and landing aircraft when the enemy found them and attacked.

Aboard the two American carriers the pilots rushed to their ready rooms for briefing. Deck crews began warming up the engines of the fighters and bombers. At 8:38 A.M. Admiral Fitch ordered a general attack from both ships.

Above the Japanese task force, Commander Robert Dixon took over the watch and circled around in the cloud cover, keeping an eye on the Japanese ships and radioing back to the *Lexington*. The Japanese combat air patrol soon discovered his presence and began chasing him. He ducked into a cloud and then into another. For two hours Dixon played tag with the Japanese Zero fighters. His gunner was tracking the Japanese as they came in firing on them when they came within range. Then Dixon would zoom off to make another pass.

The planes of the *Yorktown* were the first to launch. At 9:24 24 dive bombers, 6 fighters, and 9 torpedo bombers took off. Shortly after 9:30 *Lexington*'s 24 dive bombers, 10 fighters, and 12 torpedo planes began taking off, too.

Even as the American planes headed out from their carriers, the task force was preparing to fight off a Japanese air attack. The *Lexington* had intercepted a Japanese report giving the course, speed, and position of the American task force. So Admiral Fitch knew that he had been discovered, too.

With that report, the Japanese attack force, which had not been flying in the right direction, was directed to the American position and began preparing to attack, but the Americans got in the initial blow.

The *Yorktown*'s dive bombers arrived over the Japanese fleet first. They came at 17,000 feet and began to circle. According to doctrine, they were waiting for the torpedo planes to come up to launch a joint attack, but the TBD torpedo planes were slow and lumbering. Down below, Admiral Hara saw the American planes and began to take defensive action. There was no surprise here at all. First, he launched more fighters to augment the combat air patrol. The Japanese cruisers and destroyers moved in a fan pattern around the carriers, and the big antiaircraft guns opened fire at long range.

The torpedo bombers lumbered up about half an hour after the dive bombers. Somewhere back there were the *Lexington*'s planes, which had responded to the first radio message about the Japanese position and had then found that it was wrong and had to correct. In fact, the *Lexington*'s dive bombers never did find the Japanese; they flew around until they got low on gas and then headed back for the task force.

Meanwhile the Japanese were moving against the Americans. Just three minutes before the *Yorktown* torpedo planes arrived over the Japanese carriers, the *Lexington*'s radar picked up many aircraft coming in from the north. The Japanese were about to attack.

———

Lieutenant Commander Joseph Taylor of the *Yorktown* dive bomber squadron led the American attack. The torpedo bombers zoomed down to come in low, while the dive bombers stayed high to plummet down and drop their bombs.

The torpedo bombers were split into three divisions; each division started from an attack point, and then each pilot chose his own point and angle of attack.

On the sea, the carriers were maneuvering in beautiful *S* formations as they zigzagged to avoid the American attack. Lieutenant Commander William O. Burch, Jr., started down with his dive bombers, dropped to 2,500 feet, and released his bomb. The others followed. Below Burch could see the S-shaped wake of a carrier. It was the *Shokaku*, and a bomb fell on her flight deck, near the island. Then Burch began to pull out of his dive, with the shells of the Japanese antiaircraft guns bursting all around him.

Ensign J. H. Jorgenson was pounced on by Zero fighters, especially after an antiaircraft shell damaged his left wing and made the plane vulnerable. Three Zeros came in like sharks. Bullets banged a tattoo against the armor of Jorgenson's seat. Other bullets tore away his telescopic sight, smashed into his instrument panel and wrecked it. Several bullets grazed one leg, and a bit of shrapnel in the foot made him eligible for the Purple Heart medal. Jorgenson's gunner was rattling away with his machine gun, and he shot down one Japanese fighter. The other two were still there, though, and others came in from dead ahead. Jorgenson began firing his forward guns, and one Japanese Zero turned away, smoking.

_____

Lieutenant Commander Burch had ducked into a cloud and climbed. From above he watched the progress of the attack. He saw six hits on the carrier and thought he saw three more bombs hit but could not be sure.

Lieutenant Commander Taylor thought he saw three of the nine torpedos dropped by his men as they hit the carrier, and he flew home to report that he was sure the carrier was so badly damaged that it sank.

It was true that the *Shokaku* was badly damaged. When Admiral Hara's flagship, the *Zuikaku*, emerged from a squall a few moments after the attack, he saw fires rising above the flight deck. They were being extinguished, however, and by the time the *Lexington*'s torpedo bombers and fighters arrived, they saw below them two carriers, neither apparently damaged. The American fighter planes engaged the Zeros, successfully drawing them off from the torpedo bombers. Lieutenant Commander James H. Brett, Jr., led the torpedo bombers in their attack. Brett, too, flew away with the conviction that they had sunk one carrier. They had not, unfortunately. They had narrowly missed two cruisers, the *Kinugasa* and the *Furutaka*, but neither had sustained serious damage.

With the carrier *Shokaku*, however, it was a different story. The American attack had killed 100 of her crew, and 50 had been wounded. She had big holes in her deck, and several bombs had penetrated into the hangar deck and left planes twisted and mangled. But the torpedo bomber crews were wrong: She had no holes below the waterline.

Damaged as she was, she was still seaworthy and could return to Japan for repairs. Admiral Hara conferred with Admiral Takagi, and they sent her back. On their return from attacking the American carriers, her planes would have to land on the *Zuikaku* or find land bases.

The Japanese fighter planes chased the American carrier planes all the way back to their ships, where the survivors found the cover of the American combat air patrol. The battle was vigorous. The American fighters did their job, protecting the bombers; several fighters were shot down, but so were several Zeros. Finally the Americans approached their carriers. By this time, the American pilots found that their situation, too, had changed.

The Americans had reached their target first, but the Japanese had not lost any time. They had followed the American scout planes back to the American carriers. Captain Elliott Buckmaster, the skipper of the *Yorktown*, launched all available planes. All of *Lexington*'s contingent were in the air. At 11:11 A.M. the lookouts could recognize the shapes of the planes that were coming in. The first batch, 15 miles away, were torpedo planes. Six miles away the planes broke up into individual attacks. Up above, the Japanese dive bombers were preparing to come down as the torpedo planes came in.

Seven torpedo planes attacked the *Yorktown*. Captain Buckmaster ordered full right rudder aboard the *Yorktown*. The resulting move split her away from the *Lexington* and her protective three cruisers and three destroyers. Captain Buckmaster then began such violent maneuvers with the big aircraft carrier that even old battleship men in the fleet were impressed. The cruisers and destroyers found it hard to keep up.

The desperate maneuvering worked: Every torpedo missed, although some were very, very close. The *Yorktown* was attacked by 14 dive bombers, and 13 of them missed. One bomb, dropped at 11:27 that morning, did hit the ship. It was 12 inches in diameter and weighed about 800 pounds. It was an armor-piercing bomb and had a delayed action. It dropped through the steel flight deck, down through the gallery deck, the hangar deck, and the first, second, and third decks and finally exploded in a storeroom 50 feet inside the ship. That deck was armored below with steel 1½ inches thick so there the bomb did no damage except to bend the plating. Above that deck, however, the bomb did an enormous amount of damage and started some fires. Forty men were killed and 26 were wounded, but the *Yorktown* still moved at 24 knots, and she could still maneuver. The gunners and the planes above fought off the Japanese planes, and finally they flew away.

Simultaneously that morning the *Lexington* was under attack by the Japanese, particularly after the *Yorktown* split away from her. The Japanese used many different kinds of bombs against the *Lexington*. A 100-pound bomb went down the "stacks." A 500-pound bomb hit the boat pocket on one side and demolished that. Five other bombs, including a 1,000-pound bomb, hit the ship at other places; that 1,000-pound bomb made mincemeat of Admiral Fitch's cabin. And the ship was also struck by two torpedoes.

At around noon, Captain Frederick Sherman announced to the fleet that the *Lexington* had been torpedoed, but except for the oil slick she was trailing, many who looked at her would not have suspected it. She was riding on an even keel, and as the Japanese attackers left, she seemed to be well under control. She could still make 24 knots, although she had suffered serious damage below and many casualties. She began landing her aircraft.

———

So the battle ended. Admiral Takagi was told by his pilots that he had won a great victory; both American carriers were sunk, they said. So he steamed away from the area, worried about the condition of *Shokaku* and the loss of more than 30 of *Zuikaku*'s planes. They would have to go to Truk to pick up more pilots and aircraft.

Aboard the *Lexington* Admiral Fitch and Captain Sherman were sure that the damage was under control and that the ship could be put back into working order again. Then at 12:47 P.M. came an enormous explosion from deep in the bowels of the ship. Later speculation was that gases had built up in the motor generator room and had finally blown up. The most serious effect was the partial destruction of the ship's firefighting system. A second explosion followed, knocking out the ship's service telephone system.

Even so, it seemed that the serious damage could be controlled. But by 3:00 P.M., the aircraft of the *Lexington* that were still in the air had landed on the *Yorktown*. At 4:30 the engineering area was abandoned, and the ship went dead in the water. Destroyers came alongside and took off the wounded. At 5:00 P.M. Admiral Fitch spoke to Captain Sherman:

"Well, Ted, let's get the men off."

And that was the order to abandon ship. Boats came alongside, ships came alongside, and men jumped into the water until 300 of them were swimming. From that point on the *Lexington* was rocked by further explosions.

By 6:00 P.M. the *Lexington* was listing 30 degrees, and her flight deck was aflame from one end to the other. The destroyer *Phelps* fired three torpedoes into the carrier to sink her and then a fourth, but still she floated. The destroyer fired a fifth torpedo, but just as the torpedo was moving, the *Lexington* sank in 2,400 fathoms of water.

So the Battle of the Coral Sea ended, and the Japanese claimed a great victory. Captain Mineo Yamaoka, the senior staff officer of Admiral Hara's Fifth Carrier Division, said that here was proof that the Japanese had fought the Americans in the first big carrier battle in history and won. He remembered what Admiral Yamamoto had said back on the deck of the *Akagi* before the fleet had started for Pearl Harbor: The Americans would be the most determined and most skillful adversaries that the Japanese had ever met. Well, they had met the Americans, and they had defeated them in the carrier battle. Certainly little old *Shoho* had been sunk, but this was not a serious loss. Certainly the *Shokaku* had been badly damaged, but she could be repaired. The Americans had lost two fleet carriers, however, and the Japanese had shown their superiority in the air. It was all very satisfactory.

There were discrepancies in this version of events not recognized by Captain Yamaoka in his euphoria. The Japanese had sunk one, not two, American carriers. And the one American carrier they had not sunk would be available to fight again very soon. The *Shokaku* and the *Zuikaku* were both going to be laid up for weeks and would be unable to participate in the coming battle, already planned, in which Admiral Yamamoto was to sail to Midway Island, lure out the American fleet and its carriers, and complete the job left unfinished by Admiral Nagumo at Pearl Harbor.

And there was one more point not even considered by Captain Yamaoka but extremely important to Admiral King and General Douglas MacArthur: Because of the damage done to his aircraft carriers,

Admiral Inouye had decided to call off the Port Moresby invasion. The Tulagi seaplane base had been destroyed, too. So, although the Japanese claimed victory and the Americans did not, the result was certainly a strategic defeat for Japan. For the first time since the juggernaut had begun rolling on December 8, 1941 (Tokyo time), it had been stopped at the Battle of the Coral Sea.

8

Midway

In Tokyo the admirals were of two minds. Several months earlier Admiral Yamamoto had submitted the plans for the invasion of Midway Island and of the Aleutian Islands off the coast of Alaska. Six fleet carriers and at least two light carriers were to be employed in this attack, whose primary purpose was to draw the American fleet out of Pearl Harbor and destroy it. The operation followed Admiral Yamamoto's firm belief that the only way the Japanese could avoid final defeat in the war was to win a quick victory and persuade the Americans that the war was not worth the effort.

Following the setback in the Coral Sea—and it was certainly recognized as such in the highest Japanese naval circles, Admiral Ryunosuke Kusaka had suggested that it was time for the fleet to take a breather. The fliers were tired. They had been under the tension of action almost constantly since the fleet sailed for Pearl Harbor in November. The Hawaii attack, the foray into the South Pacific, the expedition against the British at Ceylon—all had taken their toll. The ships needed refit, and the carriers needed new planes.

Admiral Kusaka suggested that the Midway operation be delayed for two months. He also recommended that the battle experience gained by the pilots of these operations be passed along to others. The pilots would go ashore to train others and thus expand the force of naval aviators.

Others in the naval general staff remembered only too well how Jimmy Doolittle's B-25s had raided Tokyo and other cities in April, and there was a feeling of urgency in the air. The picket line of ships that were to give early warning of attack had been extended 600 miles east of Japan. But Admiral Yamamoto did not think this was enough. He felt a strong sense of responsibility for the person of the emperor, and as long as the American carriers could range the seas, the emperor and all Japan were in danger.

Admiral Yamamoto responded that the plans for Midway were too far along to change, and the suggestions of Admiral Kusaka were shelved. Despite the losses and damage that had caused the Japanese to drop the carriers *Zuikaku* and *Shokaku* from the Midway operation, Yamamoto was seeking the "decisive battle" with the Americans, and so sure was he that he would achieve it that he came along on this operation himself in the flagship *Yamato*.

The Japanese fleet began moving out on May 26 for the operation that was to begin on June 5 with an air strike against Midway. If all went well, the island atoll would be taken. Then it could be used as a future base for operations, even including the occupation of Hawaii advocated by some members of the general staff.

———

At Pearl Harbor in May, Admiral Nimitz knew that something important was brewing. The radio traffic indicated an operation that would be much larger than the Coral Sea move. Nimitz's radio intelligence staff had broken the Japanese naval code well enough to get the gist of messages. Nimitz had a hunch that the target was going to be Midway. One of his officers suggested that one way to find out for sure was to tell the Japanese that Midway was short of water, so a message to that effect was sent in the clear. Sure enough, back came a message from the Japanese to the fleet, noting that the target area was short of water.

Knowing and doing were two different matters, however. Nimitz had only three carriers available to contest the Japanese effort: Admiral Halsey's *Enterprise*; the *Hornet*, which he had taken on the Doolittle raid; and the *Yorktown*, which had been damaged by a bomb in the Coral Sea.

On May 26, Admiral Halsey steamed into Pearl Harbor. Nimitz intended to put him in charge of the coming Midway defense operation, but Halsey had a bad case of shingles and was in no shape to go. So

Admiral Chester W. Nimitz, who supervised the whole Pacific Fleet in the war against Japan in the central Pacific. (*National Archives*)

Admiral Isoroku Yamamoto. He was the architect of the attack on Pearl Harbor, and yet he had always counseled against war with the United States. (*National Archives*)

On the flight deck of the *Enterprise*, March 1942, the anti-aircraft guns were ready. (*National Archives*)

Admiral William F. Halsey carried these B-25 medium bombers to the seas off Japan, and then Lieutenant Colonel Jimmy Doolittle led them in a raid on the enemy. It was a portent, in 1942, of things to come.   (*National Archives*)

At the Battle of the Coral Sea in May 1942, the carrier *Shokaku* was damaged, but not sunk. This was the first step in Allied aggressive action in the Pacific war.   (*National Archives*)

The Japanese were hurt at the Battle of the Coral Sea, but not so badly as the Americans, who lost the carrier *Lexington*. (*National Archives*)

The carrier *Yorktown* was damaged and finally sunk by a submarine at the Battle of Midway, June 6, 1942. (*National Archives*)

Admiral Chuichi Nagumo of the Imperial Japanese Navy. Although the world considered the attack on Pearl Harbor to be eminently successful, Admiral Yamamoto knew it was a failure because Nagumo was too timid to stay and attack the American carriers. (*National Archives*)

Admiral Aubrey W. Fitch, one of the earliest aviators and an advocate of aggressive air action. (*National Archives*)

Vice Admiral Frank Jack Fletcher in 1942. An admiral of the old, or battleship school, he adhered to the doctrine, "Never risk the carrier." (*National Archives*)

This is what it was like when a bomb burst on the flight deck of the carrier *Enterprise* on August 24, 1942, during the Guadalcanal sea battles. The photographer was killed by the blast. (*National Archives*)

In the battles for Guadalcanal the Americans lost two carriers. This is the *Wasp* going down on September 15, 1942. (*National Archives*)

Japanese dive bombers attack the U.S. carrier *Hornet* on October 26, 1942, during the Battle of Santa Cruz off Guadalcanal. The *Hornet* was sunk in this battle. (*National Archives*)

Rear Admiral Frederick Sherman with Commander Henry Caldwell, his air group leader, aboard the *Saratoga* in 1943. (*National Archives*)

The men of the carriers were proud of their ships, and they kept records of the number of Japanese planes shot down the gun grews. (*National Archives*)

The new U.S.S. *Lexington* at sea in April 1943.   (*National Archives*)

Preparing bombs for loading aboard the U.S.S. *Yorktown* in November
1943.   (*National Archives*)

An F6F Grumman fighter moves up the deck aboard the carrier *Yorktown*.
(*National Archives*)

Four escort carriers in division formation, steaming ahead at sea. They were
small, but the Japanese often mistook them for fleet carriers. This photo was
taken in January 1944 from the deck of the escort carrier *Manila Bay*.   (*National
Archives*)

Admiral Nimitz chose Rear Admiral Raymond Spruance to take over Task Force 16. Spruance was not an aviator, but he was a level-headed and very competent officer, and he would have the assistance of Halsey's air-minded staff.

On May 27 Admiral Fletcher returned to Pearl Harbor with the *Yorktown*. How long would it take to repair the damage, Admiral Nimitz asked. About three months, said Admiral Fitch. They had three days, said Admiral Nimitz. And an army of 1,400 workmen replaced the crew of the *Yorktown* as she went into drydock. Admiral Spruance sailed with his two carriers on May 28 and the repaired *Yorktown* sailed on May 30 to meet the other ships off Midway.

———

The Japanese, coming across the Pacific from the north, had expected that their June 5 air raid on Midway would draw the Americans out of Pearl Harbor. They had no idea that the Americans would move before then. They had sent ahead a number of submarines to form a picket line and warn the fleet when the Americans came forth, but the American fleet slipped out before the I-boats got into position.

The Japanese had also planned to begin reconnoitering Pearl Harbor by air on May 30. They sent submarines and flying boats to French Frigate shoals, within easy air range of Hawaii, where they were to operate. When the Japanese units reached French Frigate shoals, however, they found two American seaplane tenders there and a number of PBYs. So they moved away.

On Midway, the defenders prepared for action.

On June 3 a search plane from Midway spotted the advance units of the Japanese fleet, a minesweeping group, about 500 miles from the atoll. That afternoon nine B-17 bombers were sent from Midway to bomb the Japanese ships. They came in at 20,000 feet, as they were used to doing in Europe, and it was easy for the ships to outmaneuver the falling bombs. There were no hits.

———

Admiral Nagumo, again in charge of the carrier operations, moved on toward Midway, supremely confident this would be another easy victory. "Although the enemy is lacking in fighting spirit, he will probably come out to attack as our invasion proceeds," Nagumo told the fleet. He was so sure of his advantage that he was careless in his preparations.

The first attack wave was launched from the four carriers: *Akagi, Kaga, Hiryu,* and *Soryu,* at dawn. The planes carried high-explosive bombs for use against land installations. Immediately a second strike force was assembled on the decks of the carriers, this time armed with torpedoes and armor-piercing bombs for use against ships in case the American fleet were found.

Normal procedure would have called for a careful search of the whole area before the attack force took off. But Admiral Nagumo was confident that the American carriers were still at Pearl Harbor. Only seven planes were assigned to search from north to south on the eastern side, facing Pearl Harbor. Two planes from the cruiser *Tone* and two from the cruiser *Chikuma* were to fly to the east. The *Tone* had catapult trouble that morning, and her planes were late in getting off. One of the *Chikuma*'s planes had engine trouble. Therefore, if they had moved swiftly and surely, the Japanese would have found the American fleet; they in fact did not find it.

Admiral Nagumo did not worry. "The enemy is unaware of our presence in this area," he said, "and will so remain until after our initial attacks on the island. It is assumed that there are no enemy carriers in the waters adjacent to Midway. If the enemy fleet counterattacks, we will be able to destroy it."

And so at 4:30 on the morning of June 4 Lieutenant Joichi Tomonaga led 36 fighters, 36 level bombers, and 36 dive bombers toward Midway. Halfway to the target, the attack force was sighted by a PBY which radioed Midway. Immediately everything that could fly was put into the air: fighters to wait for the attack and bombers to find and strike the enemy fleet. Unfortunately, the 26 American fighters were not very effective. When the Japanese came in, 17 of the American planes were shot down, and seven more were damaged. The Japanese lost only six planes.

The American bombers from Midway found the Japanese fleet, but they were not effective either. Four B-26 medium bombers attacked, and two were shot down. Six torpedo bombers attacked; they hit nothing, and five were shot down. The B-17s came in at 20,000 feet again and hit nothing.

———

Lieutenant Tomonaga surveyed the results of the bombing of Midway and decided that another strike was needed to finish the job. Admiral Nagumo, whose search planes had found nothing important, agreed with him. It was 7:15 A.M., and none of the search planes had yet sighted the enemy. The torpedoes and armor-piercing bombs were removed from the planes on the decks of the carriers, and high-explosive bombs were put on. The process would occupy more than an hour, they thought. A few minutes later, Nagumo's decision seemed to be confirmed when another attack from Midway planes was fended off. Once again the land-based aircraft accomplished nothing.

However . . .

At 7:20 one of the *Tone*'s seaplane pilots reported that he was at the limit of his 300-mile outward search and that he had just sighted 10 ships. They appeared to be the enemy, he said, but that was all he could tell them. The report did not upset Admiral Nagumo; it was too brief and too vague. The rearming of the carrier planes with weapons to strike Midway's installations continued.

At about 8:00 A.M. more B-17s came over the Japanese carrier fleet and bombed. Again the captains of the ships avoided the bombs easily, and there were no hits. At 8:30 the B-17s flew away. Planes from Lieutenant Tomonaga's first attack force began landing on the carriers.

Then came the surprise. The other pilot from the *Tone*, who had finally reached the end of his search line, reported that he saw below an enemy aircraft carrier! Admiral Nagumo immediately ordered the planes of the second attack force to take off the high-explosive bombs and restore the torpedoes and armor-piercing bombs for use against the carrier. At top speed, the job was accomplished in 25 minutes, and Nagumo ordered the fleet to move northward and engage the enemy.

The enemy—the Americans—were already in action. Early in the morning, Admiral Fletcher, commander of the American forces, had launched a scouting force to the north. The Japanese carrier force was discovered at 6:00 A.M.

Admiral Spruance was informed, and he turned his two carriers toward the enemy position. He intended to steam to a point about 100 miles from the Japanese, and then launch his planes. Captain Miles Browning, however, Halsey's chief of staff, suggested that the strike ought to be made immediately. That way, Browning said, they might catch the Japanese when their carrier decks were full of aircraft just returning from the Midway strike. So the planes of *Enterprise* and *Hornet* were launched: fighters for the combat air patrol, and dive bombers and torpedo bombers to hit the enemy.

The first American planes to find the Japanese ships were those of Torpedo 8, the torpedo squadron of *Hornet*. Even though the slow TBD bombers had no fighter protection, they were ordered to attack immediately. The 15 torpedo bombers bored in, in two plane sections, attacking from various angles. Up above, the Japanese Zeros, which were at high altitude waiting for either dive bombers or torpedo planes, spotted the American bombers and swooped down on them. One by one the TBDs fell into the sea. Not one of them managed to put a torpedo into the Japanese ships, and of the whole squadron only one pilot, Ensign G. H. Gay, survived the attack. His plane was shot down and his radioman-gunner died, but Gay got out and into a rubber raft and floated around, watching the rest of the action.

The *Hornet*'s dive bombers did not find the carriers. They ran out their fuel, and then had to go back to the *Hornet* for more.

Then, as Ensign Gay watched, the torpedo bombers from the *Enterprise* came along. It was about 9:30 A.M. The *Enterprise* bombers attacked, much the same as had those from the *Hornet*. The results were also almost the same, except that four of the 14 TBDs managed to survive and get back to their carrier. They scored no hits.

The dive bombers of *Enterprise* were now approaching the *Kaga* and the *Akagi*. It was 10:05 A.M. The Japanese fighters, which had swooped down on the *Enterprise*'s torpedo planes, were still down low, either attacking stragglers or climbing to get altitude, when the American planes came in high, peeled off, and attacked the carriers. At the outset they were virtually unopposed. The *Kaga* took four bombs, the *Akagi* took three, and both carriers were soon ablaze, with fires from their ammunition and fuel supplies adding to the trouble.

Admiral Nagumo immediately recognized disaster. There was no way the *Akagi* could be saved. He told his staff he intended to go down with his ship, but they persuaded him to go aboard one of the cruisers, the *Nagara*, to continue to direct the battle. Both the *Kaga* and the *Akagi* burned, exploded, and sank. Then the *Yorktown* dive bombers found the *Soryu* and bombed her. Soon she too was a hulk.

Only the fleet carrier *Hiryu* remained in action for the Japanese. Just after noon, her dive bombers found the American carrier *Yorktown* and attacked. They put three bombs into the carrier and started fires that took two hours to bring under control. The *Yorktown* even launched her second strike of the day. Just afterward, however, the *Hiryu*'s torpedo bombers arrived and slammed two torpedoes into the *Yorktown*, jamming her rudder to the left and causing her to list 23 degrees. Admiral Fletcher moved his flag to the cruiser *Astoria* and turned command of the American fleet over to Admiral Spruance.

Now it was again the turn of the planes of the *Enterprise*. Her second strike found the *Hiryu* at 5:00 P.M. and attacked. Four dive bombers scored hits on the *Hiryu* and soon, she, too, was dead in the water.

The *Yorktown* went dead in the water, and Captain Buckmaster ordered the men to abandon ship. The Japanese planes went back to *Hiryu* to report, rearmed, and went out again. This time Lieutenant Tomonaga reported that they found another carrier and torpedoed it. The fact was that they had found the *Yorktown* again, attacked, and failed. From this second attack, half of Tomonaga's planes failed to return.

The planes of the *Yorktown* landed aboard the *Hornet* and the *Enterprise*, thus providing replacements for the aircraft and pilots lost during the day's attack. By nightfall, the two American carriers of Task Force 16 were ready for another battle, but Admiral Spruance was a very conservative man. He did not want a night engagement, so he took the task force east, and then south, and then back west, making a box movement that was designed to keep him away from the enemy but that would return him by morning to the Midway area. He suspected, obviously, that the Japanese would opt for a night battle.

Admiral Yamamoto did want a night battle. He was sure that his surface ships were more than a match for those of the enemy and that his battleships could do what the Japanese carriers had failed to do: break the back of the American fleet.

Admiral Nagumo did not want any more battle at all, however, and he gave orders for the task force to withdraw from the Midway area. As he did so, Nagumo had not yet reported to Yamamoto on the loss of all four of his fleet carriers. Actually, *Hiryu* was still afloat, although burning and abandoned.

When Admiral Yamamoto heard that Nagumo had ordered withdrawal, he was furious. He relieved Nagumo from command then and there and put Vice Admiral Nobutake Kondo in charge of the Midway invasion task force. His instructions from Admiral Yamamoto were to move to Midway and begin a bombardment to draw the American fleet into action. Later, when Admiral Yamamoto had the word that all four of his carriers were out of action, he canceled the order.

———

At 7:00 A.M. on the second day, a plane from the Japanese light carrier *Hosho* sighted the burning *Hiryu*. In a burst of hope, Admiral Yamamoto ordered the destroyer *Tanikaze* to investigate, but before *Tanikaze* could reach the position, the *Hiryu* sank.

That morning, threatened by American carriers and with only the light carrier *Hosho* to protect the Japanese fleet, Admiral Yamamoto gave the order to withdraw to the northwest. Admiral Spruance was now ready to fight again in day battle. The American submarine *Tambor* sighted the Japanese fleet 90 miles west of Midway and began tracking. The Japanese knew she was there and began maneuvering to prevent her from getting a clear shot. In the process, the Japanese cruisers *Mikuma* and *Mogami* collided. Both ships were damaged, and their speed was reduced. They headed home for repairs but could not keep up with the fleet.

Admiral Spruance made a bad guess that day. His planes and submarines indicated that there were two groups of the Japanese fleet, one west of Midway and the other off to the northwest. He chose to chase the northwest group, but all his scout planes could find were two destroyers. The day brought no success at all, only tragedy and confusion; that proved his contention that the Americans were not ready for night carrier action. The strike force that went out in the afternoon found nothing, and when they returned to the carriers, darkness had already fallen. One *Enterprise* plane crashed in the water astern of the carrier because the pilot did not know how to land at night. Several planes landed on the wrong carriers.

On the morning of June 6, Admiral Spruance decided to move west on the theory that Yamamoto might have gone that way—heading straight for Japan instead of northwest. He was wrong again, but the error was mitigated by the discovery by search planes of the crippled cruisers *Mogami* and *Mikuma*, each traveling with destroyer escort about 40 miles apart. Admiral Spruance's dive bombers attacked and sank the *Mikuma* and damaged the *Mogami* so badly that she barely made port in Truk and was a year under repair.

Admiral Fletcher had high hopes of bringing the crippled *Yorktown* home to be repaired to fight again.

The destroyer *Hammann* was detailed to stand by her, waiting for tugs to come and tow the carrier. A Japanese submarine found the two ships that day and torpedoed them, sinking both.

And so the two fleets headed homeward, one having won a glorious, almost miraculous victory, and the other having suffered a disastrous defeat. The commanding officers of the *Hiryu* and *Soryu* both went down with their ships, and Admiral Yamaguchi, the division commander, also chose to die. Admiral Nagumo said he, too, was going to go down with the *Akagi*, but loyal staff officers persuaded him to change his mind. For his place in history, Admiral Nagumo might have been better off committing *seppuku* (ritual suicide), for after Midway his career was in shards. Never again did he command a major assault force. Ultimately he was sent to Saipan to command the land-based air forces there, and he perished in July 1944 in the last desperate days of the defense.

Admiral Yamamoto knew that Nagumo's carelessness had turned almost certain victory into defeat. If Nagumo had taken the usual precautions ordered by Japanese fleet procedures, the American carriers would have been discovered on June 4, and the Japanese carriers would not have been surprised. The Battle of Midway then might have taken an entirely different turn.

The American torpedo bombers were hopeless. Almost all three squadrons were destroyed, and they did not score a single hit on any carrier. The four carriers were sunk by American dive bombers. The Japanese torpedo bombers were superb; they stopped the *Yorktown* with two torpedoes. And the Japanese Zero fighters were superior to the American fighters.

The Americans did have the advantage of intelligence. They knew the Japanese were coming, and they were able to mass their forces accordingly. It was surprise, however, that caused Admiral Nagumo to lose the battle that day, surprise brought about by an arrogance, which in turn had its roots in the successes of the recent past. There was another factor: If Admiral Yamamoto had been able to follow his original plan, and use the carriers *Zuikaku* and *Shokaku* as well as the other four, the Japanese still might have won the battle, destroyed the three American carriers instead of just one of them, and occupied Midway.

That is not to say that the outcome of the war would have been any different had not Admiral Nagumo erred so seriously on June 4. The American carrier-building program was speeding along, and the Japanese could in no way match it. From this point on they would have to make do with half measures, using every vessel that could be converted for air use, whereas the Americans launched one fleet carrier after another.

No, a Japanese victory at Midway would not have won the war for them as they had hoped. The American public would still not have knuckled under. Rising up from defeat after defeat in the Pacific so far, the public had responded with a will, determined to avenge the "perfidy" of Pearl Harbor; and the most important American weapon of World War II, her enormous industrial capacity, would still have turned the tide in the end.

───────

When the two fleets got home, their respective navies issued communiques. The American communique gave the American public what it had long awaited, news of a great victory, and press and public responded jubilantly.

The American fleet had lost one aircraft carrier, the *Yorktown*, and one destroyer, the *Hammann*, and 147 planes had been destroyed, most of them because the aircraft were inferior to those of the enemy. The airmen of these American carriers were America's cream of the crop, almost all of them well trained and highly experienced.

The same was true of the Japanese, but their losses were greater and as it would turn out, their losses were never replaced. As noted earlier, before the Midway battle Rear Admiral Ryunosuke Kusaka had suggested to Admiral Yamamoto that the Midway battle be delayed for a while. He explained that after Pearl Harbor, the wearing and long campaign in the South Pacific, which involved so many air strikes against the Australian-American defenses, and the foray into the Indian Ocean to attack the British fleet off Ceylon, the carrier force was exhausted. Why not delay the Midway operation for two or three months? That way, as Kusaka said, the pilots who had gained so much experience in the early battles could be brought ashore and turned into instructors to pass their skills and knowledge along to new men. The ships could be refit, and the aircraft properly repaired or replaced. Then the fleet would be ready to give its best efforts once more.

Admiral Yamamoto was obsessed, however, with the idea that Japan must strike immediately and throw the Americans into a state of shock so that they would not have time to get their enormous industrial capacity into gear. He was counting on the destruction of American morale as the only hope for Japanese victory. He was probably right, although even another defeat at Midway would hardly have done the job. But a defeat at Midway, plus an occupation of the Hawaiian islands might have persuaded President Franklin Roosevelt, himself totally preoccupied with the war against Hitler, that the Pacific was not worth the candle.

As noted, Admiral Kusaka's suggestion was ignored, the Japanese fleet was sent into battle under a commander known to be a timid man, and Midway was lost. Three hundred and thirty-two Japanese planes were lost on the four fleet carriers that were sunk, and one heavy cruiser was sunk. One heavy cruiser and two destroyers were damaged. The most important damage was human. Several brave and valiant senior officers were lost, including the aggressive Admiral Yamaguchi, who had counseled for the second strike on Pearl Harbor. And more than 400 aircrewmen were lost, including the pilots of the 332 downed planes. It was a loss from which the Japanese naval air force would never recover. Before Midway the Japanese navy refused to carry out Admiral Kusaka's proposed training program; after Midway they could not. The only highly experienced airmen left were those of the *Shokaku* and the *Zuikaku*, and they were needed for operations, not for training.

And so Japan suffered an enormous defeat at Midway, a defeat whose roots were in the Battle of the Coral Sea, one that would negatively affect the conduct of Japanese naval operations from June 1942 until the end of the war. The Japanese carrier strike force was destroyed here, and Japan did not have the resources to rebuild it.

The Japanese, with the exception of Admiral Yamamoto, who now had to know that his chance for victory was gone, although he never admitted it, were not aware that the tide of war changed at Midway. One reason was the secrecy about the whole failure imposed by the Imperial Japanese Naval General Staff. When the Combined Fleet came home, all officers and men were cautioned against talking, and most of the men were reassigned to shore bases and other ships with no opportunity to go home. The news of the defeat was withheld from the Japanese press and public. The communique said only that an American carrier had been sunk (true) and another damaged (false), that the Japanese had won a glorious victory by invading the Aleutian Islands (questionable), and that a naval battle had been fought off Midway (true). Not even General Tojo, the chief of the Japanese government, was told that the four carriers had been lost and the battle had ended in defeat. It was more than a month before he learned the facts. And the army was never told either the extent or the importance of the defeat. Thus the arrogance of a victory attitude continued in Japan when there was every reason for the opposite.

9

Attrition

From the outset of World War II, Winston Churchill saw the need for small carriers that would operate in conjunction with destroyers to sink German U-boats. The problem in 1939 was that Britain's shipbuilding capacity was stretched tight and the Americans were not yet building warships.

The U-boat problem became more severe in 1940 after the fall of France. The Germans then had the use of all the French ports, and the range of the U-boats was extended by thousands of miles. The worst part of the problem was The Black Hole—the mid-Atlantic air gap. In the beginning, aircraft patrolled and escorted convoys as they left Britain, but they could go only about a third of the way across the Atlantic, then had to return. The same was true on the other side. This left an area in which the convoys were protected only by their escorts—and there were not enough escorts available to do the job.

The first British move was to convert a number of merchant ships to "Catapult Armed Merchantmen." These ships carried Hurricane or Fulmar aircraft that could be catapulted off to fight a U-boat, but there was no way of retrieving the planes. Theoretically, the pilot would ditch alongside his own ship or another ship of the convoy. There are few accounts by survivors of this force because too often the plane got completely away from the convoy, ran out of fuel, and the pilot found a watery grave.

The pilots had their best chance of survival on the run down to the Mediterranean. Once the convoys passed by the French ports and reached the Iberian Peninsula, the pilot could catapult, fight his fight, and then have a fair hope of landing in Spain, Portugal, or North Africa.

The battle in the Mediterranean was very hot that summer of 1942. The Italians had invaded Greece and bogged down, and the Germans had felt impelled to bail them out. The Germans also invaded Crete, and General Erwin Rommel had arrived in North Africa to help the Italians in their desert war against the British. Soon Rommel was winning victories. For the British, maintaining the lifelines to Gibraltar and Malta was essential. This meant an ever stronger presence of the British fleet must be maintained, and for air power the British had to rely on carriers even more because they had lost most of their bases in the Mediterranean.

Malta was almost constantly besieged by German aircraft, and her own air force had to be resupplied. The carriers brought in fighter planes. After the sinking of the *Ark Royal* in November 1941, the carrier force in the Mediterranean consisted of the old *Argus* and HMS *Eagle*, a carrier of the vintage of the *Hermes*. In spite of the decision of 1939 that carriers would not be used to escort convoys, in the case of Malta there was no alternative. The carriers served two purposes: to ferry planes to Malta and to protect the convoys from air and submarine assault. On one convoy the Sea Hurricanes of 801 and 813 Squadrons shot down nine Italian planes and damaged a dozen more, losing only two planes in the fight.

The Germans began to wage a special air war against Malta, and the island was really in danger of capture. The only way to resupply the aircraft needed for the island was to bring them by carrier or crates aboard merchant ships. The distances were too great to fly them from bases. In two years after August 1940, carriers delivered 718 aircraft to Malta in 25 different operations.

In August 1942, a special convoy was sent to Malta, so special it had its own name: Operation Pedestal. Four aircraft carriers were loaded with planes for Malta and sent out escorted by two battleships, seven cruisers, and two dozen destroyers. The carriers were the *Eagle*, the *Furious*, the *Indomitable*, and the *Victorious*. On August 11, the convoy was very near Malta, having survived assaults by scores of enemy aircraft.

Lieutenant Commander Helmut Rosenbaum's *U-73* was in the area. "I never saw so many British flags before," he said. He tracked the convoy for a long time, and finally settled on *Eagle* as his target. Most of the time he kept the U-boat at periscope depth, but occasionally he had to dive deep as a destroyer came whizzing by. One destroyer was very close—only 80 yards away, one crewman estimated.

At about 1:00 P.M. *U-73* managed to penetrate the destroyer screen. Several of the destroyers were fueling and vigilance was relaxed for a bit. Rosenbaum brought the U-boat to within 500 yards of the carrier and fired a spread of four torpedoes, which struck at 1:15. The carrier *Eagle* went down in only eight minutes.

The next day, the *Indomitable* was hit by three bombs from enemy aircraft and suffered from near misses by four others. Unlike many British carriers, the *Indomitable* had an armored deck so she was not destroyed. Most of the *Indomitable*'s airplanes were able to land aboard the *Victorious*.

———

Through such heroic efforts, repeated time and again by ships of the Royal Navy, Malta was saved in its period of greatest threat, which finally ended with the Allied invasion of French North Africa and the defeat of the German and Italian forces.

By that time the sea war against the Axis powers had begun to turn around. One reason was the development, slow at first but escalating rapidly, of the escort carrier.

The first real escort carrier was the *Audacity*, a captured 6,000-ton German merchant ship that was given a flight deck and four arrester wires. In the summer of 1941 she began escorting convoys, and on her first voyage was responsible for the destruction of one long-range German Condor bomber.

Soon *Audacity* was assigned to the Gibraltar convoys, because Admiral Dönitz had moved a number of submarines down to the Mediterranean and the approaches outside the straits. In the second week of December 1941, *Audacity* sailed with Convoy HG 76, bound from Gibraltar to England. It was a big convoy, 32 ships in nine columns, escorted by 16 destroyers, corvettes, sloops, and *Audacity*.

On the night of December 14, a scout plane from *Audacity* spotted a U-boat on the surface six miles off the convoy. The plane dropped depth charges and calcium light to mark the spot. The U-boat got away, but it did not attack the convoy that night. At 1:35 the next morning the same pilot found another U-boat on the surface and forced it to crash dive. The pilot could not attack because he had used up all his depth charges on that first U-boat.

Later that morning another *Audacity* aircraft attacked another U-boat, which was also forced down, although it did not sink. The rest of the day was quiet, and the Grumman Martlet (Wildcat) aircraft of the *Audacity* did not fly. As one of the pilots said, "Flying had to be kept to a minimum, as there was always a bigger risk than in other carriers." The reason was the flight deck, which was about half the length of that of the *Ark Royal*. That meant every landing was a hot one.

The next day, December 16, the *Audacity* was asked to fly a dawn antisubmarine patrol. Her planes found a U-boat at 9:25 A.M., 22 miles away. Escorts went after it and so did planes from the *Audacity*. Machine gunners aboard the U-boat shot down one Martlet. The escorts, however, sank *U-131*.

On the morning of December 18, planes from the *Audacity* found two Focke-Wulff scout bombers and attacked them. They damaged one Focke-Wulff, and both enemy planes then fled. The next day, December 19, two more Focke-Wulffs appeared. The *Audacity* pilots shot one down and damaged another. By now, because of enemy action and accidents of landing, the aircraft complement of the *Audacity* was reduced to three planes. All three were in the air late in the afternoon. Two of them spotted a Focke-Wulff, very low above the water, and shot it down. The third plane sighted a submarine and reported to the convoy commander.

———

On the morning of December 20, the Martlet fighters were up again, chasing away Focke-Wulffs and looking for U-boats. Several of the U-boats were trailing the convoy. At 9:00 A.M. on December 21 one of the air patrol discovered two U-boats lying together about 25 miles astern of the convoy. The Germans began firing with their Oerlikon guns. The pilot found that the Germans could not fire at an angle sharper than 70 degrees, so he came straight down on the submarines and shot three men off the plank laid between the two U-boats, which separated quickly, dived, and went away. Later that day the aircraft reported two more U-boats.

———

The night of December 20–21, the U-boat pack closed in on the convoy. The *Audacity* was off by herself for the night, but she was unlucky. To try to confuse the U-boats, the convoy escort commander had staged a mock battle, using star shells and tracers, and *Audacity* was suddenly silhouetted against all this light. She was spotted by Lieutenant Gerhard Bigalk, the commander of *U-751* as he was spinning his periscope around, looking for a target.

Here is part of Lieutenant Bigalk's account, as broadcast over German radio: "The whole area was as light as day. The other U-boats must have been attacking. Ten or 15 rockets hung over the U-boat as if spellbound. The destroyers nearby started firing tracer bullets, and suddenly I saw in the light of the tracer bullets and the rockets a large aircraft carrier lying in front of us."

U-751 fired several torpedoes at *Audacity*. The first torpedoes wrecked the engine room, and the carrier coasted to a stop. The men on deck of the carrier sighted the surfaced submarine. The U-boat attacked again. The men on deck saw more torpedoes coming and lay down on the deck. Lieutenant Bigalk continued: "There, a hit forward, 20 meters behind the stem. A great detonation with a gigantic sheet of flame. A short time afterwards, another detonation, the middle, again a great column of fire. Hardly had the column of water subsided when a strong detonation was observed forward. Probably ammunition or fuel had been hit. . . ."

One torpedo had struck under the bridge, and another in the wardroom. The *Audacity* began to sink. Ten minutes later she was going down, and men were jumping into the water. One of the planes slipped its moorings on the canted deck, and dropped over the side on top of some of the swimmers. Most of the men were rescued, but Britain's first escort carrier had gone down to a watery grave.

———

More escort carriers were coming. The next was the *Archer*, built in the United States for Britain from a converted merchant hull. Four more escort carriers of this class came along, one by one. Britain was about to begin the convoys to Russia to help the Soviets who had been attacked by Hitler in the summer of 1941. One of these escort carriers, the *Avenger*, was sunk on a Russian convoy run on November 15, 1942. She was the fifth British carrier to be sunk by a U-boat.

The Americans built a number of small carriers for the British and many more for themselves, using converted merchant hulls. This was never a satisfactory solution to the problem, and in 1942 Henry Kaiser, the industrialist who was already building merchant ships for the American government, offered a whole new design for an auxiliary carrier. He proposed to build 30 of these, mainly for use in the Atlantic convoys to fight U-boats.

The American navy, still in the hands of the battleship admirals, said no. Kaiser went to the U.S. Maritime Commission with the plan, and the director of the Maritime Commission went to President Franklin Roosevelt, and the admirals were overruled. The American program of building escort carriers began to gather force.

It took Kaiser nine months to build the first of this class of ships, called CVE by the U.S. Navy. The first was christened *Casablanca*.

The building time had been far too long, however. So Kaiser set up an industrial system to build aircraft carriers. He constructed a city—Vanport City—on swampland between Portland, Oregon, and Vancouver, Washington. Soon it was Oregon's second largest city. Kaiser adopted new techniques, such as welding plates for hulls instead of riveting them. The shipyards worked around the clock in three shifts.

And so the carrier program continued apace. In about a year, the construction time for a "jeep carrier" (so-called because of its small size) was down from 241 days to 171 days. (Later it came down to 70 days.) And by 1943, because of the escort carriers and the formation of hunter-killer groups of carriers and escort vessels, the heyday of the U-boat was ending.

10

The South Pacific

The Japanese defeat at Midway put a serious crimp in the Imperial General Headquarters plans to move southward and threaten Australia, but it did not end them. The Japanese still expected to capture Port Moresby and thus gain control of all New Guinea, which was to be the stepping stone to Australia. Because the army did not know of the defeat at Midway, the generals were unconcerned, and they went ahead with their planning.

So, for that matter, did the Americans, and their planning included a future amphibious operation that was to strike against the Santa Cruz Islands and Tulagi, the latter still in Japanese hands. Just when and where the American operation was to be staged was a bit vague, but Vice Admiral Robert L. Ghormley was brought back from London, where he was watching the European war. He was given command of the South Pacific operation, which was to be distinct from General Douglas MacArthur's Southwest Pacific Command in Australia.

In May, the American military buildup was proceeding at deliberate speed. Admiral Wilson Brown had been joined at San Diego by Marine Major General Holland Smith, with orders to establish amphibious training. Rear Admiral Richmond Kelly Turner had been assigned as commander of the first amphibious operation. It was all occurring in an orderly fashion.

On May 22, an army reconnaissance plane flying over Tulagi spotted strange activity on Guadalcanal Island across Lunga Channel. Soon the Americans learned that the Japanese had ordered to the area two units of Pioneers—their equivalent of the U.S. Navy construction battalions (the Seabees)—which were to go to Guadalcanal. Aerial observation showed that the Japanese had already set up a tent city there and that they were burning the grass on the central plain in what seemed to be preparations to build an airfield.

When Admiral King received that information, he saw immediately what the Japanese were up to. They were planning to construct a forward air base. Then it would be no trick for them to stage planes down from Rabaul, the big Japanese base on New Britain Island, and to attack Australia and the sea lanes around it, thus raising hob with the American reinforcement of the island continent and making it difficult to launch an offensive from there.

So King decided that the Americans must speed up their planning and attack within the next month. When Admiral Ghormley had this information and was ordered to begin moving, he was aghast. He communicated his concerns to General MacArthur, who for his own reasons agreed that the navy plan for an assault on Guadalcanal was foolishness. Admiral King had the support of the other members of the Joint Chiefs of Staff, however, and he insisted that the operation go ahead as planned. The soundness of Admiral King's stubborn insistence was immediately justified. By the end of July 1942, the Japanese had completed their airfield. From his flagship at the fleet anchorage in Kagoshima, on Kyushu Island, Admiral Yamamoto gave orders that the first bombing mission against Australia was to leave Rabaul on August 14, work its way down the Solomon Island chain to Guadalcanal, and then attack. The assault on the island continent was to begin in earnest.

Admiral King demanded even more speed, men, and equipment to counteract the Japanese move. Late in July the U.S. Navy moved 17,000 marines from various bases toward the South Pacific. On July 8 the concerned commanders met to discuss their roles in the coming invasion. Admiral Turner would be in charge of delivering the troops to the island, and then General Alexander Vandegrift would take command of the fighting. Vice Admiral Frank Jack Fletcher would protect the landings with the carriers *Saratoga*, *Wasp*, and *Enterprise*. From the beginning, however, it was clear that Admiral Fletcher had little stomach for the assignment. He came right out at the meeting of commanders and announced that he agreed with Admiral Ghormley that the whole operation was cockeyed, hasty, and doomed to failure. Then he told the others that he would stay on the scene, protecting the invasion, for only 48 hours, and then he would take no further responsibility. It was hardly the sort of performance to instill confidence in the troops.

The invasion force of 175 ships was at sea on August 4 and steamed along under squally skies for two days. On the morning of August 7 the South Pacific sky cleared as the ships went to general quarters and the carriers launched their first strike at 6:00 A.M. Some of the planes were to hit the Japanese seaplane base located on Gavutu and Tanambogo Islands, which were connected by a causeway. Some were to hit the airfield at Guadalcanal, and some would work over Tulagi, preparatory to landings there.

The planes set out, but they found that the pickings were slim. They had caught the Japanese so much off guard that the Japanese preparations for manning and protecting the new Guadalcanal base had not been completed. Had they waited another month, the story of the struggle for Guadalcanal might have been quite different. But now the Americans had the advantage of total surprise.

Planes from *Enterprise* were to attack aircraft on the Guadalcanal field, but they did not find any aircraft. They were to attack PT boats at Lunga Point, but they did not find any PT boats. They did strafe buildings at both places, but they saw very few Japanese. Most of the people assigned to the area were still at Rabaul.

———

Planes from the other carriers struck the big seaplane base on Gavutu. They destroyed nine single-engine floatplanes, one four-engined Kawanishi flying boat, and eight smaller seaplane bombers—every single plane on Gavutu.

Still other carrier planes hit Japanese troop installations on Tulagi. Lieutenant Frederick Mears, flying a torpedo bomber from *Enterprise*, searched around Santa Isabel Island for targets, but all he could find was a 75-foot cargo vessel. He wasted his torpedo on her (he missed) and then strafed the small vessel, which fought back with a single machine gun.

The marines landed on Tulagi and Guadalcanal with very little opposition. The Japanese had indeed been surprised, and within an hour the Japanese radio station on Tulagi signed off with salutations to the emperor and apologies for not driving the enemy away.

The first Japanese reaction to the Guadalcanal invasion came from the air. At 8:30 A.M. on August 7, 27 twin-engine Japanese bombers took off from Rabaul airfields. They had been scheduled to bomb Australian forces on New Guinea and were loaded with bombs, not torpedoes and armor-piercing bombs that could be used against warships. They were accompanied by 18 Zero fighters. Near Florida Island, the Japanese force ran into the fighter contingent of the *Enterprise*, and a melee began. The American F4F fighters attacked the bombers and shot down several of them. Then the Zeros got into the fight, and the F4Fs broke off to take refuge in the cloud cover, as they had been instructed to do. Even this early in the war, the carrier tacticians had evolved a manner of fighting Zeros to best advantage, using the hit and run technique, not trying to turn with the more maneuverable Japanese planes. Still, one F4F was badly shot up and another was shot down.

A more effective display of the disparity between the two planes was given that day over Santa Isabel Island, when three F4Fs were shot down in short order by 10 Zeros. On August 8, six fighters from the *Enterprise* were shot down by the Zeros. At the end of the day, Admiral Fletcher counted his losses: 21 planes. There, for him, was confirmation of the wisdom of his announced intention of withdrawing to safer places than these waters around Guadalcanal. He headed south, away from the fight. Thus Admiral Fletcher helped set up the August 8 Battle of Savo Island, at which a Japanese cruiser force surprised the Allied cruiser force, sinking four cruisers and damaging another and also two destroyers. Had Fletcher remained at Guadalcanal, his planes probably would have found the Japanese.

For nearly two weeks, Admiral Fletcher moved around, completely wasting time and effort, well outside the danger zone, keeping his carriers safe from risk. He gave absolutely no help to the marines, who were attacked several times a day by Japanese aircraft, and at night by Japanese warships that shelled Guadalcanal at will.

Admiral Ghormley ordered Fletcher to attack the Japanese destroyers and other ships that came to bombard Guadalcanal every night. Fletcher refused. So the only help that the carrier force gave the marines came on August 20 when the escort carrier *Long Island* flew off 19 F4F fighters and 12 Douglas SBD dive bombers from a point south of the San Cristobal Islands. These planes landed at Henderson Field, as the Americans called that Japanese-built airfield on Guadalcanal, and became the nucleus of what would come to be known as the Cactus Air Force. They had absolutely nothing to do with the carrier task force or with Admiral Fletcher.

At Guadalcanal, Fletcher gave a prime display of how not to use aircraft carriers in warfare. This potentially powerful weapon was reduced to steaming around in circles by the timidity of its commander. Fletcher was still circling around south of Guadalcanal, accomplishing nothing and alibiing his failure by saying that he wanted to conceal the presence of his carriers. Admiral Nimitz seemed to accept that explanation. On August 17, Nimitz reinforced Fletcher by sending the carrier *Hornet* to the South Pacific.

And as for the argument about "concealment," Fletcher did not conceal the presence of the carriers for long. On August 20 a Japanese flying boat spotted the carrier force 500 miles west of Bougainville. Unlike Admiral Fletcher, Admiral Yamamoto was looking for a fight. He had sent major fleet elements to the South Pacific to seek battle. The fleet was escorting a number of transports toward Guadalcanal as the Japanese worked to reinforce their presence there. When Admiral Yamamoto learned of the presence of the American carrier task force, which he suspected was lurking somewhere in the area, he told Kondo to leave the transports and seek a fight. The Japanese fleet fueled at sea and made ready for action.

Admiral Fletcher was ordered to attack, and he sent the *Saratoga* air group out to find the enemy, but the American planes did not immediately find the Japanese fleet. Admiral Fletcher then concluded that the Japanese were not around, and he sent the *Wasp* away to the south to fuel. Again he was playing very cautiously, almost as if relieved that he would not have to engage the enemy.

He was also very distrustful of the PBY search planes. One PBY had reported a Japanese force, and Fletcher had launched a group of bombers only to have them fly around for hours and never make contact. Therefore, he had begun to believe that the Japanese were well outside his own area of operations.

As of August 23, Fletcher's American force held a considerable advantage over the air power of the Japanese fleet that was steaming to find him. He had 215 planes available on three carriers, whereas the Japanese had only 177 planes on their three carriers, the *Ryujo*, the *Shokaku*, and the *Zuikaku*. By sending the *Wasp* away to refuel when she could have refueled at sea, Fletcher cut his own force to 176 planes, giving the Japanese a slight advantage.

The Japanese advantage was increased considerably when the *Saratoga*'s planes spent the night of August 23 at Henderson Field following a late attack on Japanese shipping. The Americans were not very good at night carrier landings, and so they were ordered to land at Henderson and rejoin their carrier the next day. Thus on the morning of August 24, with the Japanese nearby, Admiral Fletcher had only the 87 planes of the *Enterprise*. The dawn search employed 23 of those planes, and they found nothing but a surfaced submarine. With the dispatch of that scouting force, Fletcher then had only 28 bombers left for an attack.

The Japanese had two aims in seeking battle with their carriers. First, the light carrier *Ryujo* was to go 190 miles east of Guadalcanal and there support the naval contingent led by Rear Admiral Raizo Tanaka, which was bringing the transports and four destroyers full of troops to reinforce the Japanese on Guadalcanal. The *Ryujo* would, in effect, also act as "bait" for the American carriers. If they took the bait and came up to attack the *Ryujo*, then the planes from the big fleet carriers *Shokaku* and *Zuikaku* would pounce. After the troops were landed on Guadalcanal, and after the American carriers were destroyed, then the Japanese fleet was to move in and knock out Henderson Field. The troops would then attack, and once more Guadalcanal would be Japanese.

The important matter for both sides was to find the enemy carriers, and find them first.

Japanese and American search planes were out looking. On the morning of August 24 at 9:35 a PBY patrol bomber sighted the *Ryujo*, with three other warships, about 150 miles northwest of Guadalcanal. The PBY reported this, but Admiral Fletcher, still convinced that there were no Japanese fleet elements in the area, refused to believe it. Because he had previously been given some misinformation by a PBY report, now he chose to believe that the land-based air searches were all futile. So he did nothing. It was a dangerous attitude at best.

This particular PBY continued to shadow the *Ryujo* and reported in again an hour later. Still Fletcher refused to believe. His disbelief was heightened when the *Saratoga* search planes began straggling in, having seen nothing that morning. The reason, which Admiral Fletcher did not consider, was that the *Saratoga* planes had a limited range and turned back at the end of 200 miles on their search legs. The Japanese carriers lay 100 miles farther out.

———

Meanwhile the Japanese were looking. At 11:30 A.M. a Kawanishi flying boat came within 20 miles of the American carriers. Four planes of the American combat air patrol spotted the bomber, chased it, and shot it down. The plane had already reported on the American position, and Admiral Chuichi Nagumo, in command of the Japanese carriers *Shokaku* and *Zuikaku*,* did believe and acted. In less than an hour the first attack wave of 27 bombers and 10 fighters left the two big carriers. Almost immediately a second strike was ordered.

———

Admiral Fletcher, meanwhile, was still circling around, nursing his grudge against the PBYs. Then, at noon, another PBY reported on the *Ryujo* position. Reluctantly, after this third sighting, Fletcher decided he would launch his own search planes to confirm or deny the reports.

At 1:00 that afternoon, aboard the *Ryujo*, Admiral Tadaichi Hara ordered the first attack on Henderson Field, and 15 Zeros and six two-engined bombers took off to attack. The American carriers were now close enough to the *Ryujo* for the ships' radar to see the blips of the planes on the screen as they took off, circled, and headed for Henderson Field.

At last Admiral Fletcher was convinced that there were Japanese out there, and he ordered the *Saratoga*'s air group to attack. The

———

*After his failure to do the job properly at Pearl Harbor, his similar failure at Trincomalee, and the disaster at Midway, Admiral Nagumo had been reduced in effect to commanding a carrier division.

Enterprise planes had been sent off on the second search mission. The *Saratoga* pilots were tired. They had already flown five hours that day, but they manned their planes.

The fact was, however, that Fletcher had made a gross error in sending the *Wasp* off to refuel with a Japanese fleet bearing down on him. Now he did not have enough planes to do his job.

———

Shortly after 2:00 P.M. the Japanese planes from the *Ryujo* began to attack Henderson Field. The Cactus Air Force, that ragtag collection of marine, army, and Australian fighter planes, took to the air. They attacked the bombers, and the Japanese Zeros attacked them. Most of the Japanese planes were shot down, and the Americans lost three F4Fs.

The *Ryujo* launched more planes, mostly fighters, for protection from the attack the Japanese had known was coming since that PBY had begun shadowing them early in the morning.

The first planes to attack the *Ryujo* that day were B-17s. They came in from their Australian base and bombed, but as usual they did not hit anything.

Then, just after 4:00 P.M., *Saratoga*'s air strike planes arrived: dive bombers and torpedo bombers. The dive bombers peeled off and made the first attack against *Ryujo*. As they screamed down, the escort vessels ringed the carrier and their antiaircraft guns began to spit. The Zeros protecting the carrier came up to do battle, but the Americans were above them and the U.S. fighters had the advantage for the particular American hit-and-run attack that was so effective against Zeros.

Then the American torpedo planes attacked, using a technique they had learned from the Japanese at the Battle of the Coral Sea. Two planes came in together, one on each bow of the ship. That way, no matter which way the carrier turned it was likely to catch a torpedo.

The dive bombers scored several hits on the carrier with their armor-piercing 1,000-pound bombs. The torpedo planes came in and claimed some hits. Japanese observers aboard the destroyers did not see any, but it did not matter because 10 minutes after the first bomb struck, the *Ryujo* was in a sinking condition. The fires were uncontrollable, and she was listing to starboard. The flight deck was canted so that it nearly touched the water.

The captain of the *Ryujo* radioed the pilots of the Henderson Field strike to land at Buka because he could not handle them. The radio of the strike leader had been shot out, and so the pilots came in anyhow and ditched alongside their stricken carrier. They were rescued by destroyers, which were also rescuing the crew of *Ryujo*. As darkness fell, two more B-17s came over and bombed, but they did not hit anything. The *Ryujo* still floated although she was burning, listing, and dead in the water. Captain Tadao Kato was the last man off the ship. More planes arrived and ditched alongside, and more pilots were rescued. Then the *Ryujo* sank.

Shortly after Admiral Nagumo had ordered his first air strike against Fletcher's carriers, two planes of the *Enterprise* search mission had come across the Japanese carriers and bombed. They did not hit anything, but they reported their adventures to Admiral Fletcher.

The admiral was now suffering for his mistakes. If he had kept *Wasp* with him, he might have attacked the Japanese immediately. But he had sent the *Saratoga*'s planes against the *Ryujo*, and the *Enterprise* planes were on the search; he did not have enough bombers to make an attack, he reasoned. Actually he had 12 torpedo bombers and 13 dive bombers aboard the two carriers, but he was reluctant to use these last reserves. Instead, he concentrated his fighters in the air and on the decks of the carriers to repel the Japanese attack he knew was coming. The two carriers separated and gathered their escort vessels around them to concentrate the antiaircraft fire.

At 4:25 P.M. Admiral Nagumo's first strike arrived. The Japanese had found the American ships easily by following the *Enterprise* planes back from their search missions.

Finally, Admiral Fletcher mustered the courage to attack the enemy and sent off his last bombers and fighter planes, just a few minutes before the Japanese bombers began to attack his ships. Again, he blundered. The bomber pilots had not been briefed about this hastily called mission, and none of them had any navigation equipment aboard. It was a mistake a real aviator would not be likely to make, but Admiral Fletcher was a retreaded battleship man, not an aviator.

―――――――――

Over the American fleet the weather was fine and clear, with a 14-knot wind. The fighters scattered and looked for the enemy. First contact was made 133 miles out when an American pilot reported he saw 36 bombers at 12,000 feet. But he did not see the Japanese planes that came in low and high and managed to sneak through the fighter screen and approach the carriers.

There were so many blips on the radar screens that the *Enterprise* radarmen could not tell who was friend and who was foe. But at 5:00 P.M. the crew of a 20-millimeter antiaircraft gun spotted the Rising Sun insignia on a plane diving down from 12,000 feet.

The Japanese began their attack. A number of bombers chose *Enterprise*; some took on the battleship *North Carolina*. A near-miss to the carrier *Enterprise* caused the aft end of the flight deck to buckle and rise about a foot, but that was the sole damage done by the first Japanese bomb. The Japanese kept boring in. A bomb struck the No. 3 elevator and penetrated three decks before it exploded, killing 35 men and knocking out part of the ship's power. It also created a 3-degree list. Two more bombs did more serious damage and started more fires. Some near-misses also started fires.

All this occurred within four minutes. Then the Japanese turned and headed back for their carriers.

The Americans did not have the planes to do much damage. The *Saratoga* group, operating without instructions except to find the enemy, did find the main group of surface ships and the seaplane carrier *Chitose*. Near-misses from the American planes damaged *Chitose* so that she had to go back to Truk for repairs.

That was the end of the action. The *Enterprise* had to go back to Pearl Harbor for repairs to the damage done her.

So the battle was an American victory with one Japanese carrier sunk, but it was not a decisive victory. Admiral Nimitz was disgusted with Admiral Fletcher's timidity and so indicated. If Fletcher had not been so concerned with fueling under ideal conditions, had he not sent the *Wasp* away at precisely the wrong moment, he might have had a decisive victory and sunk the two big Japanese carriers. Now, Fletcher still had two carriers in the South Pacific, but so did the Japanese, who also had many bases. The odds were still in favor of the Japanese because they had a mighty surface force in the area.

For the next few days the Japanese shelled Henderson Field at will. The American land-based air forces fought back and, wonder of wonders, for once the B-17s hit something, sinking the Japanese destroyer *Mutsuki*. Altogether the land-based air forces commanded by Admiral

John McCain—not the carrier forces—prevented the Japanese from reinforcing the island. From the standpoint of the Guadalcanal defenders, the best thing to come out of the carrier action was the attachment of many of the *Enterprise*'s aircraft to the Cactus Air Force as the carriers sailed for Hawaii.

━━━━━

Admiral Fletcher's carrier force was soon back up to three, with the arrival on the Guadalcanal scene of *Hornet*. That superiority lasted two days, until the Japanese submarine *I-26* got through the American destroyer screen and torpedoed the *Saratoga*. She had to go back to Pearl Harbor for repairs, and flew off her planes. Thus the Cactus Air Force got another 20 fighters and 9 dive bombers. And Admiral Fletcher got called back to Washington by an irate Admiral King. Not even the patient Admiral Nimitz felt like alibiing Fletcher's timidity any further. What was needed in the carrier force were fighting admirals, not fueling experts. Very shortly Fletcher was put out to pasture.

In September the carrier task forces were ordered to support Admiral Turner's attempt to reinforce Guadalcanal. The *Hornet* and the *Wasp* moved to an area south of the island, but there the submarine *I-19* was waiting for them. The sub fired six torpedoes and had the enormous good luck to sink the *Wasp* with three of them, to damage the battleship *North Carolina* with one and the destroyer *O'Brien* with the fifth, and then to get clean away in the confusion. The *Wasp*'s Captain Forrest Sherman and his men fought the fires valiantly, but they could not put them out. Ultimately the carrier was abandoned and sunk by torpedoes fired by American destroyers.

━━━━━

So the American carrier force in the South Pacific was now down to one. Just then Admiral Yamamoto sent three more carriers to the South Pacific, making the ratio five Japanese carriers to one American.

The carrier actions also put an end to the career of Admiral Robert Ghormley, for he had backed Admiral Fletcher in his reluctance to commit the American fleet to attack. In October, Admiral Nimitz relieved Ghormley and sent in the *Hornet* with Admiral Halsey. Two days later the *Hornet*'s planes were committed to battle, helping to defend Henderson Field, as the carrier planes should have been doing all along. Soon the carrier *Enterprise* joined up, bringing the American carrier contingent back to two.

Meanwhile the carrier *Hiyo* developed engine trouble and had to be sent back to Truk for repairs, which brought the Japanese force down to four carriers.

Halsey sent his carriers out to seek battle, and on October 26 a search plane spotted the Japanese carrier force: the carriers *Shokaku* and *Zuikaku* and the light carrier *Zuiho*. They were still commanded by Admiral Nagumo, who matched Admiral Fletcher in timidity. On October 21, when a scouting PBY had bombed and very nearly hit *Zuikaku*, the Japanese fleet was moving south toward the Americans, but Admiral Nagumo turned around and moved away from the enemy.

The American carrier force was now under the command of Vice Admiral Thomas Kinkaid, who was a fighting man and who was seeking battle. He was steaming north, too, looking for the Japanese, and reached a point west of the Santa Cruz Islands and southeast of the Solomons.

After that PBY attack on the Japanese carrier, other PBYs continued to shadow the Japanese forces. On October 26 Admiral Halsey ordered Kinkaid to attack, and Kinkaid did. Just after 5:00 A.M. an air search went out to find and bomb the Japanese. About 85 miles out, the planes from the *Enterprise* found a Japanese bomber. The Japanese, too, were searching. The Japanese found the Americans first, about 200 miles from their own task force. An air strike force left the Japanese carriers almost immediately.

It was not long before American scout bombers also found the Japanese carrier force, and a 500-pound bomb dropped by one of the scout bombers wrecked the flight deck of the light carrier *Zuiho* and made it impossible for her to recover aircraft.

Admiral Nagumo ordered the planes of the *Zuiho* into the air to be recovered by the big carriers, and sent the light carrier back to Truk before the battle was well begun.

The Japanese planes found the American carriers and attacked first. Planes from three carriers came after the American fleet. The Americans launched later but headed for the enemy, and the two groups of airplanes passed each other in midair. Japanese fighters attacked the

American planes and wiped out half the strength of the *Enterprise* task force before it ever reached the Japanese carriers.

When the Japanese attacked the *Hornet*, the plane of the flight leader, Lieutenant Seki, was hit and he made the immediate decision to sacrifice himself and strike the carrier with his plane as a huge bomb. The plane bounded off the smokestack, started a fire on the signal bridge, and smashed through the flight deck where its bombs blew up. Then the Japanese put two torpedoes into the *Hornet*'s engine room. Three more bombs hit and started fires. A Japanese torpedo pilot, having dropped his torpedo and missed, dove his plane into the ship. It exploded near the No. 1 elevator shaft, starting more fires.

Other planes attacked the *Enterprise*. One torpedo fired at the carrier hit the destroyer *Porter* and damaged her so badly that she later sank. One bomb went through the *Enterprise* flight deck and hit near the forward elevator. Later, an attack by the planes of the *Junyo* scored a near-miss that jammed up the forward elevator so it would not work, and one of *Junyo*'s planes bombed the battleship *South Dakota* and did serious damage. Another damaged the cruiser *San Juan*.

For their part, the American pilots did well. They bombed the carrier *Shokaku* and three 1,000-pound armor-piercing bombs damaged her flight deck so severely that Admiral Nagumo sent her back to Truk. *Zuikaku* picked up the *Shokaku* planes.

———

The fight lasted all day, but the carriers were not hit again.

Then, at day's end, Admiral Kinkaid had a serious problem to resolve. The carrier *Hornet* was fighting her fires. The carrier *Enterprise* was heading away from the scene of the action as quickly as she could go, Admiral Kinkaid being fearful that he would lose the last operational American carrier in the South Pacific. He was requested to provide air cover for the crippled *Hornet*, whose captain said she could be saved, but he refused to do so. Admiral Murray, commander of the *Hornet* task force, then had to decide what would be done with his carrier.

Admiral Nagumo might have sent another strike to hit *Hornet*; she was dead in the water and had no air protection whatsoever. Nagumo knew nothing of all this, however; he was aboard *Shokaku*, which was speeding away to Truk. When Admiral Yamamoto read the dispatches and saw that Nagumo had failed to finish off a damaged carrier, he was furious. Land-based aircraft from Rabaul were ordered up to attack *Hornet* and scored more bomb damage.

Now, it was apparent aboard the *Hornet* that they were not going to get any help and that the Japanese knew of their situation. At 5:00 P.M. their fears were proved out. Six fighters and four bombers from *Junyo* (which was not commanded by Admiral Nagumo but by the far more aggressive Admiral Kakuji Kakuta) bombed *Hornet* again. Admiral Murray ordered the *Hornet* abandoned, although she was still not severely damaged except that her engines were out. Destroyers tried to sink her with torpedoes, but she was so stout that they could not, and for the first time in the war the Americans abandoned one of their warships to the mercy of the enemy. Two Japanese destroyers did find the *Hornet* that night, directed by the fires still burning aboard the abandoned carrier, and they torpedoed and sank her.

Admiral Yamamoto's furious complaints to Admiral Nagumo about his timidity caused the carrier admiral to leave the *Shokaku* and return to the battle scene that night in a destroyer, but he might as well have kept on fleeing, for the *Zuikaku* did not find the *Enterprise*, which had fled much earlier.

Yamamoto was angry because Nagumo had failed to take advantage of his victory and pursue the damaged *Enterprise*. It was the last blow. Now Admiral Nagumo was recalled to Japan on the advice of Admiral Yamamoto and ordered to command of the Sasebo Naval Station, a shore job in which he could do no further harm.

The Japanese had won a signal victory at Santa Cruz, but they had failed to exploit it, and because of Nagumo's timidity the Americans still had one damaged carrier left in the South Pacific. She was repaired soon to operate again and participate in the naval Battle of Guadalcanal, in which four American destroyers and two cruisers were sunk, three cruisers disabled, and two destroyers damaged. The *Enterprise* planes did serious damage to the cruiser *Isuzu* and the already disabled *Kinugasa*, which later sank.

The odds in terms of ships and carriers definitely favored the Japanese now but would not for long. As Admiral Yamamoto had predicted gloomily at the outset of the war, the most effective weapon the Americans had was their productive capacity, and much of this had been turned to the manufacture of aircraft carriers and aircraft.

The Japanese were unable to match this productive capacity. One big carrier, the *Nagano*, was building, but that was all. As for planes, the Japanese aircraft production was barely able to keep up with losses. In fact, the struggle for Japan settled down to a land-based air fight because Admiral Yamamoto had to commit his carrier planes and their experienced pilots to the Rabaul air force. So the carriers really did not fight again in the South Pacific struggle. And on the American side, the planes of the *Enterprise* were committed along with those of the Cactus Air Force to keep the Japanese from reinforcing and re-supplying Guadalcanal.

Land-based air might did the job the American carriers had failed to do in the early days of operations. By the end of 1942 the Japanese air force at Rabaul was in very bad shape, replacement planes were almost impossible to get, and Guadalcanal's skies were more or less serene.

Elsewhere, the carrier was changing rapidly. Most of the carrier commanders who had gone into the war at the task force command level had already been replaced. The great exception was Admiral Halsey, whose fighting qualities transcended those of any other admiral. During the Guadalcanal and later Solomons campaigns, this fact was appreciated by his superiors and by the American public. Halsey had come in to command the South Pacific when defeat seemed very likely indeed. So many mistakes had been made that the American naval forces were extremely ragged, and the marines ashore at Guadalcanal were being worn down day by day by naval and aerial bombardment. Attitude was everything. Halsey took the slender resources offered him and used them with great vigor. He tried to force the carrier battle, but the Japanese preponderance at the moment was still too great for him. Still, in the end he triumphed in the South Pacific and would go on to lead the carrier-oriented fleet in some of its days of greatest glory.

11

The Modern U.S. Carrier

After Guadalcanal was lost and the remnant of the Japanese army forces evacuated the island at the beginning of 1943, the Japanese aircraft carriers played no further major role in the battle for the South Pacific. For one thing, Admiral Yamamoto did not have the aircraft or the pilots available to use the carriers. Second, the Japanese possession of land bases made the use of carriers in the battle for the central and northern Solomons and for New Guinea unnecessary.

Furthermore, in April, the Japanese navy suffered a great disaster. The Americans learned through breach of the Japanese naval code that Admiral Yamamoto was making an inspection tour of front-line air bases in the South Pacific for morale purposes, and the American high command staged an ambush at Buin. Half a dozen P-38 fighter planes shot down two twin-engine bombers. One, carrying Admiral Matome Ugaki, Yamamoto's chief of staff, fell into the sea, and Ugaki was saved. The other, carrying Admiral Yamamoto, fell into the jungle, and Yamamoto died. He was succeeded in command of the Combined Fleet by Admiral Mineichi Koga, one of his disciples, but Koga had neither the resources nor the imagination of Yamamoto, and the aggressive use of carriers was never again undertaken by the Japanese.

The Americans, however, found ever more use for their carrier forces. As Admiral Yamamoto had so gloomily predicted, American production was beginning to show early in 1943, and carriers were beginning to come off the ways. By the fall of 1943, several new

118

carriers had been added to the fleet, the new *Essex* class, 27,000 tons, the new *Independence* class, 11,000 tons, and the escort carriers.

Rear Admiral Frederick C. Sherman was down in the South Pacific with Task Force 38, which was built around the old *Saratoga*, once again repaired, and the brand-new light carrier *Princeton*. And the Americans had new aircraft: the F6F Hellcat was a better airplane than the Zero, and the TBF torpedo bomber was better than the Nakajima 97.

————

At the end of October 1943 the Americans were ready to launch an invasion of Bougainville Island, not far from Rabaul. The capture of Bougainville would be an important step in the isolation of Rabaul, the biggest Japanese base in the South Pacific and the center of all Japanese military activity there.

Admiral Koga knew the invasion was coming, and at Truk he assembled the strongest force he could to send down to Rabaul. It consisted of a number of cruisers and destroyers but no carriers. The carriers *Shokaku*, *Zuikaku*, and *Zuiho* were at sea, training new pilots in the safety of Japanese waters. Most of the old pilots and planes had been taken from those carriers to augment the 11th Air Fleet at Rabaul, and by this time a good number of the pilots had been lost. Admiral Koga was operating on the principle that the South Pacific islands under Japanese control made the use of the carriers unnecessary. So his large force heading for Rabaul was led by the heavy cruisers *Myoko* and *Haguro*. After he had dispatched the force, Admiral Koga had some second thoughts and called for the dispatch of the three aircraft carriers to join operations, but the carriers were far away and it would take them many days to refuel, rearm, take on provisions, and sail for the south.

————

On November 4, an Allied search plane flying over Rabaul noted a buildup of Japanese naval shipping in that harbor. The cruisers *Takao*, *Maya*, *Atago*, *Suzuya*, *Mogami*, and *Chikuma* were all there, along with *Myoko* and *Haguro*, several light cruisers, and many destroyers. The pilot notified Admiral Halsey at Espiritu Santu. What Halsey needed just then was a powerful fleet task force to offset the Japanese buildup, but there was no chance of his getting it. Admiral Nimitz back at Pearl Harbor was just preparing for the invasion of the Gilbert Islands, which would begin in three weeks, and all the big ships were committed to that operation. Halsey did manage to secure the one task force, Rear Admiral Frederick Sherman's Task Force 38, which had been lent to him just for the Bougainville invasion. Nimitz had expected it back in time for the Gilbert operation, but when Halsey explained the problem, Nimitz let him keep the force longer.

That very day, November 4, Halsey issued orders to Admiral Sherman. He was to make an air strike on Rabaul on November 5.

When the orders were given, pilots began to groan. Rabaul was one of the most tightly defended installations in the world, its harbor ringed with antiaircraft guns and its air space protected by planes from half a dozen airfields. Earlier the Japanese had claimed it was invulnerable to attack, and although the Americans did not believe that tale, they knew it was going to be tough. It would be particularly difficult because Admiral Sherman had only 22 dive bombers and 23 torpedo bombers to send against this Japanese fleet, and he had only 52 fighter planes to provide combat air patrol for the fleet and to protect the bombers. Admiral Halsey said that Task Force 38 would be supported by planes from General Kenney's Southwest Pacific Air Command, but that meant heavy bombers coming from Australia, and they would not arrive until around noon. By that time the carrier strike would have either succeeded or failed.

Task Force 38 reached the launch point, 230 miles southeast of Rabaul, at 9:00 A.M. on November 5. The planes took off, and when the strike neared a point about 50 miles from Rabaul harbor, they were in perfectly clear skies. They could see the eight heavy cruisers and 20 light cruisers and destroyers lined up.

Commander Henry Caldwell, the leader of the air strike, had his fighters high above the bombers for protection. The formation stuck together as it came in over the harbor's two volcanoes, and only then did the bombers peel off, the dive bombers to pick their targets and scream down, the torpedo bombers to go down on the deck and come in low.

The Japanese antiaircraft gunners held their fire, waiting for the formation to break. They waited too long, however, and when the planes did peel off, they were already attacking. The Japanese fighter planes also waited too long, and when they attacked, they found that they were being shot at by their own antiaircraft guns, along with the Americans. The surprise to the Japanese was complete. Several of the ships had just come in from Truk that very morning and were fueling when the American planes attacked. The antiaircraft fire was the most intense that these pilots had ever seen, surpassing their gloomy expectations. Virtually every plane was hit repeatedly; it was a tribute to the construction of the American fighting aircraft that they held together.

Commander Caldwell knew that he and his men had to hit hard and then get out fast if they were to get out at all. So they did just that. One plane bombed the cruiser *Mogami*. Only one hit was scored, but the heavy bomb penetrated into the engine room and started many fires. One magazine blew up. Nineteen men were killed and 41 wounded. Another plane bombed the cruiser *Maya*. The bomb dropped down through her main smokestack, wrecking the boiler room below. Seventy men were killed and 60 wounded. Two bombers managed to hit the cruiser *Takao*. She was holed below the waterline by a bomb that landed directly alongside, and her steering was wrecked. Her casualties were 23 killed and 22 wounded.

Three bombers made near-misses on the cruiser *Atago*. Others made near-misses on the destroyer *Wakatsuki*. The light cruiser *Agano* lost her forward turret, and the light cruiser *Noshiro* was hit by a torpedo. The destroyer *Fujinami* was also hit by a torpedo.

Then, in a few moments, the Americans were gone. They had lost five fighter planes and five bombers. In view of the defenses, it was remarkable that any of the planes got home that day, and those that made it back to the carrier were so badly shot up that some planes had to be jettisoned. Commander Caldwell's TBF was riddled as he directed the operation from on high. Zeros came after him, and it was all he could do to evade. One of his crewmen was killed and another wounded, but somehow he got the plane home. Lieutenant H. M. Crockett of the *Princeton* brought his fighter limping in and had to be helped out of it because he was wounded. The handlers counted more than 200 holes from bullets and shrapnel in his plane.

That day, when the attack was over, Admiral Koga counted his losses. They were enormous in the sense that his attempt to send a task force against the Americans at Bougainville had to be abandoned.

Six of his cruisers and half a dozen destroyers would have to go back to base for repairs. Some of them could be handled at Truk, but the *Mogami* was so badly hurt that she would have to go back to Japan for a long, long stay in drydock.

The result of the American air strike by that single force from those two carriers was comparable to the British success at Taranto against the Italians. A very small force, suffering minimal losses, had completely stopped a major Japanese naval operation.

———

In the summer of 1943 it became necessary to reorganize the whole American aircraft carrier command system for the same reason that the Japanese had reorganized their carrier command in 1941. The scale of operations planned for the Pacific beginning in 1943 demanded the operation of many carriers under one task force.

By midsummer six fleet carriers, five light carriers, and eight escort carriers were ready for operations, and Nimitz made plans to organize this force into Task Force 50. To lead this force, Admiral Nimitz chose Rear Admiral C. A. Pownall, a naval aviator. The force was known in the fleet as the Fast Carrier Task Force. At more than 30 knots, the only ships that could keep up with the new carriers were the new battleships and cruisers, and so the older ships would be relegated to a new task: offshore bombardment of enemy positions under attack.

Late in August, Admiral Pownall took part of his Fast Carrier Task Force out for a raid on Marcus Atoll. It was really a shakedown cruise, practice for the carriers in armada operations. The carriers involved were the new *Yorktown*, the *Independence*, and the *Essex*. The planes from these carriers delivered five attacks against minimal opposition. In fact, no Japanese aircraft ever left the ground during the fight.

After this raid, Admiral Pownall had a talk with Admiral Spruance, who had been chosen by Admiral Nimitz to command the Fifth Fleet, the armada that would stage the invasion of the Gilbert Islands as the first move in the campaign to cross the Central Pacific Ocean and reach Japan. Spruance told Pownall that Pownall would command the carrier force.

Pownall then went to see Vice Admiral John Towers, deputy to Nimitz, and an airman. He passed on Spruance's remark, but Towers had not been informed of Nimitz's new plans and he snorted at the idea of a commander of carriers. The carriers were distributed among the task forces, he said, and there was no need for an overall commander.

On November 13, however, when the air strikes against the Gilberts moved into high gear in preparation for the coming invasion, Admiral Spruance put Admiral Pownall in charge of Task Force 50, which was divided into four groups. Admiral Pownall, in the *Yorktown*, personally led also the new *Lexington* and the light carrier *Cowpens* in what was called Task Group 50.1. Rear Admiral Arthur W. Radford, in the *Enterprise*, led Task Group 50.2, which included the light carriers *Belleau Wood* and *Monterey*. Task Group 50.3 was commanded by Rear Admiral Alfred E. Montgomery in the *Essex*, with the *Bunker Hill* and the *Independence*. Task Group 50.4 was Admiral Sherman's command, with the *Saratoga* and the new light carrier *Princeton*, which had performed so admirably in the South Pacific.

The escort carriers, which were not nearly so fast or so heavily manned as the others, were to be relegated to the task of direct support of the landings. They would stay right offshore and protect the ships that were landing men, and they would attack tactical targets ashore to assist the landings, while the big task groups would range farther afield, seeking battle with Japanese fleet units if they came out, and destroying Japanese island bases so that they could not send planes to attack the landing forces.

That was the idea of the carrier men. Unfortunately, it was not the idea of Admiral Spruance, who saw in the carriers a primary weapon for protection of the invasion force, and was much more concerned about that than he was about battling the Japanese fleet.

The Gilberts operation at sea went relatively smoothly. One lesson was learned, however, when the first escort carrier was lost in this operation. She was the USS *Liscome Bay*, flagship of Rear Admiral Henry Mullinix. Mullinix was commander of the air group that consisted of the *Liscome Bay*, the *Coral Sea*, and the *Corregidor*. The force was off Makin Island, prepared to begin operations on the first day of the landings. The *Liscome Bay* was at general quarters, getting ready to launch planes when she was torpedoed by the Japanese submarine *I-175*. The torpedo (or torpedoes—some swore it was two) struck near the bomb stowage compartment, exploding and blowing the insides out of the little carrier. The whole after portion of the

Liscome Bay simply vanished, and debris began raining down on other ships in the flotilla. The ship sank almost immediately, and Admiral Mullinix and about 650 men were lost. Only 272 men were rescued.

The lesson learned here was the need for increased antisubmarine vigilance in the vicinity of an invasion landing, a vigilance that had to be multiplied at night and had to include the carriers.

The light carrier *Independence* of Task Group 50.3 was also torpedoed during the invasion of the Gilberts, but not by a submarine. Late on the afternoon of the first day, the task group was attacked by a force of 15 twin-engine torpedo bombers. Most of them chose the carrier *Independence* as their target. The captain managed to outmaneuver half a dozen torpedoes, but one caught the *Independence* in the stern. She took a strong list, but several compartments were flooded and the ship was righted. The fires were put out and the damage repaired enough so that she could travel under her own power back to the United States for repairs.

———

After the successful invasion of the Gilbert Islands, the carrier force was almost immediately employed to strike at the Marshall Islands, which would be the next target of American attack in the Central Pacific. On December 4, 1943, they hit Kwajalein Atoll, damaging the cruiser *Isuzu* and blowing up a big transport. They did not destroy the Japanese air forces in the area, however, because the Japanese were expert at the art of camouflage, and they had many aircraft concealed in revetments.

There was another, more important reason, revealed by the aerial photographs interpreted by the naval intelligence men aboard the carriers. Admiral Pownall was another shy carrier force commander who did not like to take risks. All during the assault he had been worried about the emergence of a major Japanese air assault on his carrier task force, and after this one strike, although urged by several of his carrier captains to hit again, Admiral Pownall decided to get out of the area fast, before nightfall.

Captain J. J. Clark especially wanted to go back and take another slap at the Japanese, but Admiral Pownall refused. He said the pilots were too tired, following the Gilberts operations, so he took the task force home. That night, however, the Japanese planes Pownall had left on the fields did just what he feared they would do: They attacked the task force, and put a torpedo into *Lexington*. It was also just what the young Turks of the carrier force had been warning about: The only defense of a carrier is a good offense. If they wiped out all the enemy planes in the area, then they could not be attacked. Half measures would always bring trouble, they said.

———

The task force went back to Pearl Harbor, where the captains, led by Jocko Clark, began to complain to members of Nimitz's staff about Admiral Pownall. "Nervous Nellie," they called him, charging that he was afraid to put his carriers at risk.

Admiral Nimitz had strong feelings on that subject. So did Admiral King. They had been burned repeatedly by the timidity of Vice Admiral Frank Jack Fletcher in the past. Nimitz also recalled very well his surprise when he arrived at Pearl Harbor to see how much the Japanese attackers had left undone. He did not know then that it was because of Admiral Nagumo's timidity, but he could surmise as much. And from those experiences, King and Nimitz had evolved a doctrine for the fleet: Carriers must be risked. The United States could not do serious damage to the Japanese unless it took carriers into Japanese waters and attacked briskly. Pownall obviously did not agree with that doctrine, and so a bitter controversy began. Out of it came the relief of Admiral Pownall as task force commander. The job was given to Rear Admiral Marc Mitscher, another airman. The principle was established: The new American carrier fleet would become an attack fleet in every sense of the word.

———

In January 1944, the carrier task force rested at Pearl Harbor and was augmented by still more new ships. The older vessels and their aircraft were examined and tested, while the sailors and airmen had a breather following two months of strenuous action. The air attack to soften up the Japanese bases in the Central Pacific was continued by planes of the land-based American air force. Now that the Gilbert Islands had been captured, the heavy bombers from the South Pacific could be staged up through the Gilberts to attack forward targets.

In the middle of January, the carrier task force was dispatched again on a series of raids. Task Force 50 now consisted of six fleet carriers, six light carriers, eight fast battleships, heavy cruisers, light cruisers and destroyers. Behind them came service ships, including repair ships and oilers. These were protected by destroyers and escort carriers. So the Fast Carrier Task Force was like a traveling circus, using its own supply train.

On January 23, Admiral Richmond Kelly Turner, amphibious commander, sailed, leading some 84,000 troops toward the Marshall Islands.

The Fast Carrier Task Force hit the air bases in the Marshalls on January 29. Rear Admiral J. W. Reeves's group was led by the carrier *Enterprise*, and that group attacked Maloelap. Rear Admiral Montgomery attacked Roi. Rear Admiral Frederick Sherman's group struck Kwajalein. Rear Admiral S. P. Ginder's group attacked Wotje. By the time the American invasion force arrived, Japanese air power had been eliminated, most of it on the ground. The Japanese were usually surprised, for even this late in the war their radar was elementary and in many places did not exist at all.

———

In the air, the Japanese learned that the Zero had now been outclassed by the F6F Hellcat fighter plane. The airmen could now argue (and did) that having knocked out the Japanese air defenses of the Marshalls, they had done their job and should be allowed to move elsewhere to strike bases farther away, thus keeping the Japanese from sending air missions to strike the attacking ground troops and naval vessels. Admiral Spruance, commander of the Fifth Fleet, was a very conservative man, however. He saw the mission of the carriers as a protective one, to cover the invasion, and at the Marshalls that is what it was.

The invasion of Majuro and Roi-Namur came on January 31. It was followed by the land attack on Kwajalein the next day. Eniwetok Atoll was to be invaded on February 17, after several air strikes by two of the carrier air groups. The air strikes were duly made. For four days Admiral Ginder's planes worked over Eniwetok. The danger came from farther afield, however, and on February 12 the truth of the airmen's contention that they should be bombing other places was proved: At 2:30 A.M. six four-engined Japanese flying boat bombers from Saipan bombed the airfield at Roi, now held by the Americans. They blew up the biggest ammunition and supply dump in the Marshalls, which contained 80 percent of the supplies for the Roi garrison. For two weeks thereafter the Roi garrison lived on emergency rations until shipments could be brought in from Pearl Harbor.

So even the battleship men were convinced that the airmen had a point. Admiral Harry W. Hill, commander of the forces invading Eniwetok, made sure that Admiral Marc W. Mitscher would make a major air strike on the big Japanese base at Truk before the February 17 invasion of Eniwetok.

The day after that bombing of Roi, the Fast Carrier Task Force was moving toward Truk. Admiral Mitscher left three carriers to protect Eniwetok from air attack that could originate elsewhere, such as Saipan. On the morning of February 17 the carriers sent their planes to attack Truk.

At sunup the Japanese were surprised by 70 American fighter planes. About 30 Japanese fighters scrambled to meet them. Thirty of them were shot down, whereas the Americans lost only four planes. As the fighter sweep returned to the carriers, the bombers came in with fragmentation bombs and incendiaries to attack the airfields and plane storage revetments. They did well. From aerial photos the interpreters decided that there had been about 365 Japanese planes at Truk and that the air strike had destroyed two-thirds of them.

The big disappointment to the carrier men was that they did not find the Japanese fleet in the harbor at Truk that day. The reason was that the whole Japanese defense perimeter had been moved back, even before the loss of the Gilbert Islands. The new Japanese defense line ran from the Marianas to the Philippines. Truk and Rabaul had both been written off, which meant that they would be defended by the men stationed there but that no major Japanese effort would be made to reinforce these areas. That being the case, Admiral Koga, chief of the Japanese Combined Fleet, had moved the forward base of the fleet back to the Palau Islands, 1,000 miles to the west. All that remained at Truk on February 17 were a handful of destroyers, two auxiliary cruisers converted from merchant ships, and several supply and repair ships.

That meant there were plenty of targets. In two days the American carrier bombers flew 1,250 missions, dropping 400 tons of bombs on ships and nearly 100 tons of bombs on the airfields and shore installations. They wrecked 200,000 tons of Japanese shipping, including half a dozen tankers, already in very short supply in Japan.

The major cost to the task force was the torpedoing of the carrier *Intrepid* by a Japanese torpedo plane. She did not sink, but she had to go home for repair and was out of action for six months.

While the carriers attacked Truk, the surface forces steamed through the other islands of the atoll, seeking surface ships to sink. They found the light cruiser *Katori* and the destroyers *Maikaze* and *Nowake*, which had been late in steaming away from Truk. Carrier planes attacked the ships first and damaged them. Then the cruisers *Minneapolis* and *New Orleans* sank the *Katori* in about 15 minutes, and two American battleships went after the destroyer *Maikaze* and sank her. The *Nowake* got away.

———

So the Truk raid was an enormous success for the fast carriers and caused a major change in American war plans. In Washington, the Joint Chiefs of Staff had planned an assault on Truk. Now they abandoned it as unnecessary.

In Tokyo, the invasion of the Marshall Islands also brought about a change in the naval planning. The zone of inner defense was clearly delineated: from the Kuril Islands in the north, east of Honshu in Japan proper, to the Nanpo Shoto Islands (Okinawa), to the Marianas (Saipan, Tinian, Guam), and then the Caroline Islands, west of New Guinea. Truk was no longer needed and was not regarded as defensible.

Admiral Koga reorganized the Japanese fleet and renamed it the First Mobile Fleet. It consisted of the Second Fleet and the Third Fleet.

The Second Fleet was made up of the battleships *Yamato*, *Musashi*, *Nagato*, *Kongo*, and *Haruna*; the cruisers *Atago*, *Takao*, *Maya*, *Chokai*, *Myoki*, *Haguro*, *Kumano*, *Suzuya*, *Tone*, and *Chikuma*; and Destroyer Squadron 2, with 14 destroyers, led by the light cruiser *Noshiro*.

The Third Fleet, which consisted of three carrier divisions, seemed most impressive. Carrier Division 1 included the *Taiho*, *Zuikaku*, and *Shokaku*, very powerful modern carriers. Carrier Division 2 consisted of the less modern and smaller carriers, *Junyo*, *Hiyo*, and *Ryuho*. Carrier Division 3 consisted of the carriers *Chitose*, *Chiyoda*, and *Zuiho*, but the *Zuiho* and the *Chitose* were converted tankers, and the

Chiyoda was a converted naval auxiliary ship. So the strength of Carrier Division 3 was not very impressive.

Furthermore, the Japanese had lost an enormous number of pilots in the past few months. Between November 1943 and April 1944, nearly all the flight personnel of the Carrier Division 1 had been lost in the Rabaul area. The Division 2 had suffered a similar fate in the preliminaries to the landings in the Marshalls. The pilot force of the Division 3, organized in February 1944, had about three months' training.

Admiral Koga's new defense plan was called the Z Plan and called for an attack on the American fleet any time it entered the Philippine Sea, which obviously would be its next move. Island bases would supplant carriers, using the shuttle system to increase the combat effectiveness of the Japanese planes by 50 percent, said Admiral Koga.

At the end of March, the American carriers attacked the new fleet base in the Palau Islands. For two days the Americans raided the airfields and destroyed many planes. Help was sent to the Japanese from Yap and Peleliu Islands, but these planes, too, were shot down. Koga was killed on his way to Davao in the Philippines to organize defenses against the American landings on Hollandia when his plane was caught in a furious storm. So the Japanese Imperial Navy, having lost its first commander of the Combined Fleet in the spring of 1943, lost his successor a year later.

As noted, by this time the Japanese navy was so badly decimated that it no longer bore the cognomen Combined Fleet but was known as the Mobile Fleet. Even that was a misnomer. So desperate was the oil situation by the spring of 1944 that the Mobile Fleet was not mobile at all. Part of the fleet had to be kept in the Singapore area, near the source of petroleum in the Dutch East Indies. Most of the rest of the fleet remained in Japanese home waters, undergoing training.

In the spring of 1944, the Japanese fleet had no operational commander, but the defenses were being built up along the lines of the Koga plan. Ever more aircraft were funneled down to the fringes of the Central Pacific to oppose the Americans. At the end of April, Admiral Nimitz learned of the Japanese air buildup and sent the Fast Carrier Task Force out on several raids. Most important was a new raid on Truk, where the Japanese had planned to build a mighty air armada to oppose further Allied landings. In two days the American carrier planes nearly decimated this new Truk air force. Then they hit Satawan and Ponape in the Caroline Islands.

In May 1944, Admiral Soemu Toyoda became operational chief of the Japanese fleet. His first effort was to present a "victory" plan. It was called A-Go, Operation Victory. It envisaged the total commitment of the Japanese fleet to one single battle at the proper moment, when the Americans attacked the Philippines, Taiwan, or the Japanese homeland. To prepare for it, the First Air Fleet was moved to Tinian Island in the Marianas, and a new commander was appointed, Vice Admiral Kakuji Kakuta, who was promised 2,000 planes for defense of the new Japanese perimeter. The next step was to guess where the Americans would land and to be ready for it. The Japanese guessed, and they guessed wrong.

12

The Marianas Turkey Shoot

From Truk and the other big Japanese airbases in the Caroline Islands in April the American carriers moved so rapidly that they dazzled the Japanese. There were so many of them!

And with the immense success of the American carrier building program, the Japanese now faced an entirely new situation with which they were not able to cope. On April 22, 1944, Rear Admiral Daniel Barbey, commander of United States amphibious operations in the Southwest Pacific, made a landing at Biak Island off the northern coast of New Guinea. The landings were supported by the fast carriers of Task Force 58. After roaming the area and hitting all the nearby airbases, Task Force 58 then withdrew and returned to Pearl Harbor to get ready for a new major landing on Saipan in the Marianas. The Japanese military continued to believe that the main theater would be in the New Guinea area, however, and moved their air and fleet units accordingly. The reason for the Japanese belief was that the American carriers were in the New Guinea area.

Japanese naval intelligence counted no fewer than eight carriers. This was correct, but these eight carriers around Biak were escort carriers, not the fast carrier fleet, and the Japanese failed to make the distinction. So, on June 8 when the American Saipan expeditionary force arrived at Eniwetok, the Japanese were preparing to meet the American fleet off New Guinea. Admiral Jisaburo Ozawa, commander of the Japanese Third Fleet (the nine surviving Japanese carriers, split into three divisions), was at Tawi-Tawi, the East Indies base, waiting for word about the coming big battle. On June 13 he had the word from Tokyo, and it was a total surprise. The big battle would be somewhere around Saipan, said Imperial General Headquarters.

———

The Americans were preparing to attack the Marianas. This threat could not possibly be ignored. For the first time the Americans threatened the core of the inner empire.

The Pacific War now took on an entirely different cast. Before this time, the Japanese and Americans had been fighting in territory captured by the Japanese at the outset of the war. The native peoples were either inimical to the Japanese or neutral. In the Solomons, the Allies had benefited immensely from the coastwatcher brigade, made up of former planters and many, many native Melanesians. Both the Japanese and the Americans faced the difficulties of supplying everything they needed and building new defenses.

In the Marianas and the rest of the inner empire, the defenses were built, and the population of the Northern Marianas was largely Japanese. Japan had secured these islands after World War I as part of the Versailles Treaty settlement, and the native Chamorros had been largely displaced in the ensuing years. Saipan and Tinian had become integrally Japanese. Guam, which had been an American naval base before December 7, 1941, was a different matter, but Saipan was the key island.

To the Americans, Saipan and Tinian were the keys because they had good airfields. Possession of these airfields would make it possible for the Americans to bomb Japan proper with long-range B-29 aircraft. The Americans had already bombed Japan several times, and they had bombed Manchurian bases. The B-29s had come from airfields near Chengtu in western China. But as the Allies discovered, the western China airfields were too far away from Japan, being located at just about the maximum range of the B-29. That had meant the bombers carried minimal loads to make room for fuel, and they still could not reach the island of Honshu, the central core of Japan. So, as both sides knew very well, the struggle for Saipan was the most important that had yet emerged in the attack on the Japanese empire.

An American air strike against the Marianas was staged by the Fast Carrier Task Force on June 11 when Admiral Mitscher's planes destroyed 80 planes on Saipan and Tinian and another 25 on Guam. It sounded fine, but the fact was that they had hit but the tip of the iceberg. The Japanese were counting on land-based air to utilize their shuttle system of bombing from airfields, landing on carriers, and bombing again. Imperial General Headquarters had allocated 1,644 aircraft to Saipan, Tinian, Guam, Rota, Iwo Jima, Yap, and Palau. They had established a special headquarters called the First Air Fleet, which was directly responsible to Naval General Headquarters in Tokyo and not to the Mobile Fleet, and Vice Admiral Kakuji Kakuta had been placed in charge of this air fleet. In addition to this air fleet, Admiral Ozawa's Mobile Fleet, coming up from Tawi-Tawi, had 455 planes. The Americans would face a Japanese air armada more than 2,000 strong.

From the Japanese point of view, there were two disquieting factors. First was the confusion caused by the Allied activity in New Guinea. Because of the landings at Biak, Admiral Kakuta kept shifting his planes around, prepared to meet the attack from any quarter and not knowing, until June 10, just where the real threat lay.

Second was the problem foreseen by Admiral Kusaka before Midway. The failure of the Japanese to bring their experienced pilots home to train new ones, plus the enormous attrition of planes and pilots in the Solomons, New Guinea, the Gilberts, and the Marshalls, had left Japan with only a handful of trained airmen. The new breed, most of them with six months or less of training, were not equipped to undertake long missions flying over endless sea and navigating for themselves. Admiral Kakuta had already noticed that, as he shifted planes and pilots from one island base to the other, the attrition rate through accident was enormous. It would reach 80 percent of these unskilled fliers.

The Americans were back again on June 11, hitting the airbases again, and this time doing more damage than they knew. At the end of three days of air attacks on various bases where Admiral Kakuta had assigned aircraft, enemy damage plus accidental losses amounted to more than 500 aircraft. Already, before the battle was joined, Admiral Kakuta had lost a third of his land-based air force.

Down south, on June 3 Admiral Ozawa had been told that he was to put into effect Operation Kon, which meant a major attack to recapture Biak Island from MacArthur's forces. He had already made two attempts to recapture the island, with a high cost in planes and men. Suddenly, on June 13, Imperial Headquarters reversed orders: The big fight would come at Saipan. Ozawa was to disengage from Biak and hurry to Saipan—2,000 miles away—with all speed. The Americans were about to invade.

That night of June 13, Admiral Ozawa fueled the fleet at Guimaras and headed north, followed by seven tankers. They sped along, disregarding the cost in fuel, and on June 18 arrived 500 miles west of Saipan. Admiral Ozawa now began searching for the enemy, dispatching scout planes over a wide area. Sixteen seaplanes, 13 carrier attack planes, and 13 bombers went out; they soon enough reported that they had sighted four groups of American ships. The figures were amazing. The enemy fleet was enormous, the scouts indicated: more than eight large warships, plus 11 aircraft carriers.*

The Japanese still had superiority in numbers of aircraft. Even after the attrition of the past few days, the Japanese could put into the air some 1,400 aircraft for the Saipan battle, as opposed to the 900 aboard the American carriers.

Admiral Ozawa had one other advantage: range of aircraft. The Japanese had built new Type 92 fighters, Suisei bombers, and Tenzan torpedo bombers, all of which outranged the Americans. They could fly 400 miles without refueling.

The American F6F fighters had a range of less than 300 miles. The whole American concept was based on a flight of not more than 300 miles from the carrier.

And this was the key to Admiral Ozawa's strategy. He would find the enemy and strike from about 400 miles. While the Americans were still reeling from the first shock, he would steam swiftly toward them and launch the second strike from about 250 miles away. The planes would shuttle to the Saipan, Tinian, and Guam airfields, and bomb the American fleet again. Thus two strikes would become four.

---

*The actual strength of the American fleet was 14 battleships, 10 cruisers, 11 light cruisers, four antiaircraft cruisers, and 86 destroyers, plus seven fleet carriers, eight light carriers, and 14 escort carriers, a naval strength three times as great as that of Japan.

At 3:30 P.M. on June 18, Admiral Ozawa's planes reported on the American fleet, although they had seen only part of it. Rear Admiral Suemo Obayashi, who commanded Carrier Division 3, advocated an immediate attack and began to launch his planes. Several were in the air when Admiral Ozawa intervened and called them all back. The air strike would be made at dawn on June 19, he said. To strike now would be premature and would involve night landings. It was not necessary. They would wait. That night Admiral Ozawa broke the radio silence he had maintained all during the run north from Tawi-Tawi. He announced the dawn strike against the Americans and called on Admiral Kakuta for support from his land-based aircraft.

An hour before dawn, Admiral Ozawa sent off a group of 16 seaplanes to find the enemy, followed by another group of 14 scout bombers, and then a group of 11 attack bombers. At 7:00 A.M. the planes began reporting in: They had found the enemy, in three groups, each with carriers, with the nearest groups being only 300 miles east of Ozawa.

The admiral ordered the attack immediately. There was a very brief pause as flight leaders aboard the carriers came to their admirals to announce emotionally that they were all going out to avenge the disgrace of Midway and destroy the enemy, wipe him out, annihilate him. Then the pilots manned their planes and were off. At 7:30 the first attack wave was in the air. It consisted of 48 fighters, 54 bombers, and 27 torpedo bombers. The Japanese pilots and admirals who stood on the bridges of their ships and watched were determined to have a victory this day. They were bursting with enthusiasm for the battle.

In the American fleet, the atmosphere was far more restrained. On the evening of June 17, the American submarine *Cavalla* had reported on the position, course, and speed of a large force of Japanese warships that was heading east toward Saipan. The Americans thus had almost a full day's advantage over the Japanese on locating the enemy. Admiral Mitscher wanted to start moving toward the enemy, which was then some 800 miles to the west of the American fleet. But 800 miles for two fleets heading toward each other at 25 knots meant that they could be within range in a matter of six to eight hours.

The airmen wanted to steam out as fast as possible. Admiral Mitscher suggested that they could make air contact with the Ozawa fleet by late afternoon of June 18 and attack that night. Even more than the Japanese, Admiral Spruance did not want a night attack. The lessons of Guadalcanal were still too fresh in the minds of the surface admirals, for in virtually every night engagement the Japanese had defeated the Allied forces. Admiral Spruance decided against the night air attack and turned the fleet south. That way he lost contact with the Japanese. And contact was not regained—never was regained—by the carrier forces. Rather, Admiral Nimitz at Pearl Harbor found the Japanese fleet for Spruance on that night of June 18 when Admiral Ozawa broke radio silence to get in touch with Admiral Kakuta. By triangulation from receiving stations at Pearl Harbor, in the South Pacific, and in the Aleutians, the radio intelligence men were able to spot the position of the Ozawa fleet.

By that time, the ultraconservative Admiral Spruance had the fleet heading away from the Japanese, and there was no possibility of staging an air strike that night. No possibility, that is, unless the American fleet turned and speeded toward the Japanese fleet. If they did that, then Mitscher would be able to launch planes at daybreak and then attack. Mitscher so suggested, and the suggestion dismayed Admiral Spruance, who feared that the Japanese had secret carriers up their sleeves that might pounce on him from another angle. The Americans thus lost their chance to make the first strike on the Japanese. That course did not surprise the Japanese. Their assessment of Admiral Spruance was shrewd. They knew that he was a man of extremely limited imagination who would never take a chance.

———

Neither the Americans nor the Japanese had made proper use of their carrier strike forces by this point of the war, a fact for which Admiral Nimitz had to be given some responsibility. Admiral King really had a much more comprehensive concept of the proper use of carriers than even Nimitz, and Nimitz, who was essentially an easygoing man, went along with Admiral Spruance on his very limited concept of the function of a commander of an invasion force. Spruance believed that his prime responsibility was to protect the troops and supply vessels managing the invasion of Saipan. He believed this even though Admiral Richmond Kelly Turner, the amphibious commander, had told him to go ahead and get the Japanese fleet, that Turner with the escort carriers would protect the invasion forces. So by this reasoning, Spruance elected to abandon his other major responsibility—which was to use the American fleet to destroy the Japanese fleet if possible.

A number of the junior American admirals, the commanders of task groups, understood this philosophy very well. Admiral Radford, Admiral Forrest Sherman, Admiral Frederick Sherman, Admiral Ginder, and others all knew what the carriers could accomplish. And so did Admiral Mitscher, of the older generation, and so did Admiral Halsey. But Mitscher and Halsey were the only two of the top commanders who really did understand the carriers. As long as Spruance was in command, the carriers would be used as support ships and not as an assault force.

This attitude became clear that night of June 18 when instead of assaulting the Japanese fleet, Spruance suggested to Admiral Mitscher that he send planes to various island atolls to knock out more Japanese aircraft. When Admiral Montgomery, one of the task group commanders, learned of this, he was so outraged that he sputtered. He sent a hot message to Admiral Mitscher that was very near insubordination. Montgomery knew Mitscher, however; the admiral agreed with him completely, and there would be no trouble. But neither did the message do any good. Spruance was not to be changed. Mitscher simply said he would look into the matter of diverting planes to island bombing and did nothing about it, saving his strength for the battle he knew was coming, even if Spruance did not want it.

The air searches launched by the American planes in the middle of the night and at dawn produced nothing. The reason was simple: Admiral Ozawa had maintained his fleet just outside the 400-mile limit that was the end of the rope for the American scout planes. All Ozawa was waiting for in those dawn hours was word from his own searchers as to where the American fleet had ended up in its running around to avoid the night battle. He found out at 7:30 A.M. and gave the order to launch planes.

In the meantime, the air battle of the day had already begun.

Admiral Kakuta had heeded the message sent by Ozawa the night before and had brought many planes to Saipan and Tinian from Guam and Truk. At dawn the fighters and bombers took to the air and headed out for the American fleet.

The Americans learned of this when suddenly out of nowhere a Zero fighter appeared and dropped a bomb on the destroyer *Stockham*. The bomb missed, and the fighter was shot down by the antiaircraft gunners of the destroyer *Yarnall*. The attack on the American fleet, led by Japanese land-based airplanes, had begun.

· The land-based air command at Saipan now knew where the Americans were, and in a half hour a score of blips appeared on the screens of the carriers. The combat air patrol put up by the light carrier *Belleau Wood* was sent out to investigate these blips. Six fighters flew 90 miles from their carrier and orbited over Oroto Field on Guam. It was 6:30 A.M.

Below the American fighters, the Japanese were engaged in enormous activity. The American planes stayed up high at nearly 16,000 feet and watched what was happening below. Then four Zero fighters came down on them from above. A melee began. The F6F fighter planes were superior in armor, and the first passes of the Zeros did no good. The Americans got on the tails of two Zeros and shot them down. Soon American pilots were falling, too, in the furious onslaught by the Japanese.

More American planes from the carriers *Hornet, Cabot*, and *Yorktown* came onto the Guam scene, and the fighting grew even more fierce. Here, this day, the superiority of the F6F Hellcat over the Zero was proved time and again as American pilots survived tail attacks and then outturned the Japanese, outdived the Japanese, and outshot them in head-to-head contests. Only in speed did the Japanese still have an advantage and it was slight. As a fighting machine, the F6F was superior to anything but the new Type 92, and there were not many of those in the Marianas this day.

One group of Japanese pilots, who had obviously been studying the means of combatting the F6F, adopted one effective tactic: They would engage a Hellcat, come down low toward the water, then make a sharp diving turn. If the Americans followed they were likely, with their heavier aircraft, to go into the sea. If not, they were at a great disadvantage at low altitude. This tactic counted for several Japanese victories this day, and a number of American pilots who lived to tell the tale would not forget the skill the enemy had shown.

Then 8:30 A.M. came. Still the fight was being carried against the Americans by Admiral Kakuta's land-based air forces. Kakuta was bringing in more planes from Truk and Palau, and from Yap and other islands, more planes to attack the American fleet and destroy it as their admiral demanded: attack, shuttle to the carriers, and attack again.

In turn, the Americans sent more planes over Guam, these from the *Bunker Hill*. The sky was full of vapor trails, the air was so full of aircraft that near-collisions were a common problem, and the Americans were now numerous enough to try some new strategy. They lay in wait for the Japanese reinforcements coming in from the other islands, and when these planes went into the landing pattern and were committed to the runways, the Americans swooped down and shot them up. Many of those Japanese aircraft, coming all the way across the sea, then crashed into the ground of Oroto Field and were lost.

———————

The American planes that had moved to Guam were still in the air for the most part (some cripples having headed home and landed) when the second stage of the great air battle began. Admiral Ozawa had launched his first attack wave of 129 planes at 7:30 that morning. Then the Japanese waited. At 10:00 A.M. they were growing a little restless. They should have heard something from the attacking planes by this time, and they heard nothing. The plan called for the launch of a second wave at 10:00 A.M. This second group consisted of 20 fighters, 36 bombers, and 26 torpedo bombers. Another wave was supposed to launch from the *Taiho* at that time, consisting of about 20 more planes, but a flight deck accident delayed the *Taiho* launch.

Just after that second launch had been made, the radar operators of the American fleet saw on their scopes the large number of blips that indicated the Japanese strike force was approaching and was about 150 miles to the west. That gave Admiral Mitscher about half an hour before the enemy would be on him.

Mitscher then called back to the carriers all the fighters that had been sent out to search, and the ones that were low on fuel were landed and refueled. All available fighter planes were ordered to get into the air, and at 10:20 A.M. they began launching. In fact, the Japanese had an excellent opportunity, because the Americans were a little slow to react, and the decks of the carriers were crowded with planes. Instead of boring in to attack, the Japanese strike waves stopped to reorganize in the air. This delay of 10 minutes or so gave the Americans time to get more fighters up.

Soon fighters from the *Bunker Hill*, the *Essex*, the *Princeton*, the *Lexington*, and the *Enterprise* were all in the air, circling, awaiting instructions from their fighter directors and heading for the enemy. The Japanese and American aircraft began mixing up in dogfights all around the carrier groups. The American fighters simply would not let the Japanese attackers pass. By 11:00 A.M. the first Japanese raid was broken up, and not one single Japanese plane had reached a carrier. The battleship *South Dakota* did take one bomb, which killed or wounded some 50 men. The cruiser *Minneapolis* was damaged by a near-miss. Several destroyers had very narrow escapes, but not one was actually hit.

The Japanese planes now had their option. They could retire toward their own carriers, or they could land on one of the Mariana Islands. They could not land on Saipan, for Saipan was under attack, and Aslito Field was the center: It would be captured within a few hours and the runways were no longer usable. The Japanese garrison had left the airfield on June 18.

Some pilots did land on Guam, but they found that they were under fire as they landed and then strafed and bombed after they landed. Just after launching fighters, the captain of the *Bunker Hill* had also launched a bombing attack on Oroto Field.

———

Shortly before noon, the second attack force of Japanese planes started coming in toward the American ships. More American fighters were put into the air, and the melee began all over again.

At about 12:30 P.M. planes from the first attack force began to arrive back at the Japanese carriers, and as they landed, the pilots were debriefed. They had sad stories to tell. The battle area was covered with heavy clouds, they said, and so they were not able to get a clear picture of the whole scene. They did know that the Americans had put up an enormous screen of fighters and had hit the Japanese about

30 miles out from the ships. The pilots, dejected, said that the first wave had been a real failure, and that as far as each of them could tell, most of their comrades had been shot down or had limped into some airfields in the Marianas.

Out in front of the carrier force, the American fighters were busy shooting down the Japanese attackers of the second wave. Commander David McCampbell, commander of the Air Group of the *Essex*, led 11 fighter pilots to meet the second attack, and they shot down almost all the dive bombers of one whole formation long before they got near the carriers. The pickings were so good for the American fighters that McCampbell remarked finally, as he looked around, "The sky is getting short of enemy planes." And as with the first attack wave, after about an hour it was all over, and the remnants of the Japanese force limped toward the Marianas airbases.

Now the very confusion of the Japanese acted in their favor. Planes were still coming in toward the carriers from the Marianas airfields, in small units or individually, and thus they were much harder for the radar men to track. Also, the strike from the *Taiho* finally got off at noon and arrived about two hours later over the American ships.

And so the Japanese did manage to get some planes through the fighter screen. One torpedo pilot, wounded, crashed his plane into the side of the battleship *Indiana*. The new carrier *Wasp* took a bomb through its flight deck. The *Bunker Hill* was damaged by two near-misses that started fires and punched shrapnel holes through the hangar deck. It was no joke. Seventy-six men were killed or wounded by these "near-misses."

Every aircraft carrier is a vulnerable ship, partly because it is so large and noticeable and partly because the enemy prizes carriers more than any other vessel.

On June 19, Admiral Ozawa not only had to contend with the strength of the American carrier force but with the extremely powerful and numerous force of American submarines that ranged in these waters. The submarine *Cavalla* had reported the Japanese fleet's coming in the first place. Now, in the middle of the afternoon, as Admiral Ozawa was getting the bad news about the failure of his carrier strikes against the American fleet and the failure of the carefully planned "shuttle policy," he faced a new set of troubles. The American submarine *Albacore* was trailing his flagship, the *Taiho*.

The *Albacore* had discovered the fleet early on the morning of June 19 and had been trailing all day long. Her skipper, Commander J. W. Blanchard, had been awed by the size of this carrier, the largest he had ever seen (33,000 tons and 850 feet long). He hung around the edge of the Japanese ship formation, watching and waiting that morning.

As the last planes of the second strike were being launched at around 10 A.M., *Albacore* fired a spread of six torpedoes at the *Taiho*. One Japanese pilot, flying one of the new fast navy fighter planes that was so much better than the Zero (the Hamp), had just taken off when he saw a torpedo heading for his ship. He put the nose of his plane down and crashed into the torpedo. The plane blew to bits and that torpedo did not hit the *Taiho*, but another of those six torpedoes did hit forward on the starboard side of the ship.

To the officers of the *Taiho*, a single torpedo did not seem much of a problem. The ship had been built for maximum security, with cunning compartmentalization. It was a question of adjusting and flooding compartments on the opposite side and getting the damage control crews down to repair the skin of the ship. All this was done, and Admiral Ozawa was not seriously concerned about the flagship. She had scarcely slowed. The flight deck operations were unaffected for the moment, except that the forward elevator to the hangar deck had jammed.

At first that seemed to be all the damage, but when the damage control party entered the elevator pit they found it awash with gasoline. One of the gasoline storage tanks had been ruptured by the force of the explosion. Pumps were brought in and the crew tried, without success, to find the source of the leak. Then the ship's damage control officer made a fatal mistake. He decided that the way to clear the ship was to open the whole ventilation system and turn on the power ducts to blow the gasoline fumes away. This was done, but instead of blowing the fumes away, the ventilation system sucked them deep into the bowels of the ship. The fumes persisted and spread. The *Taiho* was becoming a time bomb.

At this point, Admiral Ozawa was impervious to the whole matter. He had too many other problems on his mind. First, he knew by noon that his first air strike was in deep trouble. The first returning pilots gave their sad stories of failure. And then Lieutenant Commander H. J. Kossler's American submarine *Cavalla*, which had tracked the fleet originally, caught up again and put three torpedoes into the carrier *Shokaku*. Flight operations had to be suspended. The pilots returning from the first strike had to be taken aboard the *Taiho* or the *Zuikaku*. The *Shokaku* was aflame. And then, before the agonized eyes of the admiral, the *Shokaku* blew up.

So here, shortly after noon on June 19, the Japanese carrier fleet was hard hit, although carrier battle had not really been joined by the Americans. Their only effort, because of Admiral Spruance's timidity, had been to protect their carriers and, in so doing, to destroy perhaps 200 Japanese aircraft. Despite the failure of the American carriers to find the enemy fleet, Admiral Ozawa had already lost one carrier, and a second had been damaged. The American submarines had already won the battle.

———

Admiral Ozawa, standing on his bridge, was puzzled by the failure of the Americans to attack him, but by midafternoon he had not much time even to speculate on Admiral Spruance's motivations. Shortly after the *Shokaku* blew up, an explosion shook the *Taiho*. The time bomb had gone off. A spark had ignited the gas fumes in one compartment. The first explosion set off another explosion, and that set off another, and another and another, until the *Taiho* was a mass of flames. Admiral Ozawa transferred his flag and Emperor Hirohito's picture to the cruiser *Haguro* and watched the *Taiho* burn and soon sink. The loss of life was enormous; nearly 4,000 men went down with the two carriers *Shokaku* and *Taiho*.

Two carriers had been sunk, and two-thirds of Ozawa's planes never returned to the other carriers. The battle was lost by late afternoon, and still the American carrier planes had not put in an appearance over the Japanese fleet. The American carrier pilots were still fighting the battle of Guam, engaging the planes of Admiral Kakuta's land-based air force and the carrier planes that came to land and perform their shuttle missions.

The Americans were shooting down many, many Japanese planes. The action continued all afternoon into the dusk. The Americans lost about 30 fighters that day, but the Japanese, who had sent out 370 planes from the carriers, recovered fewer than 120 of them. This did not count the destroyed land-based aircraft that had been shuttled in from outside bases and from Marianas bases. Perhaps another 200 Japanese planes were destroyed in the air that day and many more on the ground.

All day long, Admiral Spruance had persisted in his timidity, keeping the American fleet headed east, away from the Japanese enemy. It was not until 3:00 P.M., when the battle was already won by the submarines, that Admiral Spruance decided it would be all right for Admiral Mitscher to use his planes to attack. It was way too late, however. The American fleet was within a few miles of Guam, and Admiral Ozawa was totally out of their range.

What the Americans had done that day was put an end to Japanese air power in the Marianas. That was no mean feat, but it did not deal with the Japanese fleet.

That night, Spruance agreed that the Saipan invasion seemed safe enough for Admiral Mitscher to seek a fight, and Mitscher moved the carrier force swiftly westward. Because he did not know where the enemy was, he could not waste the fuel to go at flank speed but had to travel at 23 knots, cruising speed, to save oil for what might be a long hard day ahead.

On the morning of June 20 Mitscher launched his search planes, but they did not find the Japanese. The American planes flew out 325 miles, their limit, and then turned back. There was no help from Pearl Harbor this day because Admiral Ozawa was maintaining radio security. Also, Admiral Ozawa, still unsure of the results, still unsure of his enemy's plans, was skillfully staying out of range of the American fleet that night and awaiting the coming of dawn.

With morning came more disappointment for Admiral Mitscher. The Japanese fleet seemed to have vanished. By noon, several of Mitscher's staff were predicting that the Japanese had already gone home. Mitscher launched search planes equipped with belly tanks and they went out 475 miles, but still they did not find the Japanese.

Ozawa was still waiting. He had lost two big carriers, and he had only about 100 planes left on his remaining four carriers; but he was not dismayed. He had heard nothing from Kakuta to indicate the total failure of the shuttle system, and he believed that most of his planes were on Marianas airfields, safe and waiting. He was prepared to attack again and continued to be puzzled by the behavior of the Americans.

In Tokyo, Admiral Toyoda, the chief fleet operating officer, had a much grimmer picture of the battle of June 19. He had reports from Admiral Kakuta, telling of the disaster at Guam. He had Ozawa's reports of the sinking of the *Shokaku* and the *Taiho*. Toyoda then knew that the battle had been lost. He ordered Admiral Ozawa to steam toward Okinawa and in effect to break off the battle.

Early on the afternoon of June 20, Admiral Ozawa transferred his flag from the *Haguro*, which was hopeless as a command ship because of its limited communications, to the *Zuikaku*. He continued outside the American range of search.

At 1:30 P.M. Admiral Mitscher launched one more search. For two hours nothing was heard. Then at 3:30, Lieutenant R. S. Nelson had just reached the 325-mile mark that was the limit of his search pattern and was preparing to turn back toward his carrier when off to the north he saw the Japanese fleet: carriers, battleships, and other ships. He did not have time to count. He got on the radio and reported that the enemy was heading northwest at 20 knots and gave the position. Then he turned and headed for the *Enterprise*. Another five or six minutes out and he might not have made it.

———

Admiral Ozawa had decided that midafternoon that he was safe enough to fuel his ships for the run home. The fueling had begun when the intelligence officer of the *Atago* heard on the radio the excited, in-the-clear broadcasts of Americans announcing that the Japanese fleet had been found. In a few moments Ozawa had the word, and he ordered the fueling stopped. He began to prepare for the attack that was so late in coming.

The Americans again gave Ozawa time. Lieutenant Nelson's report, from so far at sea, had been garbled when it reached the *Enterprise*. Mitscher knew that the Japanese fleet had been sighted and by an *Enterprise* plane, but he did not know quite where. It was 6:00 P.M. before Nelson got back and could make a report.

Meanwhile planes had been launched from all the carriers, and they were milling about, but they did not know where to go. They headed to the west, figuring that they would correct their headings when the word came. When the word did come, the planes found that they were 300 miles away from the Japanese fleet, which was the limit of the American aircraft. Now, an attack became a dangerous matter. Could they attack and get home?

That was Mitscher's problem at 6:00 P.M., with his planes far out at sea. He could call them back and wait until the next day, but if he did this, it was quite probable that the Japanese would elude him entirely. If he went ahead, he was going to lose a lot of aircraft. The planes would come "home" at the limit of their endurance after the attack, and some of them would get lost. There would be many planes ditched at sea this night.

Mitscher did not hesitate. It was his task to put his ships and his planes at risk in order to strike at the enemy. He informed Admiral Spruance that he was launching another 131 bombers and 88 fighter planes to attack the enemy fleet.

———

The sun was on the horizon when the American planes moved in on the Japanese fleet. There was no time for maneuver or coordination of attack. If anyone wanted to get home, he had better get in and get it done with. So the planes went in over the tankers, which had been left behind when the capital ships hurried into fighting position, over the cargo ships, and to the warships. The dive bombers were at 16,000 feet, and they peeled off to attack the carriers. They peeled off in their bombing runs from 9,000 feet, and as they did, the combat air patrol launched by Admiral Ozawa began to attack the Americans. Eleven dive bombers from the *Enterprise* attacked together. Most of the bombs missed, although three were near-misses and did some damage to the *Zuikaku*. Then one dive bomber put its bomb into the stern.

Other dive bombers attacked the light carrier *Hiyo*, and two of the bombers put 1,000-pound armor-piercing bombs through the flight deck. The bombs started fierce fires, and in a very short time the *Hiyo* was dead in the water.

The Japanese fought back tenaciously with antiaircraft guns and fighter planes, and several American planes were shot down. All the Japanese carriers suffered some damage, the *Zuikaku* with its stern damaged, the *Junyo*, the *Ryuho*, and the *Chiyoda* with damage mostly from near-misses. The battleship *Nagato* was also damaged, and two tankers were sunk. But the real damage was to the aircraft again. In the fighting, many Japanese planes were shot down.

Actually, the damage inflicted by the American fleet on the Japanese fleet was minimal, compared with what it might have been. Admiral Spruance had been holding Admiral Mitscher back for so long and demanding attacks on the Marianas airfields that when the word finally came about the position of the Japanese fleet, the American bombers were all loaded with bombs and no torpedoes—thus no torpedo attacks on the Japanese fleet, for which Admiral Ozawa could be grateful. Also, late in the afternoon, as the American fleet steamed swiftly toward the Japanese, Mitscher had asked permission to let the battleships and cruisers make a night surface attack on the Japanese fleet. Admiral Spruance, with his typical timidity, had refused.

At that same time, Admiral Ozawa had ordered Admiral Kurita, his own battleship commander, to make just such a night attack on the Americans. Admiral Kurita had responded with alacrity and launched 10 float planes to find the enemy. There was no question of worry about night landings here. When they found the enemy, Kurita would rush in and strike. As the night wore along, Admiral Ozawa had reminders from Tokyo about retirement, and at 11:00 P.M. he finally ordered Kurita to turn around and join the carriers heading for home.

———

Admiral Mitscher considered launching another air strike, but Admiral Spruance and the weather were against him. Mitscher would have had to turn into the wind to recover his planes, and that meant he would have had to turn away from the incoming planes and away from the Japanese. All this was very complicated, and given Spruance's attitude—satisfaction that the Marianas invasion forces were safe from attack and no real interest in the Japanese fleet—Mitscher found that about all he could do was try to recover as many of the planes of his one air strike as possible and rescue as many downed airmen as possible.

The Americans, having attacked, and having sunk one carrier, had to disengage quickly from the battle and hurry to try to get back to their carriers. Not all of them made it, even though Admiral Mitscher braved the danger of air or submarine attack by lighting up his carriers so the fliers could see them from far away and at least come into the fleet orbit to ditch.

When all the planes that were going to land had landed, Admiral Mitscher counted noses. He had lost 100 of the 216 planes sent out in the attack on the Japanese. Two hundred and nine men had gone into the water, and only 101 of them had been rescued by the end of the night. Admiral Mitscher suggested that the fleet turn toward the enemy again and proceed.

Now that the battle was over and Admiral Spruance was certain that the Japanese fleet had retired, he was not worried about proceeding. So he let Mitscher have his way. Besides, said Spruance, they might find some cripples that way.

Cripples? Why not the Japanese fleet? That was what admirals were for, to fight sea battles, not to worry about protecting land invasions when the amphibious commanders were confident enough, or to search for cripples when the enemy fleet was still at sea, rather than search for the fleet. It was a measure of the American naval high command's attitude toward the war that Admiral Spruance was never faulted.

Back at Pearl Harbor in the meetings of the air officers, however, there was a good deal of criticism of Admiral Spruance. Most of the carrier captains and junior admirals faulted him for timidity. A great chance had been missed in the Philippine Sea, they said, a chance to wipe out the Japanese fleet. And, of course, it had been missed not once but twice, and both times because Admiral Spruance refused to let Mitscher go after the Japanese when there was a chance to do so.

The Battle of the Philippine Sea represented a complete contrast with the Battle of Midway. At Midway, Admiral Yamamoto had set out to draw the American fleet out of its hiding, force it into battle, and wipe it out. Yamamoto hoped for a quick victory that would bring the Americans to the peace table. The Japanese failed really because of the carelessness of Admiral Nagumo, just as Nagumo's timidity had lost the opportunity at Pearl Harbor.

When the Americans set forth to invade the Marianas, Admiral Nimitz knew that this course would bring an opportunity to destroy the Japanese fleet because the fleet was sure to appear to challenge this drive into the inner empire.

Admiral Nimitz had the wrong commander in place. Admiral Richmond Kelly Turner was extremely competent, and he knew that he could manage the Saipan invasion without any more help from the Fast Carrier Task Force than he had been given. He had the old battleships, cruisers, and the escort carriers to do his job. So the fleet commander should have been overweaningly concerned with the destruction of the Japanese fleet.

Admiral Spruance was not vitally concerned with the Japanese fleet, however. He was concerned lest the Saipan invasion get into trouble. In fact, the invasion did get into trouble on the land, and the reserves had to be committed much earlier than any one wanted. That was not a problem that could be resolved by the air fleet, though. One cannot escape the feeling that Admiral Spruance served Admiral Nimitz very badly by refusing battle twice.

The fact is that the American plane losses for the damage done to the Japanese fleet were extremely high, 100 planes for one small carrier and damage to other ships. It was the most disadvantageous ratio of the entire war. As it turned out, the late-day air strike of June 21 was hardly worth the effort, given Spruance's attitude toward the whole affair. The battle had already been won by two American submarines, which had sunk two major carriers and, in effect, wiped out the Japanese carrier attack force as a major fleet weapon. After the Battle of the Philippine Sea, the Japanese Mobile Fleet no longer existed as a unit. The carrier force now consisted of the lone fleet carrier *Zuikaku*, the light carriers *Junyo*, *Zuiho*, and *Ryuho*, and two strange ships, once battleships, whose afterturrets had been cut out to permit installation of short flight decks. These were the *Ise* and *Hyuga*, and they were now called part of the carrier fleet. Besides these there were the converted ships *Chitose* and *Chiyoda*, and these were all that were left of the once-proud Japanese carrier force.

There was one other—the enormous *Shinano*, 71,000 tons. She was still under construction and would be until November 1944, but then her life was to be extremely short. She was sunk by an American submarine while still making her trials and never saw action.

The Battle of the Philippine Sea marked the real end of the Japanese navy as an effective force. There would be one more great naval effort from the remnants of the fleet, and it would be met by the Americans very promptly at Leyte Gulf, with Admiral Halsey in command of the American battle fleet. If he had been in command at the Battle of the Philippine Sea the outcome would almost certainly have been different. The Marianas Turkey Shoot would have proceeded as it did, but the carrier attack forces would have been employed from the outset to find and destroy the enemy. That was the sort of commander Halsey was: a man to find and destroy the enemy where ever he might be. Soon enough he would have his chance.

Vice Admiral Marc Mitscher on the
bridge of the carrier *Lexington* in
June 1944.   (*National Archives*)

Admiral Jisaburo Ozawa. He was the last
commander of the Japanese air fleet, and
watched the remnants destroyed by
Admiral Halsey's planes at Leyte.
(*National Archives*)

The ships around the carriers would put up an enormous barrage under attack.
Here a Japanese plane attacking the carrier *Kitkun Bay* on June 18, 1944, has just
been shot down.   (*National Archives*)

The U.S.S. *Gambier Bay*, smoking in the background, was the only American carrier sunk by naval gunfire from enemy ships. She was sunk in the Leyte Gulf battles of October 25, 1944, when the Japanese tried to destroy the American landing forces. (*National Archives*)

A Japanese Zero fighter with a suicide pilot aboard makes a run on the escort carrier *Suwannee* during the Battle of Leyte Gulf. (*National Archives*)

Ulithi atoll, which the Allies occupied in the fall of 1944, was so big it could accommodate the whole American fleet if necessary. Here six carriers steam into the area.   (*National Archives*)

Admiral John S. McCain and Admiral William F. Halsey confer in Halsey's cabin off the Philippines in December 1944.   (*National Archives*)

These are the 40mm anti-aircraft guns of the carrier *Hornet*, in action off Japan in February 1945. (*National Archives*)

The U.S.S. *Franklin* on March 10, 1945, just after a hit by a Japanese dive-bomber. (*National Archives*)

Firefighting aboard the carrier *Enterprise* after she was hit by a suicide plane on March 20, 1945. (*National Archives*)

SB2C bombers dropping bombs on Japan in July 1945. Halsey's carrier ranged around Japan for several weeks just before the enemy surrender. (*National Archives*)

The U.S. carrier *Boxer* teams up with Air Force and Marine planes on June 23, 1952, for the biggest air raid of the Korean war. Five major hydroelectric plants were knocked out, including the world's fourth largest, at Suiho. (*AP/Wide World Photos*)

A U.S. Navy Phantom fighter-bomber prepares to touch down on the carrier *Independence* after a September 1965 strike in South Vietnam. Following the carrier is the destroyer *Stoddard*. (*UPI/Bettmann Newsphotos*)

U.S. Marines in battle gear dash across the flight deck of the U.S.S. *Valley Forge* to helicopters that will take them to a battle area 35 miles south of Da Nang, February 1966. (*AP/Wide World Photos*)

Off the coast of North Vietnam in October 1968, U.S.S. *Coral Sea* flight deck crewmen hustle through the discharge from a steam catapult which has just propelled an A3 Skywarrior on a bombing mission. (*UPI/Bettmann Newsphotos*)

A Sea King helicopter hovers above H.M.S. *Hermes* to airlift ammunition for distribution to other ships preparing to reinforce Britain's naval blockade of the Falklands in April 1982. (*UPI/Bettmann Newsphotos*)

A U.S. F-14 Tomcat takes off from the deck of the U.S.S. *America* in the central Mediterranean on April 16, 1986. That morning American war planes launched a bombing attack against Libya. (*AP/Wide World Photos*)

The deck of America's newest aircraft carrier, the U.S.S. *Theodore Roosevelt*, is filled with war planes prior to the start of joint exercises with the French navy in the Mediterranean on February 5, 1989. One month earlier, U.S. planes shot down a pair of Libyan MiGs in the region. (*AP/Wide World Photos*)

The Air Battle of the Philippines

The results of the Battle of the Philippine Sea were 100 percent negative for the Japanese. On the way home to Japan, Admiral Ozawa stopped off at Okinawa and surveyed his fleet, or what was left of it. The loss of the fleet carriers was painful to observe. So was the loss of two oilers, very much in demand and short supply. Of his other ships, several had to be sent back to Japan for repairs or for heavy maintenance.

Ozawa was so totally discouraged that he tried to resign as commander of the Mobile Fleet, but back in Tokyo Admiral Soemu Toyoda would not accept his resignation.

In the Marianas the battle continued, and much of it was fought in the air. Admiral Kakuta's land-based air forces had not given up the struggle, and the carrier pilots of Task Force 58 were kept flying and attacking, particularly that central base of Japanese operations, Orote Field on Guam. Task Force 58 continued flying daily missions until the end of June and continued to destroy Japanese aircraft in the air and on the ground. Admiral Kakuta had to be given credit for stubborn performance. Against great odds, he kept funneling aircraft into the Marianas, only to see them shot down one by one.

For the month of July, the carrier task groups alternated. Some went back to Eniwetok for rearmament and provisioning, while others stood duty off the Marianas and kept shooting down Japanese planes. The escort carriers flew mostly ground support missions, hitting tactical targets for the infantry ashore.

The attack on Guam began on July 21. Again there was air activity,

151

but it soon dropped to a trickle as the Americans hit the airfields. Now Admiral Kakuta had to bring his planes in from points far afield, and soon there were not many planes flying. The task force planes were then detailed to ground support missions, and toward the end of July that was about their only work. By August 8, the Guam campaign had worn down to the point at which the fast carriers were no longer needed.

Then it was back for some work on the ships and some new planes and some new pilots and some training, for the next big operation to be staged by the Americans was already on the drawing boards. It was to be the return to the Philippines of General Douglas MacArthur.

Before the MacArthur return could be made, however, some more effort was going to be needed in the area. Although the Japanese fleet had been worn down, and the Japanese carrier air force had been hard hit in the Battle of the Philippine Sea, the Japanese still had plenty of airplanes and plenty of airbases in the Pacific. Indeed, airbases and planes were to be the key to the new Japanese defense plan.

After the Philippine Sea air battle, the Japanese expected a major new invasion within the next few months. It could be in the Philippines. It could be against Japan itself. Or it could be against Formosa. In any event, the defense would be basically the same. The full force of the Japanese fleet and air forces would be cast against the enemy in what was called Operation Sho—*Sho* meaning "victory." The key to the defense would be the Japanese aircraft carriers, now reduced to the single fleet carrier *Zuikaku* and the three light carriers *Junyo, Ryuho*, and *Zuiho*, the *Chitose* and the *Chiyoda*, and the hermaphrodite battleship-carriers *Ise* and *Hyuga*. The numbers indicate more strength than the carriers actually had. Together they could not mount a full complement of aircraft, and most of their pilots were so sadly deficient in training that every carrier takeoff and landing was likely to end in misadventure.

———

After the Battle of the Philippine Sea, the American carrier force was further augmented and now dominated the U.S. Navy. Fortunately for those who wanted to make maximum use of carriers during the coming operations, Admiral William F. Halsey replaced Admiral Spruance in command of the fleet. The reason for the change was the naval planning for future operations. Admirals King and Nimitz were looking to the ultimate invasion of China and Japan, and they knew that two huge invasion fleets would be needed. Spruance was to command one of them, and Admiral Halsey the other. At the moment, the Americans did not have enough ships and planes to outfit two huge fleets, so the ships and sailors of the two fleets were the same; only the commanders and staff officers were different. Admiral Spruance and his staff, called the Fifth Fleet, went ashore to plan for a new operation. Admiral Halsey and his staff of the Third Fleet began operating the naval armada. It was a propitious change in view of the problems that lay ahead, for Halsey had none of Spruance's timidity and was willing and eager to put his ships at risk to meet and defeat the enemy.

"Thank Heaven that Halsey and Mick Carney [Halsey's chief of staff] have stepped into the driver's seat," wrote Admiral John Towers, Nimitz's deputy. He felt that the change was a victory for the airmen over the "battleship men," which indeed it was. Admirals King and Nimitz had been forced to reassess their operations in view of a major decision made by the president of the United States that summer. Until that time, the war against Japan had been carried by the navy, through the submarine campaign and through the drive into the Central Pacific. General Douglas MacArthur, who had been so highly publicized at the time of the fall of the Philippines, had been pushed into a back seat. In the summer of 1944, however, after the invasion of France by the Allies had succeeded and it was seen as only a matter of time before Germany was defeated, the Joint Chiefs of Staff had begun assessing their plans for the Pacific. General MacArthur had managed a meeting at Pearl Harbor between himself, Admiral Nimitz, and President Roosevelt, and there he had presented a strategic case for the invasion of the Philippines as the next step. That invasion, of course, would be under the command of General MacArthur, because had he not promised the people of the Philippines "I shall return" when he had been so unceremoniously ousted and forced to flee by PT boat from Corregidor in 1942?

The invasion of the Philippines was regarded by the navy as a grandstand play, but it appealed to President Roosevelt for several reasons, not the least of which was that he was running on the Democratic Party ticket for an unprecedented fourth term in office that year 1944, and some Republicans were already talking about

MacArthur as a viable candidate to oppose him. Furthermore, the potential melodrama of a MacArthur returning to Manila in triumph appealed to the president's sense of history. The public relations value of a "return" with promises to honor the granting of independence to the Philippines almost immediately should be enormous in undercutting the whole Japanese empire in the Pacific. Small matter if the Philippines could be very easily bypassed in favor of a landing much closer to Japan, on the China coast or on Formosa. President Roosevelt opted for the MacArthur plan, and the control of the Pacific War passed in that meeting from the navy to the army. There would be one more major naval invasion operation, at Iwo Jima, conducted by marine troops, but except for that the navy's role was now relegated to that of the past: to protect the invasion forces and to challenge the enemy on the sea and in the air. Thus, once more, an aggressive admiral was wanted in command of the fleet forces. And that was Admiral Halsey.

The invasion of the Philippines was set for the last week in October 1944, and an enormous armada of ships was beginning to assemble in the South Pacific. The first step was to be the invasion of the Japanese fleet base in the Palau Islands on September 15. Peleliu would be the invasion target.

On September 6 the American carrier force was in the area, sweeping across the Palau Islands of Babelthuap and Ngesebus and all other places in the area where airfields existed. The islands seemed strangely deserted, the enemy fleet was not in evidence, and even the airfields were strangely short of aircraft. No planes were encountered in the air, and few were seen on the ground; but the American attackers sprayed the area with napalm bombs, burning installations and some aircraft, and strafed buildings and gun emplacements. They struck the harbors and burned a number of barges.

Peleliu was hit on September 7, and although there was antiaircraft fire, there was no aerial opposition. More than 500 plane raids were made on Peleliu that day, and the pilots came back to say that it seemed that the Japanese were not really interested in defending the area.

After four days of bombing and strafing Peleliu, Angaur, Babelthuap, Koror, and Malakal, it was apparent to Admiral Halsey that the Japanese had many troops in the Palaus but that they were saving their air strength as much as possible for something else. He took note.

During the second week of September, the Third Fleet ranged off Mindanao. Its object was to knock out the southern Philippines airfields so that no planes could be staged to the Palaus for the defense after the invasion began. The American air attack caught the Japanese entirely by surprise. Many planes were destroyed on the ground at Lumbia and Cagayan airfields, major bases. Here is the reaction of one Japanese naval officer, preserved in the Japanese Naval Records.

This morning at Cagayan south airfield, the Korea base squadron's main force and the 66th Squadron's leading units were deployed around the field. At about 8:00 A.M. at an altitude of 3,000 meters (9,000 feet), a group of ten American bombers approached. As we watched when they were directly above, about half of them suddenly rolled over and dived, coming down in single file to attack the planes and the seaplanes moored at the base. This was the beginning of a systematic enemy attack, and as we watched, our aircraft were destroyed one by one. As if in a daze we saw them catch fire and burn.

During the four days from September 9 to 12, the American carrier task force ranged all around the southern Philippines. Starting on the second day, the Japanese did send up air opposition to counterattack, and they did send out search planes to try to find the American fleet so that bombers could attack. The fighters were overwhelmed by the number of American planes aloft, though, and the American F6F fighters were a very good match for anything the Japanese could put into the air. The new Japanese Shiden fighter was perhaps a better aircraft, faster and more maneuverable, but the difference now was in the quality of pilots. After the Battle of the Philippine Sea, Japan had few experienced pilots left, and the difference showed in these air fights in the southern Philippines as the Americans triumphed time after time.

Off the coast of Mindanao the American planes found a large convoy of coastal vessels carrying ammunition, fuel, and supplies, and they worked that convoy over thoroughly. The planes ranged all around Mindanao, attacking shipping, sinking an escort vessel, striking dock facilities, and still they met almost no Japanese opposition in the air. One big patrol plane was sighted and shot down by American fighters. But Japanese fighters? They were few and far between in the air. On the ground, the American airman soon learned to look closely, and they often found aircraft that at first had not appeared to be there. At the Damagusto airfield on Negros Island, one squadron of bombers sighted about 50 single-engined planes cleverly concealed beneath trees away from a runway. They bombed with 100-pound demolition bombs and destroyed at least half of them on the ground. The photos they brought back showed 11 planes actually burning at the moment of photographing.

Literally hundreds of Japanese aircraft were destroyed in these four days. Before the raids, the Japanese naval air force in the southern Philippines had been a formidable force. Afterward it was virtually nonexistent. The Japanese could not even mount enough scout planes from Mindanao to conduct air searches for the American fleet that was moving so swiftly around the Philippines shores.

This sustained air raid in the southern Philippines was the most sophisticated use of carriers yet devised for the softening up of a target for invasion. At Cebu, for example, on September 11, Japanese Fighter Squadron 30 with 31 planes, and Fighter Squadron 31 with 30 planes, were up to strength. The planes were gassed up and had been equipped with long-range fuel tanks because the squadrons had been selected to attack as soon as the long-range search planes found the American fleet that morning. But the search planes never took off, and so Squadrons 30 and 31 waited and waited. They waited, and the Americans found them at about 9:30 that morning.

There was virtually no warning. The Japanese had some radar in the southern Philippines, but all the installations had been destroyed on the first day of the big raid, and none had been repaired. Suddenly, almost without any warning at all, the American planes swooped down on the airfield. The pilots jettisoned their volatile long-range tanks on the airfield and hastened to take off. Four planes from the Squadron 31 did get into the air, but they were shot down. Then the other planes were shot up as they came streaming along the runways. In this first wave, none of them got off the ground, but cartwheeled, groundlooped, and crashed, to burn. After that first wave, several planes of Squadron 31 did get into the air and engaged the enemy. One Japanese plane rammed an F6F, and both pilots went to their deaths.

American attack followed attack, all day long. By the end of the afternoon, what was left of the two squadrons moved down from their pitted runway and destroyed air installations to Sarabiya airfield in the Bacolod area. Thirteen planes from Squadron 31 had survived the massacre. Sixteen planes from Squadron 30 had survived. On the evening of September 12, half a dozen pilots from these two squadrons announced that they were going to go out that very night and attack the enemy carriers. They did not know where the carriers were, of course, but they persuaded the commanding officer of the base that they must do something and he let them go.

What did they intend to do? It seemed certain that they were prepared to make suicide dives into American ships, for they were that keyed up with a sense of failure and self-sacrifice. No American ships were destroyed that night, and no one ever heard from these pilots again. The base command took the affair seriously enough, having given it the operational title Kanshi Go, which can be translated as Surveillance Operation but can also be translated as an act of suicide in defiance. This was September 12, 1944. The concept of the *kamikaze* ("divine wind") would not become highly publicized for another six weeks when Admiral Takajiro Ohnishi adopted the suicide attack in desperation when given responsibility to defend the Philippines without any planes. But the roots of sacrifice were already buried deep in the Japanese consciousness, as Operation Kanshi Go proved.

———

On September 13 the carrier task force turned its attention to Negros Island, in the Visayan group. Nearby Cebu, once buzzing with Japanese aircraft, was now silent, but many planes were found on Negros. Commander David McCampbell, leader of the *Essex* carrier planes, looked down that day and saw about 20 Japanese planes parked at the Bacalod air complex in revetments of camouflaged positions. He had become expert in identifying the marks of camouflage. As the Americans approached, once more surprising the Japanese on the ground, some of the planes moved to take off, but the Americans hit them either before or just as they became airborne, and they went crashing down onto the field. So many planes were hit this day that they did not even count the planes that did not burn, although they too may have been destroyed by strafing. There were planes on the fields, but they had no gasoline. The *Essex* men counted a dozen twin-engined bombers and seven single-engined fighters on the ground.

After that, the *Essex* fighters formed up and looked around. There were a dozen of them. They spotted a single "Oscar"—a Japanese army fighter—and the pilot gave battle. What chance did he have, one against 12? In a few minutes Commander McCampbell had shot him down.

They encountered a few more planes that day, and shot them down too. Then the Japanese did offer some real opposition, and before the day was over McCampbell's fighters encountered about 40 enemy planes (at one point he was fighting five all by himself). They shot down 21 of them, losing only one F6F in the process. The reason for the disparity was in both the quality of aircraft and the quality of enemy pilots. Many of the Japanese, although willing, were extremely unskilled and lacking in thorough training.

At the end of that day, after air strikes by many American planes, photographs showed only about a dozen aircraft remaining in the huge Bacolod air complex. The same sort of finding was made at Fabrica, Saravia, and San Pablo airfields in the Visayan area of the Philippines. Another section of Japanese air power had been destroyed.

Back at the fleet flagship, Admiral Halsey assessed the situation as of September 13. His planes had made 2,400 individual flights in the past two days. They had struck every airfield in the south and central Philippines, and they had wiped out all the opposition they found. Admiral Halsey suggested that since the Japanese fleet had abandoned the Palau Islands and since the whole southern area had now been decontaminated, the invasion of the Palau Islands could very well be scrapped. The invasion had already been put in motion, however, and it was not stopped. Peleliu was invaded on September 15. Another invasion was launched against Morotai. The Palau invasion proved to be both unnecessary, as Admiral Halsey had said, and extremely costly, and it had no effect on the coming struggle. The admirals and generals had expected an easy victory. Without air power but with much artillery, the Japanese held out in the Palau Islands long after the invasion of the Philippines, and the last Japanese did not surrender until well into 1945.

———

On September 13 the Japanese moved most of their remaining air strength from the south and central Philippines to the Clark Field complex on Luzon Island. The American fleet worked over the Clark Field complex, destroying many of the planes that had just been brought in, and then moved out again to replenish and resupply. As of September 20, the Japanese still had 300 aircraft in and around Manila. Manila Bay was full of ships, some 30 in all. In three days of air attacks, the American carrier force wiped out most of that air power, sank 17 of the 30 ships, and damaged most of the others. Then, the next day, September 24, the Americans were back in the central Philippines, striking the Visayas again just in case. Each strike found less to destroy than had the one before it—a few seaplanes, a few small ships. Admiral Halsey was more than ever convinced that he had destroyed Japanese air and naval power as it existed in the southern Philippines and that the way had been indeed paved for the coming invasion of Leyte.

———

In the third week of September, Admiral Halsey's ships had attacked Ulithi Atoll about 900 miles from the Philippines. It was taken with no opposition and would prove to be the most valuable forward fleet base the Americans would have for the rest of the war. Its huge protected lagoon anchorage was capable of handling the whole fleet.

Halsey went down there to rearm his carriers and replenish his ships. He had done the job in the Philippines. At the end of the first week of October he would undertake the fleet's second major task, the destruction of the ''air pipeline'' by which the Japanese had been bringing planes direct from Japan, by air, across the Pacific to the Philippines. The planes would take off from Kyughu, fly to Okinawa, and then make their way down the island chains to Formosa, and then along the chains to the Philippines. The installations and the planes at the airfields had to be destroyed. The most important points were Okinawa and Formosa, both housing enormous air complexes. The run into these waters put the American ships very much at risk, for this was the center of the inner empire, and it had never before been breached by any ship but one lonely submarine. The Japanese were prepared with an air armada to contest Admiral Halsey's entrance every foot of the way.

14

The Battle of Formosa

On September 24, 1944, Admiral Nimitz wrote Admiral Halsey that he was counting on Halsey to do something really spectacular in the forthcoming invasion by the American fleet of Japanese home waters on the eve of the Leyte Gulf landings.

Nimitz need not have worried. Halsey had been waiting and watching at Pearl Harbor in June when he saw Admiral Spruance throw away the chance to destroy the Japanese fleet, and Halsey had determined then that the same thing would never happen to him. Halsey wrote to Nimitz:

> I feel that every weapon in the Pacific should be brought to bear if and when the enemy fleet sorties. . . . As mentioned in my earlier plan I intend if possible to deny the enemy a chance to outrange me in an air duel [as Ozawa had outranged Spruance] and also to deny him an opportunity to employ an air shuttle against me. Inasmuch as the destruction of the enemy fleet is the principal task, every weapon should be brought into play and the general coordination of those weapons should be in the hands of the tactical commander responsible for the outcome of the battle.

Early in October, Admiral Halsey had a gut feeling that the Japanese Imperial Navy would soon be coming out to fight. He did not have any special intelligence but just his understanding, which was considerable, of the Japanese naval mentality. His relationships with the Japanese went back to the days of "the Great White Fleet" dispatched by President Theodore Roosevelt to Japan to show the American flag. There Halsey had gotten to know a number of Japanese naval officers.

As October began, the thought of destroying the Japanese fleet was very much on Admiral Halsey's mind. His major task of the moment, however, was to wipe out the enemy's ability to attack the Leyte invasion from the air, and this is what he set out to do on October 6, 1944, when the Third Fleet moved out from Ulithi toward the Okinawa area.

———————

Task Force 38, the carrier fleet, consisted of four task groups under Admiral Mitscher, and a total of 17 carriers, the largest air armada yet employed by any navy during this war.

Admiral Halsey could put up 1,000 aircraft from those four task groups, and they could fly thousands of missions or sorties each day. Never in history had there been anything quite like this carrier force. Its existence now completely overwhelmed the "battleship men" who had been the critics of the past. This was the weapon with which Admiral Halsey proposed to bring a sudden end to the Japanese navy, once the most powerful in the Pacific, crippled now by the loss of carriers. The Japanese Imperial General Staff had a different perspective: With the war coming to Japan's doorstep the carriers were no longer vital to Japan's success but could be supplanted by land-based air power. And so the Japanese navy was still a fearsome weapon, the weapon that Admiral Halsey was determined to break.

Before the surface fleet could be dealt with, the very real danger of all that land-based air power in the northern Philippines and the other islands must be eliminated as it had already been in the southern Philippines.

The first American move was a feint. Halsey sent a force of three cruisers and six destroyers to bombard Marcus Island from the sea, to suggest to the Japanese that Marcus was to be the scene of a major invasion.

The news of this bombardment electrified Japanese Naval Headquarters. It was accompanied by another little item: A Japanese scout plane from Kyushu had set out on its usual patrol on that morning of November 9 and had not come back. Actually, it had been shot down by an American patrol bomber from the Marianas, but the Japanese decided that the Americans were planning a major invasion and that the carrier fleet was out there somewhere. To Admiral Toyoda in Tokyo, the recent havoc wreaked in the Philippines plus the Marcus report added up to an invasion of the Philippines, and he set the wheels in motion for a major Japanese naval effort to stop it. As has already been mentioned, this was to be the Sho Plan. It was to involve all the major elements remaining in the Japanese fleet, which would make a desperate effort, supported by land-based aircraft, to find and destroy the American fleet in the area of the Philippines.

So the Japanese guessed correctly about the coming Leyte invasion and sent out the orders for the fleet elements to prepare to sortie. Halsey was to have his dearest wish come true. But not just yet.

———

The Sasebo naval base in Japan had issued an alert for the Ryukyus area that was based on the knowledge of that missing scout bomber. The report was slow in getting transmitted to Okinawa that day, and so the Japanese had no inkling of the coming air strike. In itself, this was an indication of the extreme value of radar, which the Japanese had only just begun to develop. Without radar, that morning of October 10, Okinawa was in for a big surprise.

———

On the morning of October 10 the task force struck Okinawa and the various other islands of the Ryukyu chain wherever they saw an airfield. One major target was the Yontan airbase, a complex of airstrips on Okinawa. The American planes came in swiftly and caught the Japanese completely by surprise. The fighters came first and strafed planes on the fields. They did not find any planes in the air, although several near the runways gave indication of a hasty attempt to get into the air. Then came the dive bombers to plaster the runways, control towers, hangars, and buildings with high explosive.

Two hours later the second air strike came in. This time the Japanese were ready, and a number of fighters came up to challenge the Americans. In fact, the Japanese put everything they could find that would fly into the air, including a number of slow trainer planes. The trainers were particularly easy pickings for the carrier pilots, and all were shot down, as were most of the enemy fighters. Both the first and second strikes also spent some time attacking shipping around Okinawa, sinking many small vessels and barges. They found some oil barges between Okinawa and Yahagi Shima and set these afire.

All day long one strike followed another, the planes coming back passing the planes going out. It was a sort of shuttle program. The Yontan complex was completely wiped out, said the air intelligence officers after the third strike, so the fourth strike went to the Southern Yontan airbase. One pilot found a new airfield at Ie Shima; he attacked and burned several planes and spread the word. At the end of the day the American carriers had flown 1,400 missions, and the Ryukyus airbases were in shambles. The Americans claimed the destruction of more than 100 aircraft. They had actually destroyed about half that number. They had also sunk a 10,000-ton freighter, a submarine tender, 13 torpedo boats, two midget submarines, three other freighters, and 22 miscellaneous small vessels. The Americans had lost 21 planes but not that many pilots and aircrewmen.

―――――――――

That night Halsey turned to his next target: Formosa.

Formosa was an even more important Japanese military and naval base than Okinawa. Much of the Kwantung Army from Manchuria had been moved down here already to participate in the final defense of the Japanese homeland, wherever the attack might come. Formosa boasted 24 airfields and the largest air command outside the Japanese home islands. Of the highly trained Japanese pilots who remained in the Japanese ranks, most were based either on Kyushu Island or on Formosa.

―――――――――

On October 11, just to confuse the Japanese and make sure they would not be ready on Formosa, Admiral Halsey sent about half the carrier task force on a strike against the Aparri airfield on northern Luzon. The planes worked over the airfield complex until they were sure there was nothing left worth worrying about.

On October 12, Admiral Halsey began the assault on the airfields of Formosa. Halsey was now invading the territory of Vice Admiral Shigeru Fukudome, who was in charge of the naval air defense of southern Kyushu, the Ryukyus, and Formosa. Fukudome's Sixth Base Air Force could put up 750 planes. Before the American raid on the Aparri airfield, the Fifth Base Air Force in the Philippines could still manage to fly 450 planes, but that number had been greatly diminished in the raid of October 11. After the disastrous battle of the Marianas, the Japanese First Air Fleet had moved to Clark Field, but it had already been hit by Halsey and its strength of 500 planes had been reduced to half that number. The softening up process was coming along very nicely from the point of view of the Americans. Now it was Formosa's turn.

The first American planes appeared over Formosa at 6:45 on the morning of October 12. This time the Japanese had managed to get scout planes out before dawn; they had located the carrier force, and they knew the Americans were coming. So when the American fighter sweep that was to precede the bombing attack appeared over the edge of Formosa that morning, the Japanese were already putting scores of planes into the air. Commander David McCampbell of the *Essex* air group was the strike coordinator that morning. He flew high, directing the activities of the 32 fighters of the first sweep. By the time they had assembled over the target area, the Japanese were ready for them at 23,000 feet. At 19,000 feet the Americans had to climb to intercept. The Japanese they were fighting on October 12, 1944, were not the same well-trained, disciplined fliers that the Americans had met first in 1941 and 1942. Although the Formosa air force was supposedly one of the finest in all Japan, most of these pilots had a faulty knowledge of battle discipline. Many of them threw their height advantage to the winds, and peeled off to attack singly. The Americans, on the contrary, remained in their four-plane divisions and at the moment of contact split off into two-plane sections so that each man had a wingman to cover his tail.

"At no time was there noticed a single friendly [fighter] alone, unless he was joining up on other F6Fs. The enemy aircraft did not follow this procedure. Consequently it was easy to pick them out and off,'' said Lieutenant Commander James F. Rigg, who led the *Essex* fighters that day.

The American fighter pilots had been instructed to stay high and avoid entanglements that would take them down below 10,000 feet where the Zeros and other Japanese fighters would have an advantage because of their maneuverability.

This first big air battle of the day was fought at altitudes of from 15,000 to 25,000 feet. This high, the F6F could match the best of the enemy's Shiden fighters.

The battle raged, so fast and so furious that no one, not even Commander McCampbell, could remember how many Japanese planes were shot down that morning. The Americans encountered a new fighter that day, the Raden, which they called a "Jack." That plane, they discovered, could outclimb the F6F at high altitude. The American pilots maintained their tight formations, however, and thus stayed out of trouble.

The Japanese fought valiantly, but many were shot down and others moved away. The Americans went on with their fighter sweep, which was designed to reduce the airfields. They attacked the Keishu airdrome and there found many fighters preparing to take off. They strafed and burned many single- and twin-engine planes, some of them in revetments. Now the antiaircraft fire proved to be the greatest problem, and several American planes were hit. Lieutenant Van Altena of the *Essex* was shot down, and his friends saw him get into his rubber life raft. Ensign Dorn, his wingman, circled the raft for a while, until he was assured that Lt. Van Altena was about to be rescued by a lifeguard submarine in the area. Then Dorn flew back toward the carriers. The circling had taken too much gasoline, though, and he never made it back. He announced that he was about 20 miles from the carrier when he went into the sea, but when the ships came by there was nothing but water.

Other fighters now arrived and began to strafe the Kobi airbase. Bombers followed. The Toyohara airfield was hit, and the bombers concentrated on the buildings and hangars. As they were coming out of their dives they saw about 100 planes parked on the field.

Planes from Admiral Sherman's carrier group hit the Pescadores Islands and Boko harbor, wiping out a considerable amount of Japanese shipping. Another air strike concentrated on the Rokko airfield complex, and the Nikosho airfield was also bombed and strafed.

As the day ended and the carriers began to batten down for the night, the air intelligence men began to count. They were quite satisfied with the results of the day's work on the Formosa air complexes.

———

The morning after the first raid on Formosa began, the Imperial General Staff in Tokyo held a conference to decide what to do and where the Americans were planning to land. The conference ended indecisively: It could be Formosa; it could be the Philippines. The wheels of Operation Sho were moving, but the fleet could not yet be unleashed.

At the moment, the responsibility was Admiral Fukudome's. He was to find the American carriers off Formosa and destroy them. He then transferred Naval Air Squadrons 3 and 4 from Kyushu to Formosa. The Formosa base air force was also put under Admiral Fukudome's overall command. And Admiral Fukudome now ordered his most effective and highly trained attack unit, the T Force, the Thunderbolt Torpedo Squadron, to Formosa to find and destroy the American carriers.

The T Force consisted of about 100 torpedo bombers of the most modern type. A number of the planes were the improved Tenzan torpedo bombers (called "Jills" by the Americans). The T Force was alerted and moved down to the Formosa airfield complexes to prepare for a night's work.

That afternoon, Japanese search planes from Formosa found three of the four groups of the American carrier force off the eastern side of Formosa and reported back. At 2:00 P.M. the first elements of the T Force took off from several airbases, moving toward the enemy. The Americans were fortunate: The sky above the carrier groups was very black, and the Japanese did not find their way to the carriers. Fifty-five Japanese planes set out that day to attack under what they called the Milky Way Plan, but in fact none of them attacked at all. And it was a sign of the state of preparedness and training of even this crack unit that of the 55 planes that set out, only 29 returned to base. Some of the others may have been shot down by American fighters on their way back to their carriers, and some may have been hit by antiaircraft fire from the ships. A number of the pilots, however, simply failed the ultimate test of navigation, and their planes went uselessly into the sea.

———

On the morning of October 13, the American Fast Carrier Task Force resumed its operations against Formosan targets. The attack this day was on the north and west sides of the island. The fighter sweep, which went out first, found very little; Admiral Fukudome was saving all the strength of his command for a major effort to be conducted on October 14. The American fighters and then the bombers concentrated on shipping; there was not much else to do.

The bad weather that the T Force had encountered had drifted over Formosa also, so that the Americans had their difficulties in mounting attacks. The attacks that day were not very successful—too few targets seen—and the concentration in the afternoon was once again against the Nanpo archipelago shoto, the Ryukyus Islands, not far away and a constant source of potential trouble. The last attack of October 13 was against the Kagi airfield on Formosa. Here, in clearing weather, the Americans did manage to find a number of Japanese aircraft on the ground and destroy them.

By the end of the day, Admiral Halsey was well satisfied. His pilots had made a lot of claims about kills. Halsey knew that some of the claims were exaggerated, but the photographs showed that the major Japanese airfields were in bad shape, the hangars were twisted and burned, the runways were badly pitted, and many many skeletons of burned-out aircraft littered the ground. So Halsey was ready to go back to Philippine waters and do whatever had to be done there to finish up the job.

———

The Japanese had other plans.

On the night of October 13, Admiral Fukudome launched a major attack against the American fleet off the Formosan shore. It was scheduled to arrive just as darkness fell over the carriers, for the Japanese perceived that this was their own most vulnerable moment of the day.

The idea was for the Japanese to find the Americans, hide in the clouds until darkness fell, and then attack. And that is the course they followed. That night, the planes of the T Force attacked again, torpedoing the Australian cruiser *Canberra*.

———

After the strikes on Luzon on October 11, the carrier groups had hit Formosa on October 12. But on October 13, one group had been sent back to the Philippines to make sure the northern Luzon fields did not generate opposition. Thus on October 13, the carrier *Franklin* was off northern Luzon. She was attacked by four Japanese torpedo planes but managed to evade all four torpedoes and shoot down the enemy aircraft. Then late in the day, she was attacked by something else.

Rear Admiral Masafumi Arima, the commander of the 26th Air Flotilla of the Japanese navy's First Air Fleet, had personally decided to show the way to help the navy win the great victory that had to be won in the Philippines. Against all orders, the admiral took off from a Luzon airfield, came over the *Franklin*, and deliberately crashed his bomber into the carrier. It exploded with a roar and a cloud of flame and smoke, and did some damage to the *Franklin* but not enough to put her out of action.

That day, October 13, 1944, marked a new episode in the war of the carriers. Admiral Arima was the first suicide pilot who had really planned his attack. The name *Naifu* ("Knife") had been painted on the side of his plane before it took off on this death mission.

Even as Arima went to his death, Vice Admiral Takajiro Ohnishi was on his way from Japan to the Philippines to take over and reorganize the naval air defenses there. Admiral Toyoda had come down from Tokyo on an inspection tour a few days earlier, and he had seen that the defenses were in terrible shape and that Vice Admiral Kimpei Teraoka had a defeatist attitude toward the war. So Teraoka was sent back to Japan where his skills would be useful in running a training command, and Admiral Ohnishi, one of the most aggressive of Japan's naval officers, took over the air defense of the Philippines.

As Admiral Ohnishi journeyed to the Philippines, he realized that there was virtually nothing left to work with. His worst fears were realized a few hours later when he arrived in Manila.

Meanwhile the Battle of Formosa went on. The Australian *Canberra* was dead in the water. Some navy men wanted to abandon the ship and get on with the task force business, but Halsey said no, he would get that ship back to Ulithi for repairs, and he set about doing so.

The recent air strikes had taken their toll. The next day, Halsey could put only about 250 planes into the air, but that he decided to do. These should keep the Japanese busy, and prevent them from making any further attacks on the *Canberra* until the Americans could get her under tow and out of the way.

So, on the morning of October 14, three of Admiral Halsey's carrier air groups sent strikes toward Formosa. The *Canberra* was taken under tow by the American cruiser *Wichita* and, at the agonizingly slow speed of four knots, the ships began to move south.

In Kyushu, Admiral Fukudome told his commanders to ignore the American air strikes on the island except to make sure that they were able to attack the foreign invaders. The task for the day was to "annihilate the remnants of the enemy." That statement was partly Japanese military hyperbole. Another part was a real belief that in the two attacks of the previous days the T Force had managed to sink two carriers and damage other ships. The Japanese pilots were even more exaggerated in their claims than were the Americans.

A decision was made at the highest level, and this meant Admiral Toyoda's Tokyo command, that maximum effort was to be exerted against the Americans in the Formosa area. If Toyoda wanted to go into his reserves, he could employ 1,000 planes, and now he decided that was the thing to do. The T Force had lost about 30 planes in the first night's attack. It was to be given full strength and then go ahead on the evening of October 14.

From Formosa the Japanese gathered their forces. They were seriously disturbed that day by another factor. Admiral Halsey had called for help from the south, and from the Marianas up came 100 B-29 aircraft to attack Formosa. They hit in the afternoon, and for two hours they blasted the southern half of the island.

During the late afternoon, the American task groups began to feel the pressure. All around them Japanese "snoopers" were found. Several were shot down, but others seemed to take their places immediately. It was obvious that something was about to happen.

For this day's effort, Admiral Fukudome had assembled 430 planes, from airfields in southern Kyushu for the most part. On that morning of October 1 they had moved out of Kyushu and headed for Formosa. The Formosa airfields had been hard-hit, but they were still useful as staging points, and most of them still had supplies of aviation fuel buried underground.

At 3:00 P.M. the Japanese had the word that the American fleet was about 60 miles southwest of Ishigaki Island off Formosa. And that's when the attack plan was finally organized.

Very shortly afterward, Japanese planes began to attack every one of the four carrier air groups. The attacks continued throughout the night. As the Japanese planes that did return from these attacks came back to their Kyushu airfields, they reported on glowing successes. They had sunk three or more carriers, they said. They had sunk three or four cruisers and many destroyers.

Just after 5:00 P.M. the radarman of the carrier *Essex* reported a whole new set of "bogies" heading in. This unit consisted of about a dozen planes. The call for general quarters came 10 minutes later, and men began running. The first torpedo bomber launched its torpedo, and *Essex*'s emergency maneuvering began. Within three minutes, after brilliant maneuvering, the action was over. Four torpedo planes had been shot down by the antiaircraft gunners, and the rest had veered away.

The same sort of action was occurring with all the other American task groups. The Japanese were attacking furiously, and they were getting shot down, but the survivors kept returning to base and reporting one sinking after another. A sort of hysteria filled the air, with each Japanese unit trying to outdo the other in claims made.

As the night wore on, the commanders in Formosa and Kyushu began to believe, and the word reached Tokyo that a great victory had been scored over the American carrier fleet. There, too, it was believed. The naval headquarters released the information to the press, citing numbers and types of ships. The press published the material, and the radio broadcast "the facts":

Continuing their furious intercepting attacks against the invading enemy air and sea forces, Japanese air units on the night of October 12
sank or damaged two aircraft carriers and two warships of unknown
category belonging to the U.S. task force in the sea area east of
Taiwan, the Imperial General Headquarters announced at 11:30 A.M.
on Friday [October 13]. Then at 3:30 P.M. the same day Imperial
Headquarters released a new communiqué additionally revealing that
the Japanese had shot down about 110 out of an aggregate of 1,100
raiders that invaded the Taiwan area the previous day. And moreover
that at noon heavy air battles were raging with enemy planes that
attacked the island on the morning of October 13.

By Saturday, October 14, the euphoria was gaining ground. The
survivors of the famous T Force, returning to their bases, boasted that
they and their missing comrades had devastated the American task
force. Imperial Headquarters issued a new communique:

Our air units are continuing their vigorous attacks against the enemy
task force in the waters east of Taiwan. The war results, including
those previously announced, up to the present (5:00 P.M.) are as
follows:

SUNK, INCLUDING THOSE INSTANTANEOUSLY
SUNK:

    3 aircraft carriers

    3 warships of unidentified category

    1 destroyer

DAMAGED:

    1 aircraft carrier

    1 warship of undetermined category.

The number of enemy planes downed over Taiwan since October 12
up to the present now totals 160.

On October 14, Admiral Halsey looked over the intelligence reports
and saw that the fleet had accomplished maximum damage to Formosan

airfields. He was running a little low on ammunition and supply, and he had the two damaged ships to worry about. Because he was due back in the Philippines in a few days to cover the Leyte landings, he decided to withdraw toward the Philippines now.

On the morning of October 15, Admiral Ralph Davison's task group went ahead to begin attacks on the Luzon airfields and prevent the Japanese from attacking the two stricken ships that were coming slowly along. Admiral Halsey had a name for them, "CripDiv One"—navy slang for Division of Cripples. Two other task groups milled around Formosa for a longer period, hoping to tempt the Japanese fleet into coming forth to fight. Admiral Toyoda could not be tempted thus, however. He had already put Operation Sho into effect, and the surface fleet was to be saved for that one big battle to be staged when the landings came, either on Formosa or in the Philippines. On Sunday, Admiral Fukudome's 6th Base Air Force sent off 100 planes to find and attack the cripples. The weather was dreadful: low clouds, almost constant squalls, and almost no visibility on the sea. Therefore the Japanese did not find CripDiv One that day.

———

The U.S. Third Fleet was now scattered over the waters between Formosa and the Philippines. Admiral Lawrence DuBose was in charge of the crippled ships, and to defend them he had three cruisers, eight destroyers, and the carriers *Cowpens* and *Cabot*. The Japanese, who sighted these ships as they moved together, got the impression that this was the main force of the fleet. Hence the term "pitiful remnants" that Radio Tokyo used as the Japanese again went after CripDiv One.

On that morning of October 15, the Japanese search planes out from the Clark Field complex near Manila discovered four carriers and support ships. Then another scout force discovered four carriers and support ships at another point. Was it one force or two? The Japanese could hardly believe it would be two different forces with so many carriers. They believed one pilot had gotten mixed up in his location. They had a lot to learn about the American fleet of the fall of 1944. For example, in Tokyo the Imperial Headquarters was referring to the commander of the American Fast Carrier Task Force as "Rear Admiral Marc Mitchell."

That day in the Philippines, Admiral Teraoka, commander of the

5th Base Air Force of the Philippines, decided to launch a major attack on the American carriers. He was antipathetic to kamikaze attacks, so he dispatched a normal strike force, sending out hundreds of planes to join those from Kyushu, Formosa, and Okinawa. They did not find the American force, however. Although the surface fleet was being saved for Operation Sho, Admiral Toyoda sent the 2nd Strike Force, commanded by Admiral Kiyohide Shima, out to find the crippled American ships and sink them. These three cruisers and their destroyers did not find the Americans either. They were, instead, found and attacked by planes of the American task force. Admiral Shima decided that there were many American carriers still about, so he turned around and went back into Japanese waters. By Sunday, October 15, even with no Japanese successes at all, the Japanese claims had still risen to the skies. Here is Imperial Headquarters Communique, 3:00 P.M. October 15:

The enemy task force in the sea area east of Taiwan is now fleeing toward the east since the morning of October 14, with our units vigorously and repeatedly attacking the enemy and enlarging their war results.

War results:

SUNK:

  7 aircraft carriers

  1 destroyer

DAMAGED:

  2 aircraft carriers

  1 battleship

  1 cruiser

  11 warships of undetermined category.

With the dual aim of cutting off the communication lines between the Japanese mainland and the Philippines, as well as crushing the fighting power of the Taiwan area, the enemy staged stubborn and persistent air assaults over the southwest group of islands [Nansei archipelago] as well as the southwestern part of Taiwan. Japanese air units in close cooperation between the army and the navy fiercely counterattacked the enemy forces over the sea east of Taiwan, blasting a total of 23 enemy warships including nine regular aircraft carriers and one battleship up to October 15.

Many daring fights are still being fought between the opposing forces and particularly during the night attack of October 12, which lasted two hours, beginning at 7:00 P.M. The Japanese units scored brilliant results by instantly sinking two enemy aircraft carriers and damaging two others. Furthermore at dusk the following day, the Japanese, furiously pounding the enemy, sank two plane carriers and one destroyer in one devastating stroke.

In the face of the continued furious attacks repeatedly directed by the Japanese units, the enemy raid forces which sustained annihilated [sic] blows after losing nine plane carriers is now fleeing toward the east in great confusion.

While continuing their relentless onslaughts upon the fleeing foe, the Japanese forces are further extending their intensive activities by enlarging the war results.

As a result of the furious Japanese attacks, the majority of the fighting strength of the American task force which appeared in the area east of Taiwan have been practically smashed, and at the same time tremendous losses have been suffered by the enemy, thus the enemy scheme and the object of his offensive in the waters off southwest Japan have been totally frustrated.

By morning all Japan believed that a major aerial victory had been scored off Formosa and that the American fleet was in flight. "The people went mad" is the verdict of Japanese war historians. The next day they really believed they had virtually won the war. On October 16 Captain Etsuzo Kurihara, the Japanese navy press spokesman, said that the Japanese had destroyed "the good right arm" of the American naval forces. "Cut the enemy's flesh by allowing him to cut your skin, cut the enemy's bone by allowing him to cut your flesh," said the captain. The Japanese had done just that, he claimed.

The score now claimed by Imperial Headquarters was 35 warships sunk or damaged. "The results," said Captain Kurihara, "were even greater than those at Pearl Harbor. Halsey's task force will be virtually annihilated before the battle is over.''

The enthusiasm was infectious. That day, Sadao Iguchi, spokesman for the Japanese Board of Information, announced that the results of the Taiwan battle showed how powerful Japan really was and that she was just now beginning to roll up the tide of battle, to reverse the defeats of the past few months. The military analyst for Domei, the Japanese news agency, said that the United States must have lost 13,000 men and at least 600 aircraft in the big battle. A mass rally was staged in Tokyo's Hibiya Park.

The fact was that about 600 Japanese planes had attacked the American forces on October 13, but in all this noise and fracas, only one American ship was hurt—the cruiser *Houston*, torpedoed by a Japanese plane. There were, in effect, two crippled ships in the American fleet, no more. The task was to get them back to the fleet base at Ulithi without any further damage, and it was a task Admiral Halsey was glad to assume. Even as the Americans moved away from Formosa, the Japanese continued to trumpet the word of their enormous victory, louder, louder, louder.

Prime Minister General Kuniaki Koiso talked about the victory, laying great emphasis on the new cooperation between army and navy air units to achieve the great results he believed had been obtained. The reason for these remarks was to promote just that unity, which in fact was sadly lacking and had been all through the war.

From Shanghai Domei reported that huge crowds of Japanese thronged the streets, cheering the enormous good news. The public bulletin boards on Nanking Road were surrounded all day long by happy, happy Japanese. From Manila, from Manchuria, from Malaya came reports of crowds marching and people celebrating.

At the rally in Hibiya Park on October 20, Prime Minister Koiso praised the armed forces for their tremendous victory and thousands of people cheered and sang. Another rally was staged in Osaka. From Hsinking, the capital of Manchukuo, Emperor Pu Yi sent his congratulations to Tokyo.

By October 18 the Japanese assessed the American loss of aircraft in the Taiwan air battle as more than 1,000. The loss of men was now brought up to 25,000.

The American fleet had moved back toward the Philippines, and the Japanese naval air forces there now claimed to have sunk another carrier and another battleship. The Japanese press on October 18 quoted Admiral Nimitz at length on the arduous difficulties that would have to be faced in winning the war in the Pacific. Nimitz, of course, was talking about the ultimate invasion of Japan proper, which was in the planning stage. The Japanese, however, continued to delude themselves that the war had really been turned around.

By October 19, the Imperial Headquarters figures of American losses had risen to 42 ships, including 11 aircraft carriers sunk and seven damaged. Actually none had been sunk and only one slightly damaged. And CripDiv One, identified as definitely destroyed by the Japanese, was steaming steadily if slowly toward Ulithi.

The euphoria in Tokyo continued. Stories were now being printed to laud the individual heroism of Japanese pilots in the great Taiwan air battle. From 20th Base Air Force came the tale of Captain Ken Saito "who participated in the attack of the night of October 14 and who is the only scout plane pilot who returned to the base." Reading between the lines, some Japanese might have wondered how all the planes could have been lost if such a wonderful victory had been obtained. The story of Captain Saito was pure heroism. As he approached the American fleet in his torpedo plane he came under fire. His account follows:

The enemy's arms were of a superior kind and almost immediately the plane I piloted was hit in the stabilizer. I opened the throttle and increased speed. Just then one of our comrade planes was seen to self blaze. Other comrade planes all roared straight ahead. I circled about the left and went to attack the enemy cruiser which came into sight when I spied an aircraft carrier some ten thousand meters ahead.

Circling around it at an altitude of a thousand meters, I released the torpedo which hit the enemy aircraft carrier amidships. It was fortunate for me that not a single enemy warship opened fire until my plane had roared past the group of vessels. Witnessing the attack the enemy opened fire immediately and my plane was enveloped in a sea of flame. The windshield was pierced with a hole 30 centimeters in diameter. The enemy carrier sank immediately.

I feel great regret for the fact that I am the only scout pilot officer who returned from the attack safely. That night our torpedo units scored such results as eight enemy vessels sunk or damaged, one battleship instantly sunk, large and small carriers sunk and destroyers and cruisers sunk.

After we had left the battle area I saw explosions on enemy vessels. The night was dark with occasional showers. The attack and counterattack continued for only five minutes from 6:32 P.M. I must admit that the enemy searchlights were accurate and that gunfire was superior.

This sort of personal account was unusual for the Japan of 1944 and generally speaking was included only as a part of the emperor's monthly list of honors for fallen heroes. The fact that a surviving army captain was interviewed had a significance: It was done to show the "great cooperation" between army and navy, and the fact that army planes were now joining the general attack on the enemy's fleet for the first time.

On October 20, the great rally at Hibiya Park attracted hundreds of thousands of Tokyoites. "A People's Rally to Renew Righteous Indignation Against the Enemy," it was called. Prime Minister Koiso spoke at length. Foreign Minister Shigemitsu spoke at length. So did War Minister Sugiyama and Navy Minister Yonai. So many people showed up that most of them could not get into the exposition hall where the speeches were made but had to listen to the proceedings through loudspeakers outside.

There was a very important reason for the rally and for the call to national action. Premier Koiso indicated it in the opening of his speech:

The decisive war which the nation has been looking forward to has at last started; the combat upon which will depend the destiny of our empire has begun. Great indeed are the war results which have been achieved in a few days as they include more than forty enemy ships blasted including aircraft carriers, battleships, cruisers, and destroyers, and thus the entire enemy task force has been annihilated. It is an event unparalleled in the history of warfare.

There was more such hyperbole, but then General Koiso's tone changed: "However the recent victories are only a prelude to the final decisive battle, and we must remember that a grand scale decisive battle is yet to come.''

The prime minister knew what he was talking about.

On October 17, as the U.S. Third Fleet moved back toward the Philippines, there was a very good reason for the move, and it had nothing to do with the Japanese claims that the fleet was "fleeing." That day the leading elements of the Leyte invasion armada arrived at the entrance to Leyte Gulf. The Japanese garrison of Suluan Island saw them coming, and saw that some ships were stopping and a small force of troops was coming ashore at this sentry point for the gulf. Before they went out to fight and die, the Japanese troops radioed the word to Tokyo. Now it was all clear to Admiral Toyoda: The big American invasion would be in the Philippines, not in Taiwan. Operation Sho was now put in motion. The "decisive battle" that Prime Minister Koiso referred to in the second stage of his speech was now very near. And in this battle, for the Japanese, the aircraft carriers were the symbol of American might. The kamikaze pilots of Admiral Ohnishi's air force were all dedicated to sinking carriers. If they could sink enough of them, they believed, they could really turn the war around.

15

The Battle of Surigao Strait

On October 18, as the Leyte invasion force steamed toward its objective, Admiral Halsey's Third Fleet moved into the optimal position for protecting the landings.

Admiral Sherman's task group spent the day fueling for the battles to come. Then the carriers of that group moved out east of Luzon Island for operations against the Clark Field complex, where most of the air opposition was likely to originate. They would join with Admiral Bogan's task group off Cape San Ildefonso. The rest of the fleet scattered around the Philippines, to be ready for whatever the Japanese might offer.

———

The Japanese were planning to offer the Americans a major battle.

After Admiral Ohnishi's arrival at Manila, he consulted with Admiral Teraoka before taking over the command of the air forces in the Philippines. He found that he had fewer than 100 planes with which to implement Operation Sho, which called for the air force to strike the enemy fleet even as the Japanese surface ships sortied in three groups to oppose them on the sea. Only 100 planes. What could be done with 100 planes?

Something had to be done, because on October 17 Admiral Toyoda had sent Admiral Ohnishi the word: The Sho Plan was in motion. The target would be the Philippines. The navy was counting on Ohnishi.

Before dawn on October 17, the Third Fleet's planes began sweeping across the Philippines, hitting the northern part. Their goal was to do what had already been done in the south: wipe out Japanese air power.

In eight days the ships of the Imperial Navy would have to do battle with the Americans. Meanwhile, the Americans were here, attacking everywhere. On October 18, they attacked Clark Field and wiped out more planes. Some new ones came in along the pipeline that began at Kyushu and ended at Clark Field, but at the end of the day, Admiral Ohnishi still had only 100 aircraft. For every plane brought into the Philippines, one had been shot down.

Ohnishi saw what he had to do, what Admiral Arima had already done. He had to organize his naval pilots into a special attack force, so that every one of those 100 planes would be effective. Each pilot must prepare to die, and he must make his plane into a directed bomb.

The kamikaze concept had emerged fullblown.

On October 18 American carrier planes were crisscrossing the skies all over the Philippines. Primary targets were again the airfields on Negros, Cebu, and Panay. The pickings were slim, because there simply were not that many Japanese aircraft left in the southern Philippines. At Tacloban, Dulag, and San Pablo airfields on Leyte, two planes were found in the air and 22 on the ground. That was all.

The confusion in Tokyo about just where the Americans were going to land—the Philippines or Formosa—had delayed the functioning of the Sho Plan. Therefore the Japanese ships, which should have been sailing on October 18 and 19, were still in their harbors, still loading, still getting ready for the great decisive battle. Meanwhile, the channels were being swept for mines, and the American assault forces were preparing to land on Leyte Island.

On October 20 the landings began before the Japanese were ready. They had hoped to have their naval forces waiting and their air forces assembled to smite the Americans mightily, but it was not to be.

Indeed, on the night of October 19, high-ranking army and navy officers met at the Navy Club in Tokyo to discuss the defense of the

Philippines. They disagreed. The navy was insisting on Operation Sho, the dispatch of the Japanese fleet for the decisive battle. The army opposed it, for the simple reason that if the navy came with its surface ships and no air cover, then the army would be forced to supply air cover, and this would prevent the army planes from being used to attack the enemy on the land.

The navy said it was now or never. The army said better never, and the discussion deteriorated into nothing at all. The navy went ahead with its plan, and the army sternly disagreed.

Admiral Shoji Nishimura would sail on October 21 with one force of surface vessels. He would move through Balabac Strait into the Sulu Sea, and then north of Mindanao through the Surigao Strait. Then he would come up on Leyte and swoop down on the American landing forces.

Admiral Kiyoshide Shima would lead a second, smaller force into Surigao Strait independently. He would then cooperate with Admiral Kurita, who had the main body of the Japanese fleet, including the two big battleships *Yamato* and *Musashi*. They would certainly strike and pulverize the Americans. The three forces would come together on October 25, and then the Americans would be driven away and the great battle won.

One other Japanese force would be at sea, the carrier force. But the carrier force was now a tiger without teeth: It had very few planes and very few skilled pilots, and its carriers were second and third line. The carrier force was really nothing much more than bait for the Americans, to draw the major elements of Admiral Halsey's Third Fleet away from the Leyte area, and thus allow Admiral Kurita's striking forces to have full play.

That was how the battle would stack up from the Japanese point of view, if everything worked well. But everything was not working well and had not been since September, when Admiral Halsey began sweeping over the Philippines airfields, knocking out the Japanese aircraft that were to support the Sho Plan.

Furthermore, the Japanese did not even know of the existence of Admiral Kinkaid's Seventh Fleet—''MacArthur's Navy''—which would prove quite capable of defending the Leyte landing forces without the help of the Third Fleet.

On October 20, the first day of the Leyte landings, American amphibious forces landed troops on the island. By nightfall they had put some 80,000 men ashore with their basic equipment. There were some air attacks on the invasion fleet that day, most by Japanese army planes, and the cruiser *Honolulu* was torpedoed. A few other ships were hit by bombs, most notably the escort carrier *Sangamon*, but the damage was minimal and did not interfere with operations.

On October 20, Admiral Ohnishi was down at the airfield at Mabalacat, talking to the best fighter squadron he had left. He told them of the kamikaze approach. Every young man knew well the story from Japanese history of the attempted invasion by Kublai Khan's Chinese and Mongol forces in the thirteenth century, when a terrible storm had sprung up and destroyed the invasion fleet. The Japanese had always claimed the storm came from divine intervention and was proof that Japan was the favorite land of the gods.

And so now the favorite land of the gods was to be saved by these brave young spirits who would make of their aircraft gusts of the divine wind and destroy the American carrier fleet that threatened their nation.

At the end of that day 24 young Japanese naval airmen had organized themselves into the first kamikaze squadron and were itching for an opportunity to give their lives for the emperor, to crash their planes into carriers.

It was October 21. Admiral Halsey was keeping a sharp eye out for the Japanese. He had the feeling that the fleet would be coming out very soon, and he was pledged to destroy that fleet, as he had written Admiral Nimitz. On October 20, American submarines had reported sighting several major Japanese warships and, although no cogent picture yet emerged, Halsey had the feeling that Toyoda's ships were already out.

That day half the carrier force topped off with fuel to make sure that there would be no hiatus in the battle, no matter what. The other half flew missions in the central and northern Philippines, but they found very little. The Japanese were saving their very slender air strength for the big push when the Japanese fleet arrived; the planes that were encountered that day were almost all army planes.

There was one Japanese casualty. Early in the morning off the invasion beach, a Japanese flight of three army planes attacked Admiral Barbey's northern landing force. One of the pilots dived his plane into the bridge of HMAS *Australia*, killing the captain of the ship and 19 others. Later that day a sad little convoy was sent back to Manus: the *Australia*, the *Honolulu*, and two escorts. Admiral Kinkaid considered that a small price to pay for the success of the landings so far.

———

On October 22, the Third Fleet kept a sharp eye out for the enemy. The Japanese were still "out there somewhere," Halsey was sure, but he did not know where.

At Brunei Bay, Admiral Kurita sailed with his battleships, cruisers, and destroyers. They headed for Palawan Passage, which runs between Palawan Island and a sea area known as "the dangerous ground" because of the many reefs and shallows that have been the graveyard of hundreds of ships. This was the most dangerous but the most direct route to San Bernardino Strait, at the northern tip of Leyte Island. Admiral Kurita planned to come around Leyte and swoop down from the north, while the Shima and Nishimura forces came around to the south and swooped north. They would catch the invasion forces in a pincers and squeeze them to death.

That night, the ships approached Palawan Passage.

Meanwhile, the American submarines *Darter* and *Dace* met on the surface near Balabac Strait. Their captains were conferring when the radar man of the *Darter* announced contact with a number of blips. The radar man was not even sure it was ships—it might be a rainstorm kicking up the fuss—but he reported it, and the two submarine skippers were alert. They parted company and began tracking the contact as it moved through Palawan Passage. The *Darter* moved in close and soon identified the battleships, cruisers, and destroyers that made up much of the Japanese fleet.

That morning of October 23 the two submarines acquitted themselves nobly. The *Darter* torpedoed the *Atago*, Admiral Kurita's flagship, and the admiral barely had time to escape before she sank. The

Darter also torpedoed the cruiser *Takao* and damaged her badly. On the other side of the column of ships, the *Dace* torpedoed and sank the cruiser *Maya*. Admiral Kurita relinquished command of the force to Admiral Matome Ugaki, his battleship commander, and the Japanese force tightened up and moved on toward San Bernardino Strait.

The most important aspect of the sighting, after the torpedoing of three ships, was the information. The submarines put out the word. The Japanese fleet was moving toward San Bernardino Strait. Admiral Halsey soon had that information, and it was just exactly what he wanted to know.

———

Also on the morning of October 23, Admiral Shima's three cruisers and four destroyers were sighted by another American submarine. The Shima force had sailed from Amami-O-shima, north of Okinawa, where it had gone to fuel after Admiral Shima had thought better of attacking the American fleet off Okinawa during the Battle of Formosa.

Shima had sailed on October 18 for Bako in the Pescadores Islands. His mission was to pick up the cruiser *Aoba* and several other vessels at Manila and take them in to join Admiral Kurita off Leyte. While Shima was at sea, however, the high command at Tokyo changed the plans, relieved Shima of his responsibility and command of the *Aoba* force. Instead, he was assigned to pick up a group of transports on Luzon and escort them to Leyte, where they would land their troops. So swiftly had the Americans moved ashore in Leyte that the army was desperate for reinforcements, and Shima was detailed to do the job.

The ships had arrived at Bako on October 20, refueled and then sailed on October 21, heading for Manila, but Tokyo again changed the plans. Shima was now to go to Coron Bay north of Palawan Island, refuel, and then join Admiral Nishimura's attack force. On October 23, while the *Darter* and *Dace* were tracking Admiral Kurita's force, Admiral Shima had arrived at Coron Bay and was not really very far away from them.

At the same time, Admiral Nishimura's attack force was also at sea. The admiral had sailed with two battleships, a cruiser, and a number of destroyers from Brunei Bay on October 22 and at 10:00

A.M. on October 23 had reached Balabac Channel. At noon he was in the Sulu Sea, heading for the western entrance to the Mindanao Sea, from which he would move toward Surigao Strait and Leyte Island.

———

On October 23, the fourth major Japanese naval force was also at sea. This was Admiral Ozawa's carrier force—four carriers, two hermaphrodite battleship carriers, three cruisers, eight destroyers, and only 116 planes with which to fight the enemy. And Admiral Ozawa understood his mission perfectly. He was bait for Halsey, and he could expect to lose his whole force, even if the Sho Plan was a remarkable success.

Ozawa had no illusions. He even referred to his young pilots as "one-way ducks" because they were so poorly trained that after they took off from the carriers, their chances of landing safely were very slim indeed.

Admiral Ozawa had sailed from Japan's Inland Sea and gathered his carriers and other ships around him. Then he set off for the waters north and east of the Philippines, to draw Admiral Halsey's Third Fleet away from what the Japanese saw as its major task: protection of the American landings.

And why should the Japanese not have that view? For in all the previous landings, staged under the management of Admiral Spruance, the carriers had never been allowed to stray because Spruance had a very limited view of his function as a fleet commander. This time it would be different. Admiral Halsey had already given notice—and Admirals King and Nimitz knew their man—that, given a chance to destroy the Japanese fleet, that is precisely what he would do. In fact, in the last King-Nimitz conference in San Francisco, this matter had been referred to obliquely in laying plans for the future. King had suggested that Spruance might be put in charge of landings when they came to Japan so that Halsey could go out and fight.

———

On the morning of October 23, the Ozawa fleet was east of Formosa, dodging submarine contacts. That night they set a course that would run them off the northern tip of Luzon Island.

That evening Admiral Halsey sent out long-range search planes to look for the Japanese fleet. Meanwhile the Japanese from the Philippines were searching eagerly for the American fleet.

On the night of October 23, Task Group 38.3 was off Polillo, Luzon. Rear Admiral Sherman was riding in the *Essex* and Vice Admiral Marc Mitscher, who had just suffered a heart attack, was riding in the *Lexington*. Most of his work was being handled by his chief of staff, Captain Arleigh Burke.

At daybreak on October 24 the task group was about 60 miles east of Polillo, and the carriers began launching planes for the day's work. One of the carriers was the light carrier *Princeton*.

That morning the Japanese found the task group, and eagerly both army and navy planes moved in to attack. Some of them followed the time-honored tactics of bombing and strafing, but the navy pilots almost all followed the new plan for suicide diving into ships, preferably carriers.

The American combat air patrol was in the air. As the Japanese began to come near in large numbers, even more American fighters were put up, and they began shooting down Japanese planes. Commander David McCampbell of the *Essex* shot down nine planes that morning, and his wingmate Lieutenant Rushing shot down six more. But scores more Japanese planes kept coming in, now that they had found this task group, and they were eager to attack. Then came the word that the Japanese fleet elements had been sighted in the Sibuyan Sea, and the American carrier captains hurried to make ready for an air strike. They were landing planes for refueling and quick takeoff at about 9:40 A.M. when a Japanese army dive bomber came in and dropped a 500-pound bomb on the *Princeton*'s flight deck.

At first the captain of the *Princeton* was not much worried by the 14-inch hole in his flight deck. But down below fires had started, and they could not be put out. For hours the men of the *Princeton* and of the cruiser *Birmingham* and other vessels fought the flames, but ultimately the ship had to be abandoned and sunk by American destroyers. The Japanese had scored on this first day of Operation Sho.

From the Clark Field area, the Japanese were launching their most important air strike of the campaign. They put everything they had into the air that day, but the carrier pilots met them just outside Clark Field, fought them all the way to the coast, and then fought them all the way back again. As the day ended, the Japanese naval air forces at Clark Field were virtually wiped out, in the air and on the ground.

———

That same day the four task groups of the Japanese fleet were sailing along on their various routes to the battle. At 8:00 that morning, a search plane from the carrier *Intrepid* sighted Japanese ships in the Sibuyan Sea: four battleships, eight cruisers, and 13 destroyers— about 25 warships in all—off the southern tip of Mindoro Island. The three task groups available (one was fueling) were ordered to find the enemy (not hard with these directions) and to strike him hard. This was Admiral Kurita's strike force, now commanded by Admiral Ugaki.

And then, in short order, the Americans found Admiral Nishimura's ships—the battleships *Fuso* and *Yamashiro*, the cruiser *Mogami*, and four destroyers—in the Sulu Sea, heading for Surigao Strait. From V Army Air Force Headquarters came the report that a long-range bomber pilot had seen another force (Admiral Shima's) near the Cagayen Islands that morning.

Admiral Halsey decided to concentrate the attacks of the Third Fleet that day on Admiral Kurita's major force of battleships and cruisers. The attack began to move. From the carrier *Cabot* went torpedo bombers and dive bombers covered by F6F Hellcats. They found the Japanese fleet, waited for other American air units to come up, and then began a coordinated attack directed by a strike commander who flew above the fight. All day long the planes attacked in wave after wave. Here is how it looked to the airmen of the *Cabot* as given in the After Action Reports:

> Lieutenant L. R. Swenson dived on what is believed to be a *Kongo-*class battleship. Interrogation indicates that he obtained a direct hit almost amidships, and slightly to the starboard side. This hit is verified by personnel of VF-19 Squadron.
>
> Lieutenant J. L. Butts, Jr., also dived on the battleship and for an undetermined reason his bomb failed to release, whereupon he re-

quested permission from the air group commander to make a second attack, which permission was granted and he made a one-plane attack on a heavy cruiser. He scored a hit or a near miss.

Lieutenant P. R. Stradley and Lieutenant JG W. P. Wodell are believed to have dived upon a heavy cruiser. The results of Lieutenant Stradley's bomb drop are not known, but it is believed that Lieutenant Wodell obtained a probable hit upon this ship.

Lieutenant JG C. H. Bowen dived through the overcast, corkscrewed around a cumulous cloud and dropped on what he described as either a light cruiser or a destroyer. He dived very low, completely blacked out himself and his crewman, to the extent that his crewman never did see the ship on which he dropped. It is not known and the question of which ship he dived on cannot be definitely settled.

A. F. Drosky, aircrewman who was riding with Lieutenant Stradley and taking pictures, said he saw a destroyer explode, break in two, and sink almost immediately. The torpedo squadron did not attack this ship and insofar as we know its exploding is unaccounted for unless hit by Lieutenant Bowen or by planes from another air group. We are not attempting to claim this ship but feel that the important thing is that it was sunk.

Inevitably, with all the commotion of 259 planes striking the Japanese force, there was duplication in the reporting of ships hit and ships sunk. It was hard work for the intelligence officers to sort it all out that day and evening and to figure out just what had been done to the Japanese center strike force.

At about noon, Admiral Mitscher sent a happy message to Admiral Halsey. The Americans had shot down about 100 Japanese planes in the attack on the carriers that early morning and now that the Japanese fleet had been found off Mindoro Island, the American strike forces were hitting them.

The Japanese Kurita fleet felt the attack first just after 10:00 A.M. Up above, Admiral Ugaki counted 30 planes coming at them. They claimed to have shot down 23 of them (which was not true), but they also saw the cruiser *Myoko* take a torpedo and fall behind the fleet. She was immediately dispatched to go back to Brunei for repairs.

Soon the big battleship *Musashi* was taking a severe beating from

American bombs and torpedoes, and the *Yamato* had taken a bomb and a near-miss that did some more damage. The battleship *Nagako* had also been hit, and the battleship *Haruna* had been damaged by a series of near-misses. The *Musashi* could not keep up and had to be left behind, escorted by two destroyers.

By midafternoon the Kurita force had reached a point 20 miles northeast of Tablas Island in the Sibuyan Sea. By 4:00 P.M. the Kurita force had sustained five separate waves of attack from the American task force, and with all the damage sustained, Admiral Kurita was feeling very glum. He took command back from Admiral Ugaki and ordered the strike force to turn around. Actually what he was doing was a feint: He hoped to take the heat from the Americans off his force by turning around now. Then in darkness he would turn back and complete his mission.

When Admiral Toyoda received that message in Tokyo, he was furious. The whole Sho Plan depended on the actions of that strike force of four battleships to smash the American landings at Leyte. Kurita should not quit now, said Toyoda.

As the Kurita force steamed back down the Sibuyan Sea they passed the *Musashi*, down by the bows, her bridge blown away, listing 10 degrees to port. She did not seem long for this world.

Admiral Kurita might have been prescient, the way he turned when he did. For not long afterward, the Americans reported to Admiral Halsey that Kurita was "fleeing" the scene. Halsey also had word that search planes had sighted the Japanese carrier force off the tip of Luzon Island. That was exciting news! To Admiral Halsey the carrier force represented the Japanese fleet. He thought of it as it had been in the old days, the combined fleet with the carriers as the strike force. He did not know that the sad remnants of the carrier force could scarcely strike anything this day. Halsey had already mauled the Japanese battle force, and now he wanted to turn against the carriers and finish the job.

As darkness neared, Kurita turned again and headed back, once more passing the sinking *Musashi*, and headed for San Bernardino Strait. Meanwhile the Nishimura force and the Shima force were both steaming through the Sulu Sea toward Surigao Strait. Admiral Kinkaid was getting ready for them. Kinkaid's orders to his Seventh Fleet read: "Prepare for night engagement. Enemy force estimated at two battleships, four cruisers, four light cruisers, and ten destroyers is reported under attack by our carrier planes in the eastern Sulu Sea. The enemy may arrive at Leyte Gulf tonight. Make all preparations for a night engagement.'' So the old battleships, left over from the days of the Pearl Harbor attack, and some cruisers and destroyers, and many PT boats, were prepared for action against the Japanese coming in along the Sulu Sea.

That night, Admiral Halsey gave the order to his three most northern task groups. They were to assemble under Admiral Mitscher and hurry northward during the night to attack the Japanese carriers and battleships in the morning.

By 2:30 P.M. on October 24, Admiral Jesse Oldendorf, commander of the battle force of the Seventh Fleet, was ready for the night engagement. The American force was ranged across the mouth of Surigao Strait like the cross of a T, just waiting for the body of the T to come up. This way, all the American ships could fire on any or all the Japanese ships as they came, whereas the Japanese could fire only their forward turrets. It was a classic advantage in modern warfare.

The Nishimura force had been bombed that day but had not sustained any vital damage. Behind Nishimura came Admiral Shima. And up north, preparing to pass through San Bernardino Strait, was Admiral Kurita, moving again, and now telling Admirals Nishimura and Shima that he expected to meet them off the southern tip of Samar Island at 10:00 A.M. the next day to launch the coordinated attack on the American beachhead.

Shortly after 10:30 that night of October 24, American PT boats operating off Bohol picked up the Japanese and made a plan to attack. They had found the Nishimura force. From the days of Guadalcanal, the Japanese were old hands at fighting PT boats, and they went after them with a vengeance. Soon the destroyers were making hits on the PT boats. *PT-152* had been hit by Japanese shells.

Just before midnight the Japanese reached a point south of Limasawa Island. There another section of PT boats attacked, but again the

Japanese turned on them in real fury, even dropping depth charges to confuse the PT boats. The Japanese moved on at 18 knots.

At 1:00 A.M. they were coming near Panaon Island, and then they would move into Leyte Gulf. All they had seen so far was a handful of PT boats. Admiral Shima knew nothing about the force of battleships and cruisers waiting for them at Surigao Strait, guns ready.

So on they came. Off Sumilon Island PT boat Section 6 attacked. The Japanese fired back at them, and the torpedo boats' torpedoes all missed.

Now into action came the American Destroyer Squadron 54 of the Seventh Fleet. At 2:42 A.M. the destroyers picked up the Japanese ships by radar when they were about 17 miles away. Ten minutes later the fuzzy blips of the ships became more clear. Two heavy ships were clearly seen on the radar (the *Yamashiro* and the *Fuso*), a slightly smaller ship (the cruiser *Mogami*), and several smaller vessels that were the Japanese destroyers.

At 3:00 A.M. the American destroyers began firing torpedoes at the Japanese, firing and making smoke to confuse the big enemy ships. At 3:09 A.M. the commander of the destroyers saw two explosions. One destroyer disappeared from the radar screen.

The American destroyermen did not really know what was happening in the darkness, but the Japanese knew. The *Fuso* took a torpedo amidships, which made the ship list to starboard and lose speed. The destroyer *Asagumo*'s bow was shot off. The destroyer *Michishio* lost her bow, too. The *Yamashiro* was also hard-hit. The *Yamagumo* was hit and sunk. Then the *Yamashiro* blew up. The *Michishio* began to sink.

At about this time the Japanese ships, five of them still moving, came under the fire of the American battleships and cruisers in Surigao Strait. But the Japanese were fighting, too. They hit the *Albert W. Grant*, and soon that destroyer was dead in the water.

It was not long before the battleship *Yamashiro* sank. The battleship *Fuso* blew up, and as dawn began to peek around the corner, the remnants of the Nishimura force turned and headed back whence they had come. There were only two ships still afloat of the Nishimura force: the cruiser *Mogami*, which was burning and smoking, and the destroyer *Shigure*, which seemed to bear a charmed life.

All this action had occurred between 3:00 A.M. and 4:19 A.M.

Right behind the Nishimura force came Admiral Shima's smaller group of ships. From 3:15 on, the Shima force was trailed and attacked by PT boats. Shima passed the wreckage of the *Fuso* and the other ships, moving at 26 knots. The Japanese ships were going very fast, and they did not see the half-wrecked *Mogami* as it came back toward them out of the dark. The *Mogami* bow crashed into the port quarter of the Shima flagship *Nachi*.

By 6:30 A.M. it was all over. The Japanese had failed to force their way through the American ships. They had lost two battleships and several destroyers. Two cruisers were badly hurt. And Admiral Nishimura had also gone to his death with the battleship *Yamashiro*. The Battle of Surigao Strait was over, and two of the four Japanese forces were out of action. They would not meet Admiral Kurita the following morning or at any other time in the waters off Samar.

16

The Battle of San Bernardino Strait

The Battle of Surigao Strait had been essentially a surface action, one of the handful during the last days of the Pacific War, but it had also involved the carriers in the beginning phases, when they had found the Nishimura force and warned Admiral Kinkaid of the coming of the enemy.

The next phase of the Battle of Leyte Gulf was to be the Battle of San Bernardino Strait, sometimes called the Battle of Samar because it actually took place in the waters off Samar. The carriers, and specifically the escort carriers, would play a greater role in this fight. The escort carriers came into their own in this battle.

As noted, on the night of October 24, Admiral Halsey had sent his three available air task groups north to find the Japanese carrier fleet off Luzon Island and to attack the next day. This departure of the carrier forces left San Bernardino Strait unguarded and enabled the Japanese force of Admiral Kurita to come through the strait. The advisability of this action has long been debated by naval officers and historians. As Admiral Halsey had already made very plain to Admiral Nimitz, if he had a chance to go after the Japanese carriers, he certainly would take it. Nimitz knew that very well. The problem was that Admiral Kinkaid, in command of the Seventh Fleet and the invasion force that was standing off Leyte, did not know what Halsey intended to do. That was Halsey's real failure—the failure of communications, for the fact is that the Seventh Fleet had the instruments of its own salvation at hand.

That night of October 24, Admiral Kurita announced to Tokyo that he intended to charge into Leyte Gulf at 11:00 A.M. the next day and wreak havoc with the American ships there. He did not then know the fate of the Nishimura and Shima forces, which had been decimated in their attempt to run through Surigao Strait. Kurita had suffered badly from the American air attacks of the past two days and the submarine attacks earlier, but he still had 22 of the 32 ships with which he had set out from Brunei Bay.

Now, as October 24 wore away, Kurita had no information at all about the fate of the Nishimura and Shima forces. One reason was the damage suffered to the communications system of the battleship *Nagato* in the American air raids. Kurita was hoping for assistance from Admiral Fukudome and Admiral Ohnishi, not knowing that the Japanese naval air forces in the Philippines had been reduced to a handful of kamikazes, and that the pipeline from Kyushu through Formosa and down to the Philippines was virtually shut off. Most of the air activity around the Philippines now was conducted by Japanese army air force planes, and they did not have much experience in dealing with ships.

That night a Black Cat, one of the PBY patrol bombers specially equipped with radar and night flying gear, took off and flew up to San Bernardino Strait to check. The pilot saw nothing because he arrived and left well before Admiral Kurita's force came.

At 11:30 that night the Japanese ships formed into a single column, and the Japanese force moved through the strait at midnight. By 12:30 they were through and Leyte lay before them. Admiral Kurita then formed his fleet on a broad 13-mile front and ran east until 3:00 A.M. At 2:30 he had a message that Admiral Nishimura was entering Surigao Strait. Then Kurita turned southeast down the coast of Samar Island, toward the Leyte landing area. At 3:35 A.M. he had a message from Nishimura reporting the sighting of three enemy ships. After that, the radio was silent for two hours. Then came a message from Admiral Shima that the Nishimura force had been destroyed! Then, because Admiral Shima was also in the process of being destroyed, there was nothing more.

———

That night, after the Battle of Surigao Strait ended, Admiral Kinkaid made some plans for October 25. He felt secure about San Bernardino Strait, assuming that Admiral Halsey's Third Fleet battleships were guarding the narrow channel and that the Japanese would never pass there. At 4:00 A.M., when Admiral Kinkaid asked his staff if they thought any loophole remained untended, his operations officer said there was one thing: No one had ever asked Admiral Halsey directly if he had left the fast battleships guarding San Bernardino Strait as he went streaking off to chase the Japanese carriers. Had anyone thought about it, he would have realized that Halsey was riding in one of those fast battleships, the *New Jersey*, and he was unlikely to stay back at San Bernardino Strait when there was a chance to smash the Japanese carrier fleet up north. That idea had not occurred to anyone on Admiral Kinkaid's staff before. Admiral Kinkaid said that was a good question, and they sent a message to Halsey asking, but that message was not received aboard the Third Fleet flagship until about 6:30 A.M.

Admiral Kinkaid ordered Admiral Thomas Sprague, commander of the half dozen escort carriers that guarded the invasion force, to send an attack group down to Mindanao early in the morning to pick off any stragglers from the night sea action. He also told Sprague to send a search up along Samar to San Bernardino Strait, just to see what was going on up there, but neither he nor Admiral Sprague considered that mission to be top priority. So the antisubmarine patrol was gotten off the carriers first that morning and then the strike to the south was gotten off, but the search to the north was not. There seemed to be plenty of time.

———

At 6:30 A.M. Admiral C. A. F. Sprague, commander of the unit of carriers called Taffy Three, which was nearest the north, sent a message to the carriers that they could secure from general quarters after the planes were launched and resume ordinary watches. There seemed to be little chance of excitement. Eight fighter planes circled the area of the carrier unit, and they saw nothing to report. Of course they did not see a great deal, for as Admiral Ugaki wrote in his diary that morning as the Japanese moved south from San Bernardino Strait, "The weather on the east coast is particularly unfavorable. It is almost impossible to determine when day breaks and scattered dark clouds accompanied by squalls hang low."

Dodging in and out of the cloud cover, the pilots of the combat air patrol watched the sun come up. Still nothing.

At 6:44 that morning, Japanese lookouts suddenly sighted the American forces off Samar: four destroyers, three carriers, three cruisers.

What they saw was the most northern element of the American invasion force: the escort carriers *Gambier Bay, White Plains*, and *Kitkun Bay* closest to the Japanese fleet, with the destroyers *Hoel, Heermann*, and *Johnston* (identified by the Japanese as cruisers), and the destroyer escorts *Samuel B. Roberts, Dennis, Raymond*, and *John C. Butler*. Down south a little, and not immediately visible to the Japanese, were the escort carriers *Fanshaw Bay, St. Lo*, and *Kalinin Bay*. And farther south, strung out among the invasion fleet, were 10 more escort carriers. It was not an inconsiderable force, recognizing that each aircraft carrier housed about 30 planes, for a total of almost five times as many planes as Admiral Ozawa could muster on his fleet up north. To put it another way, the American escort carrier fleet carried more planes than the Japanese had had in the Philippines on October 25, 1944.

When Admiral Kurita learned of the presence of the American ships he gave the order to attack.

At 6:58 the battleships opened fire at a range of about 20 miles. The Japanese fleet steamed down on the enemy Americans. Outside on the left was the destroyer screen. Then came the heavy cruisers *Suzuya, Kumano, Chikuma*, and *Tone*. Behind them were the heavy cruisers *Haguro* and *Chokai*. They were followed, inshore, by another destroyer squadron led by a light cruiser, and three miles behind steamed the majestic battleships *Yamato, Nagato, Kongo*, and *Haruna*. The surprise to the Americans was complete.

At almost the moment the Japanese guns began firing, at least three American pilots sighted the Japanese fleet. At 6:45 the alarm bell had sounded aboard the escort carrier *Gambier Bay*.

As noted, on the night of October 24, Admiral Halsey had sent his three available air task groups north to find the Japanese carrier fleet off Luzon Island and to attack the next day. This departure of the carrier forces left San Bernardino Strait unguarded.

The *Yamato* had nine 18.1-inch guns, and they were talking loudly. The major Japanese target was the *Gambier Bay*, the most northern of the American escort carriers. Soon shells were falling all around the American carrier. The first carrier to be hit was the *Kalinin Bay*, which took 8-inch shells from cruisers, and 14- and 16-inch shells from battleships. The *Fanshaw Bay* was hit four times by 8-inch shells. The *White Plains* was hit by 6-inch shells, and the *Kitkun Bay* was damaged by several near-misses.

Immediately Admiral T. L. Sprague, the commander of the force of 16 escort carriers, gave permission for all carriers to launch all planes to repel the enemy attack, and the carriers were quick to respond. The *Gambier Bay* managed to get off about a dozen planes, including several torpedo bombers. Not all the bombers were armed with bombs, and none of those on deck were armed with torpedos. They took off anyhow, and several pilots zoomed down on the Japanese fleet and fired their machine guns even if they did not have bombs. The same was true of all the escort carriers. They fought very hard although they had been surprised.

Meanwhile the air began to crackle with calls for assistance. The carrier commander asked to be allowed to bring the carrier force south for the protective cover of the battleships of the Seventh Fleet, but Admiral Kinkaid denied the request. That would bring the carriers and the Japanese down too close to the transports and the unloading area.

So the battle was fought up along the Samar coast, and the escort carriers did themselves proud. Their planes buzzed around the Japanese like bees, harrying the gunners, and occasionally scoring an important hit on the enemy ships.

The American naval air force here was not inconsiderable. Each escort carrier had aboard about 30 planes, and there were 16 escort carriers in the force. That meant the Americans at Samar could put in the air as many aircraft as Admiral Ozawa had been able to do at the Battle of the Philippine Sea. And soon enough the Japanese warships began to feel the heat of battle.

The *Gambier Bay* was targeted. At first she was hit by shells from the destroyers and cruisers, and then the battleship *Kongo* found the range. The *Gambier Bay* began taking shell after shell, and soon she was dead in the water. She broke in two, capsized, and sank.

Off Samar Island, the weather was very squally this morning, and this plus the smokescreens laid down by the carriers, destroyers, and escorts helped shield most of the fleet from the Japanese. The planes ducked in and out of the clouds. The American destroyers prepared to attack with torpedoes, as did the little destroyer escorts.

The Japanese battleship *Yamato* had come down to about 15 miles from the nearest group of ships—Taffy Three, of which the *Gambier Bay* was a part—when the captain, Rear Admiral Nobuei Morishita, saw six torpedoes coming toward the battleship. He ordered a turn that put the ship in the middle of the spread, heading away from the fight. So they sped along together, the battleship and its six torpedoes chasing, for 10 minutes before the torpedoes ran their course and it was safe for the battleship to turn back. By that time the *Yamato* was 25 miles away from the fight and out of the action for all practical purposes.

Admiral Kurita then ordered a scout plane catapulted. Its pilot reported that the Americans were retreating southward, so Kurita ordered a pursuit. The ships bore down on the Americans, and through the clouds they spied the destroyer *Hoel*, which had come forth to fire torpedoes. The cruisers and battleships immediately leveled their guns on her, and soon she was sunk.

Soon the destroyer *Samuel B. Roberts* also was sunk, and the destroyer *Johnston* was sunk after holding a whole Japanese destroyer squadron at bay for an hour. The *Heermann* was hit repeatedly. The destroyers and destroyer escorts of Taffy Three did a magnificent job, thoroughly intimidating the Japanese.

By this time the Kurita fleet was spread out over a wide area, which kept the ships from concentrating their fire on the carriers they wanted to knock out.

The American planes kept buzzing around the Japanese battleships and cruisers, and this, too, diverted the attackers. The destroyers and escorts bravely steamed in to the face of the enemy that was laying smoke and preparing to fire torpedoes.

The American planes suffered from a lack of coordinated leadership, but fortunately most of the bombers were loaded with torpedoes because Admiral Kinkaid had thought they might be needed to help with the Battle of Surigao Strait. The pilots gamely looked about for any companions, joined up, and tried to coordinate their attacks on the Japanese ships. They succeeded better than they knew: By 9:00 A.M. the cruisers *Chikuma* and *Chokai* were hit hard and losing speed and fighting ability. They were forced out of the pursuit. The destroyer *Fujinami* was assigned to help the *Chokai*, and the destroyer *Nowaki* was assigned to help the *Chikuma*. That took two more Japanese ships out of the battle.

After 8:30 the American attacking planes got a little better organized. Some landed on carriers that were not their own, refueled and rearmed, and went back to fight again. From the Japanese view, the American defense was becoming better organized and creating more difficulty.

Furthermore, Admiral Kurita now began to worry about fuel. He had used a lot of fuel getting through San Bernardino Strait, and now for more than two hours the Japanese ships had been maneuvering at high speed, which ate deeply into the fuel supply. He still wanted those American carriers, but he knew that the speed of an American fleet carrier was 30 knots and that would mean maximum speed for the Japanese battleships. (He never realized that he was facing escort carriers and not fleet carriers this morning.) Besides, as Admiral Kurita knew, his assignment was not to go after the American carriers but to destroy the American invasion fleet off Leyte. So he turned the ships toward Leyte. Just after 9:00 A.M., Admiral Kurita was reorganizing his force to swoop down on the beachhead. But the Americans were conducting a very skillful defense, bobbing and weaving like boxers before the Japanese onslaught.

———

Japanese naval historian Masanori Ito, in assessing the battle off Samar, has said:

This battle was no shining victory for the Japanese. It was, rather, a most skillful retreat on the part of the enemy. The principal reason for our failure was misjudgment of the enemy's strength, which Kurita believed to be five or six fleet carriers, two battleships, and at least ten cruisers and destroyers capable of a speed of 30 knots. His error was the result of inadequate aerial scouting. The enemy force actually consisted of six escort carriers and eight destroyers, whose group speed was no more than 18 knots.

That was also wrong. The truth, which was simply undiscovered by either side, was that the 16 American escort carriers were the equivalent in strength of half a dozen fleet carriers but were completely underestimated by the Japanese and the American navies. The escort carriers proved themselves in battle this day, as Admiral Turner had always known they would if it came to that, as they attacked fiercely and impressed the Japanese ship commanders.

———————

At 11:20 A.M., the Japanese headed for Leyte Gulf. By this time the effective warships of the Japanese totaled only 15, but Admiral Kurita was still boring in. The Japanese sped, in ring formation (for more effective antiaircraft fire), toward the gulf. Twenty minutes after heading for Leyte, Admiral Kurita's force reported sighting a battleship and four destroyers, but they ignored this diversion and went on.

Just after noon, Admiral Kurita radioed back to Japan that he was moving to execute the penetration of Leyte Gulf in spite of any more enemy aircraft attacks. The idea he was sending was that he had had plenty of enemy aircraft attacks already but was going on in spite of them. Having encountered the enemy carriers, having fought and sunk one, and damaged others, and having turned back toward the original goal of knocking out the American landing force at Leyte Gulf, Admiral Kurita was forging on. This was noon, on October 25.

Then Admiral Kurita had another thought. He was very much concerned because the air support he had expected from the Philippines had not materialized. He ordered the fleet to turn back to the north and engage the enemy fleet. By this time, Admiral Kurita knew that the carrier planes were landing on Leyte and refueling. He knew that the American ships at Leyte had landed the troops. He knew that the Seventh Fleet had many battleships in the Surigao Strait area. But as time went on and he headed north out of the Leyte Gulf position to go back to Samar, Admiral Kurita got more information from the radio. He began to realize that the Americans had many forces in the Leyte area and that he was in danger of being surrounded. To be surrounded was one thing, but to be surrounded without possibility of victory was another. Admiral Kurita therefore made the decision to go north to find the big American carrier force that was now chasing Ozawa, and to engage them and either defeat them or go to a glorious death.

The *Yamato* had almost a total supply of battle ammunition; of her total of nearly 2,000 18-inch shells she had fired fewer than 100 in the action off Samar. One of these shells could sink a fleet carrier.

That afternoon of October 25 as Admiral Kurita decided to head north to find the American carrier fleet and attack, the Japanese force was attacked by several waves of American carrier planes, again from the escort carrier force. Kurita had to reconsider. What was the source of these planes? He did not know how many escort carriers the Americans had, and basically he did not know the difference between an escort carrier and a fleet carrier. They looked much the same except in the matter of scale.

Also in the early afternoon, Admiral Kurita had some good news. A formation of about 60 Japanese planes flew over the Japanese fleet and asked how to find the enemy. Kurita could not give them much help, but their appearance gave his people an enormous boost in morale.

By this time it was midafternoon and Kurita had little information. He did not know where the American task force was located, although he believed it was up north. He had two options: either to move back through the San Bernardino Strait or to charge into Leyte Gulf. He had already abandoned the Leyte Gulf option as suicidal and foolish in view of the presence of carriers, cruisers, and battleships in force. Admiral Kurita decided to turn around, get out of the difficulty he was in, and seek battle elsewhere as soon as possible. As he later explained: "I thought we would be able to get within the range of this enemy. But his carriers were a hundred miles away. No matter how much we pursued we could not engage this [Third Fleet] force. The destruction of enemy carriers was a kind of obsession with me, and I fell victim to it."

So Admiral Kurita headed north and ultimately went back through San Bernardino Strait without finding the carriers he sought. Eventually he headed back for the base without having accomplished the mission to which he had been assigned. All this was largely because the Japanese, their naval intelligence, and Admiral Kurita's staff had not learned how to differentiate between fleet carriers and escort carriers. But were they wrong? Hardly. With the number of carriers involved and the determination of the American fliers from those carriers, the escort carriers were doing the same sort of job that the fleet carriers would have done. The real problem in assessing this engagement off Samar is that no one on either side, and not even the admirals commanding the escort carriers, realized what a fearsome weapon they really had. So long had the escorts been treated as inferior ships that the captains and admirals believed it. The fact was that they were simply smaller, not inferior (except in protective devices). Admiral McCain would later characterize the aircraft carrier as nothing more than an airbase that could be moved into the front line. The escort carriers were simply smaller airbases, and not as well built or as heavily armed as the fleet carriers, but they were effective in force. At the time of the Battle of Leyte Gulf, and for a long time afterward, the ''jeep'' carriers continued to be the most underestimated arm of the United States Navy.

The prospect of meeting them had caused Admiral Kurita, with his battle force, to turn around and desist from the Battle of Leyte Gulf, where, indeed, he might have raised havoc with the American transport and supply ships had the escort carriers allowed him to do so. The fact is that judging by their performance of the morning of October 25, it seems logical to say that the escort carriers would never have let the Japanese succeed in their invasion of Leyte Gulf. In all the talk about the ''failure'' of the Third Fleet to maintain its babysitting of the Seventh Fleet, this has largely been forgotten. Warships were built to be put at risk, and the escort carriers were no exception.

———

After the decision against penetrating Leyte Gulf, disaster came to Admiral Kurita. He had come into battle not understanding the disparity between Japanese and American air power in the Philippines that then existed. He had been living in a fool's paradise, and he had asked Admirals Fukudome and Ohnishi, the two Japanese naval air commanders in the Philippines, for assistance. He had not realized that, with conventional attack and suicide attack, they had nearly expended their total effort that day.

That night of October 25 Admiral Kurita proceeded westward through the Sibuyan Sea, actually in retreat.

And on the morning of October 26 the American carrier planes began once more attacking the Kurita force. The cruiser *Noshiro* was soon disabled. The *Yamato* took two bombs. Then came another wave of American bombers about 1½ hours after the first. They torpedoed and bombed the *Yamato*.

A third wave of American bombers arrived in late afternoon. The *Yamato* was hit again by three bombs and damaged by several near-misses. The *Nagato* was also hit and nearly missed by several planes.

That night Admiral Kurita asked the two air admirals in the Philippines to regain control of the air the next day by hitting the American carrier fleet. As if they could! Admiral Kurita may have believed that they could do so, for he had been told that he would have maximum air support and he had never received it. He must have realized by this time, however, that the reason was that the Japanese had no support to give him. Perhaps he did not. Japanese communications during this entire battle were almost nonexistent. None of the forces—the four naval forces, the air forces, or the army—knew exactly what was happening other than in its own particular area. That communications did not work at all was one of the basic reasons for the total failure of Operation Sho. And so Admiral Kurita started home through the Sibuyan Sea.

As noted, on the morning of October 26 the Americans began picking the bones of the remains of the Japanese center force hitting enemy carrier planes. The cruiser *Noshiro* was disabled by a torpedo. The *Yamato* took two more bombs. About an hour later came a wave of 30 B-24 heavy bombers from the south to hit the *Yamato*. She took many bombs this time.

A third wave of bombers came over. The *Noshiro* was sunk. The *Yamato* was hit with three more bombs, which let in about 3,000 tons of water, and soon she was down several feet, for she had taken in the amount of displacement made by an ordinary cruiser. The *Nagato* had four direct hits and nine near-misses, all of which created some damage.

The ships limped west, leaking oil and leaving a telltale trail behind them. Kurita headed into the "dangerous ground," preferring to face the obstacles of nature than the submarines that had hit him once before on the Palawan Strait passage. Finally he returned to Brunei Bay on October 28. The *Yamato* was still afloat, which seemed remarkable considering the punishment she had taken, and she was now just about the only effective surface vessel left in the Imperial Navy. And the morale of the Japanese was still high, as they painted rainbows and spun pipedreams about the future. If only they had more carriers.

Back in Japan, as everybody knew, the carrier *Katsuragi* was under construction, and the *Unryu* and the *Amagi* would soon be ready for action. Yes, said the naval men, the carrier force of Japan would soon enough be augmented and then they would show the Americans.

So came to an end the forays of the Nishimura force, the Shima force, and the Kurita force. There was one more Japanese force left to be dealt with, and Admiral Halsey was hurrying eastward, around the tip of the Philippines, to engage this group of ships: the carrier fleet of the Japanese navy.

17

The End of the Japanese Fleet

The attack by the battleships and cruisers of the Japanese fleet was not the only new experience of the escort carriers that morning of October 25. They also became the prime targets of the new Japanese naval air force, the kamikaze corps. That morning the Shikishima unit of the kamikaze corps flew out of Mabalacat Airfield. There were five suicide divers, escorted by four Zero fighters whose pilots were instructed to lead their charges to the attack area and protect them, and then to observe the results of their crash dives and to report these back to Admiral Ohnishi.

Lieutenant Yukio Seki made Japanese history that day. His kamikaze plane was a Zero, with a bomb under each wing. The other four kamikaze planes were similarly armed. At about 10:30, less than an hour after the escort carriers off Samar had disengaged from the Japanese fleet of Admiral Kurita, the kamikazes and their escorts appeared. The small carriers were very busy, taking on the planes of the *Gambier Bay* and the *Kalinin Bay*, which had been attacked.

Just before 11:00 A.M. Lieutenant Seki and his fellows moved in toward the carriers. Seki chose the *St. Lo* and zoomed down on her and crashed into the flight deck. The bombs exploded, and so did the airplane. At first the damage seemed limited, but then one explosion shook the hangar deck and another below rolled up a part of the flight deck. A third explosion tore out more flight deck and blew the forward elevator out of its shaft. The captain of the *St. Lo* then realized that the bomb had somehow set off the ship's own bombs and torpedoes and that the carrier could not be saved. Less than an hour after the

206

attack, the *St. Lo* was abandoned and sunk, the first carrier lost to a kamikaze.

Several other escort carriers were attacked that day by kamikazes. The *Santee* was damaged, and the *Petrof Bay* suffered from a near-miss by a suicide diver. The *Suwannee* was hit by a suicide plane, but she was not seriously damaged. Then the *Kalinin Bay* and the *Kitkun Bay* were both hit and damaged by kamikazes. Others attacked the *White Plains* and the *Kitkun Bay* but were shot down. Even so, the damage done by the kamikazes was serious and was so recognized. In the suicide plane the Japanese were seeking a one-for-one ratio: one plane to sink one carrier. If they could come anywhere near carrying out that plan in the future, the American naval forces were in very serious difficulty.

At the moment, the American high command had its eyes turned elsewhere. Admiral Halsey was moving at high speed toward the Japanese carrier force with the intent to destroy it. In pursuit of this end, Admiral Halsey decided that he would take the fast battleships with the carriers in case of need for a surface engagement to destroy the Japanese fleet. There was an even more compelling reason: to leave the battleships behind was to leave them exposed to attack from Japanese land-based aircraft. Halsey had had enough experience in the ability of the Japanese to bring planes down from Japan in a hurry to know that this was a definite threat.

This decision meant that Halsey was leaving San Bernardino Strait unguarded, but the intelligence available to him when that decision was made indicated that Admiral Kurita had been badly mauled, had turned around on that afternoon of October 24, and would not try to get through San Bernardino Strait. Halsey therefore sent the Third Fleet north. At 11:30 that night the three carrier groups all came together, and Admiral Mitscher took command of the battle that was to come. An hour later the carrier *Independence*, which carried night fighters, launched search planes. And just after 2:00 A.M. one of its planes located the Japanese fleet. The plane began to follow the Japanese fleet, radioing changes in course and speed.

Then about an hour later, the tracking plane developed engine trouble and had to break off and return to the *Independence*. More night searches were sent out, but they did not find the Japanese fleet that night either. And so the Halsey force steamed on, not quite sure when contact would be made. Halsey was definitely planning a surface attack as well as an air attack, and the fast battleships were out ahead of the carriers, moving in the direction they thought the Japanese had taken.

Just before 6:00 A.M. Admiral Mitscher ordered the attack force launched. It was to take station 50 miles ahead of the carrier fleet and head north. The idea was to beat the Japanese to the attack, as Admiral Spruance had refused to do in the Philippine Sea. Just before 7:00 A.M. Halsey had that message from Admiral Kinkaid's command, asking if the fast battleships were guarding San Bernardino Strait. In fact, Admiral Kinkaid had the answer by that time, because the Japanese battleships and cruisers had already opened fire on the American ships off Samar Island. Halsey replied just after 7:00 A.M. that he was not guarding anything but was preparing to engage the enemy fleet.

The messages then came thick and fast, most of them from Kinkaid, describing what was happening off Samar and asking that the fast battleships be delivered to Leyte Gulf immediately. Some messages were from lesser commanders. One was from Admiral Nimitz asking where the Halsey battleships were. The messages were confusing; some were decoded and read out of order. Even had Admiral Halsey wanted to deliver his battleships, he could not have gotten to Leyte Gulf in time to affect the outcome of the Battle of Samar. A study of the communications of the Leyte battles indicates that even with the most modern facilities, it was impossible to keep up with the coding, decoding, and transmission of messages. The messages that came to Halsey's fleet that morning could not in actuality affect the outcome of the Leyte battle but were more or less simple nagging.

Halsey soon realized that the Kurita force had indeed come through San Bernardino Strait, but he was already committed to battle against the Ozawa fleet. What he could do and did was order Admiral McCain's task group of five carriers and four cruisers, which was down south fueling, to rush to Kinkaid's side.

Admiral Kinkaid had plenty of power down there, which did indeed stop the Japanese. One of the problems of the whole affair was that before, during, and after the battle off Samar, Kinkaid and others failed to recognize the strength of the escort carrier force, a strength that

Admiral Richmond Kelly Turner had recognized months earlier. In the American navy there was still an element that regarded the battleship as the kingpin of a fleet, and the idea that a battleship force augmented by heavy cruisers could be stopped and turned about by a handful of destroyers and escorts and a flock of planes from small carriers was just too hard to accept.

Thus, even during the battle and Halsey's run north, there developed a feeling by the battleship men that Halsey had deserted his post to run off on a wild goose chase. It was a feeling that would not die and would be given credence by official naval historian Samuel Eliot Morison in his history of U.S. naval operations in World War II.

———

At 7:30 A.M. the American planes sighted the Japanese task force and counted one carrier (the *Zuikaku*), three light carriers, the two hermaphrodite battleship-carriers, and several destroyers and support ships.

At 8:40 the first planes attacked the Japanese. These were 14 fighters from Air Group 15, the *Essex*'s carrier planes. Ten of the planes carried 500-pound bombs, and the other four fighters covered them while they hit the destroyer screen around the carriers.

The *Zuikaku* launched 20 Zero fighters, which attacked the Americans, shooting down one American plane and damaging several others. The pilot of the plane shot down, Lieutenant J. R. Strane, was later rescued by an American destroyer. Then the dive bombers attacked the carriers. The dive bombers set the *Chitose* afire, and soon her insides were exploding and she was dead in the water. The torpedo pilots attacked the carriers, too. Soon the bombers of 12 carriers were concentrated on Admiral Ozawa's destruction.

Within an hour the Americans had bombed or torpedoed the *Chitose*, the *Zuiho*, the *Zuikaku*, and several destroyers and cruisers. The *Zuikaku* launched fighters for combat air patrol, but there were too many Americans and not enough Japanese to prevent successful attacks. By 10:00 A.M. the *Zuikaku* was in such serious condition that Admiral Ozawa transferred his flag to the cruiser *Oyodo*. By this time all three light carriers were in desperate condition and could not recover their aircraft. The fighters they had launched had to land in the water.

At 1:00 P.M. the Americans made their third strike on the Japanese fleet. Halsey was rushing the battleships forward to finish off any cripples and fight the Japanese surface vessels. They were only about 50 miles from the Japanese fleet. By this time, Admiral Halsey had responded to the nagging from all concerned, including Admiral Nimitz, and had already dispatched one carrier group and the fast battleships back to Leyte. Of course, the Leyte battle was already over, and in any event the battleships could not have arrived in time to make any difference. It was a fine example of the failure of the most modern naval communications system in the world. Two hours after Halsey sent away his fast battleships and one carrier task group, he had a message from Admiral Kinkaid announcing that the Kurita force had turned around and fled, and that the Americans had won the battle off Samar without Halsey. The dispatch of the battleships away from the Battle of Cape San Engano was a complete waste of time and effort, based on panic and a faulty understanding by Kinkaid of the strength of his own weapons.

Now the planes of the Third Fleet and those of the escort carriers began working over the remnants of the Japanese fleet, which was scattered all around the Philippines.

The remains of the Nishimura force headed back toward Japan, escorted by destroyers. The cruiser *Mogami*, hit hard by the planes of the escort carriers, had fallen behind. She was attacked by planes from the escort carriers and set afire. The crew was taken off, and the *Akebono* sank her with a torpedo. Her survivors were put ashore in the Philippines at the Cavite naval base.

The cruiser *Abukuma* headed for the southern Philippines to make repairs and then get home somehow. She was caught off Dapitan by a number of B-24 heavy bombers from the south, hit hard, and sunk. That was almost the complete end of the Nishimura force. One ship remained, the destroyer *Shigure*, which joined up with the remains of the force led by Admiral Shima and went home. Shima's survivors were the cruisers *Ashigara* and *Nachi*, and three destroyers. Out of those combined southern forces, the Japanese had lost two battleships, four cruisers, and three destroyers.

As soon as the escort carriers recovered from the shock of being attacked, they began to give a good account of themselves. The Kurita force was heading back through San Bernardino Strait, back through the Sulu Sea, back toward Japan. All the way, the force was harried by carrier planes.

At 10:30 on the morning of October 25, Admiral Kurita sent a brave message to Tokyo claiming that he had sunk one fleet carrier, damaged another, and sunk three cruisers. But even as the message was sent, the Japanese force was under attack. Eleven times that day the carrier planes struck Kurita's force. When the attacks finished, the cruisers *Kumano, Suzuya, Chikuma, Chokai*, and *Hayashiro* were either sunk or about to sink. The surviving ships headed for Coron Bay.

The Japanese spent part of October 27 burning the ships' dead, a mournful process. They refueled.

October 28 dawned dark and cloudy, for which Admiral Kurita could be thankful. That night at 8:00 the battered fleet units entered Brunei Bay. Waiting for them were messages from Admiral Toyoda, telling Admiral Kurita to sit tight at Brunei Bay and wait. Wait for what, he was not told. So they waited, and waited, and waited. At the end of November, they were ordered to return to the Inland Sea of Japan.

As for Admiral Ozawa, he was very lucky. All those confused messages about what was going on in Leyte Gulf, and particularly Admiral Nimitz's unwise questioning of his fleet commander in the middle of a battle, had caused Admiral Halsey to break off the surface action with the Japanese and to divert one of his task groups to the south where nothing at all was needed. So Admiral Ozawa got away, or at least a part of his force did. The *Zuikaku* was sunk. So were the *Zuiho*, the *Chitose*, and the *Chiyoda*. By late afternoon, however, Admiral Ozawa still had 12 of his 17 ships afloat.

At 8:00 P.M. on October 25 Admiral Ozawa was stalking about, turning around and seeking another engagement with the enemy, but Admiral Toyoda informed him of the failure of the Kurita mission and the destruction of the Nishimura and Shima efforts. So Ozawa headed north.

By October 26, Halsey had completely lost track of the Ozawa fleet. Halsey felt that he had been harried out of his chance to make a clean sweep of the fleet and that probably it could have been done had Nimitz not interfered. On October 27 Admiral Ozawa entered the protected waters of the Nansei Shoto, and his force of tankers at Amami-o-Shima was broken up. Part of it was sent to the Philippines for transport and guard duty. Part, including several damaged ships, was sent back to Japan for repair and refit. Ozawa moved his flag to the *Hyuga*, the hermaphrodite carrier-battleship. What a comedown for an admiral whose flag had flown proudly above the *Taiho*, the biggest and best of Japan's carriers, before the Battle of the Philippine Sea! On October 28, Admiral Ozawa took his fleet remnants back to the Inland Sea, arriving on October 29. There they were greeted with brave words about rearming and going back to sea, but nobody really believed that story.

In the battles of Leyte Gulf, the Japanese had lost 10,000 and most of the ships that sailed. Admiral Ozawa recommended the disbanding of the "mobile force," which was logical enough since the only thing left of it were the two strange battleship-carriers. He knew that the Japanese fleet had come to its effective end. So did Admiral Halsey, but Halsey was disappointed at not having been able to preside over the burying of that fleet instead of letting it slip away to sink into oblivion without fanfare.

So the Japanese fleet was gone. There were no more Japanese aircraft carriers. But there were ever more American carriers. And now for the first time since 1942 the British would again begin to play a role in the carrier warfare of the Pacific. The Royal Navy was preparing to send a Pacific Fleet out to Australia to join the battle against Japan.

18

New Carrier Strategy

By the end of October 1944, the Japanese fleet was finished as a fighting force, and that meant the American fleet could range where it would without concern for any carrier counterattack. As became very clear during the Leyte landings and the days that followed, however, the end of the Japanese fleet did not mean the end of Japanese power in the Pacific. Indeed not. The Japanese still held most of the Philippines, and their airbases extended from Japan proper all the way down. Admiral Toyoda was quite right when he said that as of the autumn of 1944 the Japanese did not really need carriers anymore. The area of battle was so constricted that the island airbases served Nippon very well indeed.

Furthermore, the development of the kamikaze concept made the utmost use of Japan's air power. The major target of the suicide pilots always was and always would be the carrier fleet. As of the time of the Leyte landings, the carriers and their supporting ships began to take quite a beating from the kamikazes. Very shortly after the landings, Admiral King was troubled enough to establish a special research and development office in Boston to come up with a solution to the kamikaze problem. Later a special task force of ships and carriers and planes was moved into Casco Bay in Maine to simulate kamikaze attacks and come up with defenses. The problem, as the investigators found straightaway, was that when a young pilot was willing to give his life in order to ram his plane into a ship, he had quite a good chance of succeeding, and except for increasing the number of antiaircraft guns, fighter planes, and vigilance, there was nothing new that could be done about it. The

Boston office continued to work until the end of the Pacific War, and never did come up with any easy answer to the kamikaze problem.

———

At the end of October, Admiral Marc Mitscher went home for a rest. His heart attack at sea had left him weak, and he was due for a blow anyhow. Vice Admiral J. S. McCain now took over management of the Fast Carrier Task Force. It would make no difference whether Halsey was running the show (Third Fleet) or Spruance (Fifth Fleet), the ships and planes and men were the same. But it was also understood that Mitscher would be back if he recovered enough. It was best that Mitscher work with Spruance, who needed an aggressive carrier commander because he was so unaggressive himself. As for Mitscher and Halsey, their styles were much the same, for both were real airmen.

———

The fleet was going to have to get used to a new way of life, it was learned soon enough. On October 30, kamikaze planes hit the carriers *Franklin* and *Belleau Wood* causing enough damage to send both back to Ulithi for repairs. The major reason for this was a failure by MacArthur's land-based air command to exercise adequate vigilance and to mount a proper combat air patrol over the fleet. The Seventh Fleet suffered more than any other unit, for it had no air power of its own other than the escort carriers, and they were widely spread out by this time.

On November 1 a destroyer was sunk by suicide planes and four others were damaged. Kinkaid asked MacArthur for more help, but it was not forthcoming. MacArthur's army air forces just were not organized yet to set up guard operations in the Philippines. The carrier force responded as best it could, but it had a responsibility to attack, not defend, and the results were not totally salutary.

Halsey's answer was to set up a series of powerful air strikes on Luzon Island, and particularly the Clark Field complex, where the kamikaze flights were originating. On November 5, Task Force 38, the carriers, hit Luzon very hard and claimed the destruction of nearly 450 planes in two days of raids. They also sank the Japanese cruiser *Nachi*, a survivor of the Battle of Surigao Strait that had been assigned by Admiral Toyoda to remain in the Philippines for convoy duty. The Japanese also took their toll. The new *Lexington* took a kamikaze aboard, and the carrier was badly enough damaged for Admiral McCain to transfer his flag to the *Wasp*.

Halsey was more than a little annoyed at the prospect of hanging around the Philippines in a defensive posture because he had wanted very much to make a swipe at the Japanese homeland in November. The presence of so many kamikazes in the Philippines kept him there, trying to wipe out the menace. The carriers could not be spared until MacArthur's engineers could build airfields and get an adequate number of land-based air squadrons into the Philippines. The army seemed to move with agonizing slowness.

In the middle of November, the carriers were still operating off the Philippines. They sank a light cruiser, five destroyers, and seven transports, and that was all very well, but it was not striking the Japanese where they lived, in Japan. The Americans lost 25 planes in this effort, but they shot down more than 80 Japanese planes.

The ratio of American to enemy aircraft was satisfactory, but the kamikaze level was not. On November 25, planes from the task force sank the Japanese heavy cruiser *Kumano*. It took a big effort to do so, but it was worth it. What was alarming was that on the same day kamikazes hit the carriers *Intrepid* and *Cabot*. That took only two planes, one for each carrier, a high and worrisome cost.

———————

In December the Third Fleet continued to roam around the Philippines area, striking targets of opportunity, softening up the Japanese defenses for MacArthur's move into Luzon. On December 17 Halsey ran into a severe typhoon, and the destroyers *Spence, Monaghan*, and *Hull* sank under the enormous pressure of the storm-swept waves. The real reason for the disaster was that, as a result of wartime attrition, many modifications had been made to the destroyers over a period of two or three years, giving them new radar, new guns, and other fighting equipment. The changes had made the ships top-heavy, and when the storm clutched them, they capsized. Some of Halsey's critics suggested that it was the admiral's fault for not having known all about that typhoon and getting away from the center of it, but Halsey's meteorologist disagreed with that view. The damage was enormous. The cruiser *Miami* was hurt, as were the light carriers *Monterey, Cowpens,* and *San Jacinto*. The escort carriers *Cape Esperance* and *Altamaha* were also damaged, and so were 22 other ships. A hundred and fifty planes were lost, most of them swept off the decks of the carriers by the waves. The typhoon loss was the worst disaster that had struck the American fleet since the Japanese victories down in the South Pacific in the Guadalcanal days.

The American navy at the end of 1944 was much better able to stand such losses, however. It consisted of 23 battleships, 62 cruisers, 371 destroyers, 378 destroyer escorts, 238 submarines, and 89 aircraft carriers. Fifteen of these carriers were of the big fleet class (including two left over from before 1942), eight were light carriers, and 65 were escort carriers. They were all portable air power, and the importance of the escort carriers was now established beyond doubt. In January, Admiral Kinkaid made the Lingayen landings on Luzon Island without any help from the big fleet, except the temporary loan of some ships by Admiral Nimitz. The air cover came from 15 escort carriers, half a dozen seaplane tenders, and land-based air forces.

———

Admiral Nimitz was not concerned with the Philippines; it was entirely an army show. The Fast Carrier Task Force was occupied with Iwo Jima and Okinawa.

The main military reason for the capture of the Marianas Islands, as noted, had been to obtain bases from which the long-range B-29 bombers could strike at the heart of Japan. Once these bombings began in November, however, it soon became apparent that more was needed: fighter bases close enough to Japan so that long-range fighters could accompany the B-29s over the target and protect them. The Japanese effort against the B-29s was becoming stronger as the war wore on. The enemy was using kamikaze tactics to ram B-29s and bring them down. And although in November 1944 the B-29s were bombing from 25,000 feet and above, higher than the range of the Japanese antiaircraft guns and higher than anything but a stripped-down fighter could go, the B-29 accuracy left much to be desired. General H. H. Arnold, commander of the U.S. Army Air Forces, wanted a base for fighter operations. The ideal base would be Iwo Jima, a volcanic rock close enough to Japan to let fighters work, and a halfway point that could serve as an emergency landing base for crippled B-29s.

As planned by Admirals Nimitz and King, on January 27, 1945, Admiral Halsey turned over command of the fleet to Admiral Spruance and went home for a rest. The real reason for the change of command was to put Spruance in charge for another amphibious operation because Admiral Nimitz knew absolutely that Spruance would never deviate from the task of protecting the invasion forces, even if every gun-bearing ship in the Japanese navy came up and sailed around him in circles. Besides, the battles of Leyte Gulf had broken the Japanese navy, and it was no longer a problem. The big problem for the U.S. Navy at the beginning of 1945 was the suicide planes, and that problem would continue until the end of the war.

———————

On February 8 Admiral Spruance sailed out with the Fifth Fleet. The object was to get close enough to Japan to enable the fast carriers to attack the Japanese airfields and aircraft factories, in the hope of curtailing their production enough to help in the coming operation against Iwo Jima.

The air strike was successful in the old sense. The carriers moved to within 60 miles of Japan's major island of Honshu before launching their planes. The Americans claimed about 350 planes destroyed in the air and nearly 200 destroyed on the ground, with a loss of about 90 American planes. That was a satisfactory ratio of losses, but the air strike was not the sort of success Admiral Nimitz had hoped for. He was expecting too much, that the fast carriers could do what the B-29s had not yet been able to do: seriously affect the production of Japanese aircraft, which was running at 500 to 600 planes a month. Despite scores of raids by big bombers on Nagoya, the home of the Mitsubishi aircraft engine, the Mitsubishi production had scarcely been affected.

After a number of attacks by the Fast Carrier Task Force and bombardment by ships offshore, Iwo Jima was invaded in February. The struggle for the island turned out to be extremely costly in casualties. The Japanese had their backs to the wall now, and their resistance was even more furious than it had been. In spite of heavy casualties, the southern airfield of Iwo Jima was captured on the second day by the Americans. In terms of the carrier force, the casualties were serious enough: the escort carrier *Bismarck Sea* sunk, the escort carrier *Lunga Point* damaged, and the big new *Saratoga* damaged. But the proof of the pudding was also there: Two weeks after the invasion began, the first damaged B-29 landed at the southern airfield following a raid on Japan, and the plane and crew were saved.

The fast carriers spent much of the late winter and early spring in Ulithi, making preparations for the coming invasion of Okinawa. Something new was being added. The British were sending four aircraft carriers, two battleships, five cruisers, and 11 destroyers to join the Americans fighting Japan. Vice Admiral Sir Bernard Rawlings was in command of the new British Pacific Fleet.

Admiral King was not overjoyed at the prospects. He was not personally a fan of the British. Furthermore, he really did not need the British in the Pacific, although not even he could deny that four fleet carriers would be useful. He had more than enough sea power himself, and Japanese sea power was nonexistent. Aside from ancient resentments, the coming of the British would only complicate Admiral Nimitz's life. The Royal Navy had its own methods of operation; communications, guns, ammunition, and just about everything else were slightly different from the American way. For political reasons, though, it was important to the British to reestablish the Union Jack in the Pacific, and the orders to accept British help had come from the office of the president and commander in chief of the navy. And so the British came.

> They say that the fleet came to Trincomalee
> Early in 'forty four.
> Heavily laden with men and with gen,*
> Bound for the Japanese war.
> There's Vic and Indom and Illustrious too,
> The Indefat came for the ride.
> You get no promotion in the Indian Ocean,
> We'd rather be back on the Clyde.**

---

*Information and intelligence.
**Song of the British Pacific Fleet, sung to the tune of the Australian war song "Bless 'Em All."

After the defeat of the British Far Eastern Fleet at Trincomalee in 1942, the carriers had not been active in the Indian Ocean until 1944. By that time many of the British carriers were equipped with American planes, and many British aircrews were being trained by the U.S. Navy at Pensacola, Florida.

In the spring of 1944, the British carrier *Illustrious* had come out to Trincomalee and had begun joint operations with the new American carrier *Saratoga*, which was lent for the purpose of familiarizing Americans and British with each other's ways. In April and May, the two carriers had conducted operations against Japanese oil installations in Sumatra and Java. Then there were operations in the Andaman Islands. In the summer of 1944 the *Victorious* and the *Indomitable* arrived, and there were more operations against Sumatra.

By November 1944, the ships were in place at their headquarters in Columbo, Ceylon, and the name of the fleet was officially changed to British Pacific Fleet. Admiral Sir Bruce Fraser assumed command. At the same time, the escort carriers *Amere, Atheling, Battler, Begum*, and *Shah* were sent out to become the East Indies Fleet, under the command of Rear Admiral Philip Vian, in the fleet carrier *Indefatigable*. The presence of Britain was truly reestablished in the Pacific.

On December 20, 1944, the British Pacific Fleet began operations with a strike on Sumatran oil facilities. In two strikes on January 24 and January 29, 1945, the fleet knocked out the Japanese oil refinery at Palembang, the most important facility in the East Indies. The British have never had much credit (they did not have many war correspondents aboard the carriers, and Admiral King was not much interested in blowing the British horn), but their carrier strikes in the Dutch East Indies were largely responsible for the desperate plight of the Japanese naval and air forces in the spring of 1945. For years American submarines had been sinking tankers, but the destruction of the production facilities was even more important. The Japanese defenders met the invading carrier planes, and 37 Japanese fighters were shot down in these two days.

After the Palembang raid, the British Pacific Fleet went back to its base in Australia for resupply. There it was joined by six escort carriers: the *Chaser, Fencer, Ruler, Slinger, Speaker*, and *Striker*. The fleet moved up to Manus, in the Admiralty Islands. This would be its forward base.

On March 17 the American carrier task force was again in action off Okinawa. The Japanese air force was out with everything it could put in the air, and at Okinawa the Americans faced an entirely new situation. For the first time, the Japanese could fight from their own home shores in Japan. The airbases in Kyushu were within easy reach of Okinawa, and so the Allied fighting forces around these islands could expect to receive the full lash of what was left of Japanese air power. And, as they were to learn, the Japanese air force could still sting very hard.

Earlier in the year Vice Admiral Matome Ugaki, once Admiral Yamamoto's chief of staff, had been appointed commander of the Fifth Air Fleet, with headquarters on Kyushu Island. His assignment was to build a new naval air force capable of stopping the American invasion of Japan. In the planning in Tokyo it was inherent that the backbone of this force would be the kamikaze suicide pilots. The new command consisted of about 600 planes located west of the Kanto Plain (the Tokyo-Kyoto area). Ugaki's headquarters would be the Kanoya airbase in southern Kyushu, on the Osumi Peninsula.

In the spring of 1945, the changes came thick and fast. After the first American carrier raid on Japan, and after the fall of Iwo Jima, the Japanese high command ordained that virtually no ordinary squadrons, army or navy, would be retained. Almost everything would be converted to kamikaze operations. The number of operations units was increased to more than 1,000.

As of March 13, Admiral Ugaki began tracking the movements of American ships. He wanted to get into the habit, because in the future he was going to launch many attacks against those ships.

On the evening of March 17 a Japanese search plane discovered the Allied task force 175 miles south of Kyushu. It was Allied this time, for the British fleet units had joined up with the Fifth Fleet. That night Admiral Ugaki ordered up his first big attack, 27 kamikazes and 25 normal torpedo bombers.

The next day the Allied carrier planes attacked the Kyushu airfields vigorously, and Admiral Ugaki sent two strike waves to hit the carriers. Task Force 58, as it was now known, with Admiral Mitscher back in command, was hit by Japanese conventional bombers and by kamikazes. The *Enterprise* was hit by a bomb, the *Intrepid* was damaged by a near-miss, and the *Yorktown* was bombed, one bomb blowing two big holes in her.

All day long Admiral Ugaki waited for news from his attack forces. He was having great difficulty in mounting strikes because the Kyushu airbases were under attack from the American and British carriers.

For the next few hours Ugaki could not figure out what had gone wrong, why his planes had been so ineffectual, for this damage to the fleet had not been done by Ugaki's pilots but by army pilots. Then he learned: The flight leaders had funked out, abandoning the strikes before they were halfway along.

And so on March 19 Admiral Ugaki sent more planes to strike the Allied carriers. That day the *Wasp* was bombed, and 101 men were killed and 269 wounded. The *Franklin* was hit very hard: one bomb wrecked the forward elevator and started fires on the hangar deck. A second bomb set fire to planes on deck, and soon the whole flight deck was aflame. On the *Franklin*, 725 men were killed and 265 wounded.

This day the Japanese hit the *Franklin* again. Two more bombs struck the ship and did enormous damage. Six separate explosions on the *Franklin* were heard aboard the *Bunker Hill*, which was 50 miles away. Later that day the *Wasp* was also hit by a conventional bomb dropped by a conventional bomber. The *Wasp* suffered 300 casualties, but she could still operate, unlike the *Franklin*, which had suffered nearly 1,000 casualties.

Admiral Davison transferred his flag to the *Hancock*. The *Franklin* went dead in the water, but so improved were the techniques of compartmentalization and damage control over those in use at the time of Guadalcanal and the death of the *Lexington*, *Hornet*, and the *Wasp*, that the *Franklin* was saved and went back to the United States under her own power.

The results of the kamikaze attacks of March 18 and 19 on the American carrier fleet were serious. For the first time in the Pacific War, morale threatened to become a problem in the American navy. The attacks on the two carriers proved the soundness of Admiral Ugaki's theory that if enough carriers could be put out of action, the American drive could be halted. The catch for the Japanese was that they had too few trained pilots and too few conventional planes in good condition. It did not go unnoticed that the damage caused to the two carriers had been done by conventional tactics in both cases, and that several kamikazes had been shot down near carriers and other ships at the same time. If American morale suffered, so did Japanese morale. The Japanese had had a heaven-sent opportunity to hit the carrier fleet, and they had failed to do their job. Ugaki was desolated.

———

Later on March 19 the American carriers began to retire. By this time, four had been hit: the *Franklin, Wasp, Enterprise*, and the *Yorktown*. Admiral Ugaki's men had done better than he had thought.

On March 20 the American fleet was again under attack, but no disasters occurred. One fighter attacked the destroyer *Halsey Powell*. Its bomb went straight through the ship and hit the bottom of the ocean without exploding. Another plane strafed the carrier *Enterprise* again. But that was all.

On March 21 the Japanese unveiled a new weapon, the *oka*, or "piggyback" bomb, which was carried by a conventional bomber to the scene of operations. Then a pilot took over and aimed the flying bomb at a target. The Japanese had great hopes for the oka, but it never really accomplished much from that first day, March 21, when several okas were sent out but none hit anything.

The three-day air battle of March 18 through 20 had cost both sides a lot. The Americans had two badly damaged carriers, and the Japanese had lost in the air 160 planes, including 69 suicide planes. On the ground, they had lost at least 50 more planes. Admiral Ugaki had to rebuild his Fifth Air Fleet.

———

On March 23 the American carriers again struck Okinawa.

On March 25 the naval bombardment of Okinawa, the softening up before the invasion by the troops, began. So again did the kamikaze attacks. Although more and more ships were being hit, the attacks did not stop the Americans or the British.

———

March 26 was a bad day for the American fleet. The kamikazes hit the destroyers *Gilmer* and *Kimberly*.

By March 31, the invasion of Okinawa was under way, and a

kamikaze hit the *Indianapolis*, flagship of Admiral Spruance. He had to move his flag to another ship, and the cruiser had to go back to the United States for repair. Indeed, the kamikazes had become the most serious problem the American navy had ever faced, and it was not getting better.

The Japanese then began a continual harassment with kamikazes called Operation Ten Go. It began with a raid by 23 planes on April 1. Captain Itsue Kobase led the first flight of five suicide pilots. It was gratifying to Admiral Ugaki, if not to the Americans, that Captain Kobase had learned all the lessons Ugaki had been teaching about determination and effort. The captain flew his plane into *LST-884* off the south coast of Okinawa that day. The tank landing ship was severely damaged. The other four kamikazes all developed engine trouble when they had gone only a few miles from the base and turned back. Later in the day those four planes, joined by one from the 65th Squadron, managed to take off. They used approved tactics, flying together until they came near Okinawa, and then separating to avoid being "bounced" by a large group of American fighters or presenting a large target to the antiaircraft gunners. They came in at dusk to attack.

One kamikaze crashed into the battleship *West Virginia*. Another smashed into the transport *Hinsdale*. A third hit the transport *Alpine*. The fourth hit the transport *Archenar*. Of the six kamikazes that had set out from Admiral Ugaki's field that day, only five had been successful. To be sure, they had not sunk any ships, but they had damaged five, several of which had to be towed to Kerama Retto, near Okinawa, for repairs. That sort of damage was extremely costly to the Americans.

From another field came a number of other kamikazes that day, planes of the Japanese army. One strafed the deck of the British carrier *Indomitable*, causing several casualties. It also strafed the deck of the battleship *King George V*. Then a kamikaze crashed into the deck of the carrier *Indefatigable*, but the steel deck of the British carrier prevented damage below, although several men were killed or injured on the flight deck. The destroyer *Ulster* was hit by a kamikaze and had to be towed to Leyte. The carrier *Illustrious* was attacked by a suicide pilot, but his aim was faulty; the plane caromed off the deck and slid into the sea, with minimal damage to the Royal Navy ship.

This first week of April was really hell for the American and British fleets off the shore of Okinawa. Every day the kamikazes came over in some force, and every day they caused casualties to ships and men. On April 2 a plane hit the destroyer transport *Dickerson*, killing 53 men and wounding 15. The ship was so badly damaged that ultimately she was scuttled. Another suicide diver hit the transport *Goodhue*, which was carrying men from the U.S. 77th Infantry Division, as part of a convoy. Another hit the *Chilton* and a third the *Henrico*. Many men of the 305th Infantry Regiment and the captain of the *Henrico* were killed. Other suicide divers crashed the transports *Telfair* and *Wyandotte*. On April 3 the kamikazes attacked and damaged the *LST-509*, the destroyer *Pritchett*, and the escort carrier *Wake Island*.

Then, for the next two days the weather was so bad that the kamikazes could not attack the Allied fleet. To the Americans and British it seemed a heaven-sent respite. Then on April 6, Admiral Ugaki launched his greatest effort yet: the beginning of Operation Ten Go, a new tactic devised by Ugaki himself. It employed the wave technique: the dispatch of hundreds of suicide planes, accompanied by hundreds of fighter planes whose job was to divert the American fighter planes and let the suicide divers complete their attacks.

On April 6, 355 kamikazes attacked the Allied fleet, coming in waves that lasted all day long. They sank three destroyers, two ammunition ships, and an LST, and they damaged nine destroyers and escorts, a mine layer, and 12 other ships. The Americans said they had shot down 486 planes that day. But the fact was that it was easier to produce planes than it was to produce ships, and the loss of life to the Japanese was 486 men. The loss to the Americans was in the thousands.

That day the battleship *Yamato*—pride of the Japanese fleet, once Admiral Yamamoto's flagship, and later the leader of the raid through San Bernardino Strait—sailed out from Kure naval base on a suicide mission of her own. Theoretically, she was to proceed to Okinawa and act as a floating artillery platform in support of General Ushijima's Okinawa defense force. Actually, she was sailing to her death in an attempt to get near enough to the American carriers to take some down with her with her big guns before she was sunk. Admiral Kusaka, chief of staff of the combined fleet (now only a headquarters), called on Admiral Ugaki and asked for air support, but Admiral Ugaki had no skilled pilots to give him. He had many brand-new, unskilled pilots who could make one-way flights, but that was not what was wanted.

So the *Yamato* sailed with several destroyers, bound to meet her destiny, without air cover. Ultimately Admiral Ugaki did send a few planes, but they came late and did no good. The *Yamato* met that destiny the following day, April 7, when at about 8:30 A.M. she was spotted by a plane from the morning search patrol of the U.S. carrier *Essex*. Planes from the U.S. task force bombed the battleship and torpedoed her repeatedly. They also sank four of the eight destroyers that had come out with her. Of the *Yamato*'s crew of 3,300 men, only 300 were rescued.

That same day, Admiral Ugaki launched another wave of *kikusui*, "floating chrysanthemum suicide planes." They approached the carriers at about 11:00 A.M., when they were fully alert after the *Yamato* affair. The combat air patrol was in the air, augmented, and very keen. The Americans shot down most of the planes, but one suicide diver got through and smashed into the carrier *Hancock*, destroying 20 planes on deck, killing 72 men, and injuring 82 others. Another crashed on the battleship *Maryland*, another on the destroyer *Bennett*, and another on the destroyer escort *Wesson*. And from this point on, the suicide attacks on the American fleet off Okinawa did not cease. There were particularly large wave attacks on April 12 and April 13, and they did enormous damage to the Allied fleet. The suicide planes came again on April 14, and again on April 15. Each time they left ships burning and sinking behind them, which had an extremely negative effect on American naval morale.

They were back over the Allied fleet on April 16 in force, and they damaged the carrier *Intrepid* and the battleship *Missouri* and sank the destroyer *Pringle*. They came again on April 17, and on April 27, 28, 29, and 30.

The American fleet was a stationary floating target, it seemed. The fleet had to stay offshore, to supply the American troops fighting desperately to capture Okinawa. That was Admiral Spruance's doctrine, and he stuck with it, keeping the carriers close at hand to supply air cover for the fleet.

In May the kamikazes raided every day that planes could fly, and in force on eight different days. They sank five ships and damaged 34. The pressure on the American fleet was enormous, and the psychological pressure on the sailors and airmen was very serious. Morale in the fleet had never been lower.

Ashore, the enormous physical power of the American forces was overcoming the desperate resistance of the Japanese defenders. Naha, the capital of Okinawa, fell at the end of May. The fighting grew even fiercer.

Shuttling between Washington and Pearl Harbor was a man who had an entirely different idea from that of Admiral Spruance on how to fight the kamikazes. He was Admiral Halsey. Admiral King's studies of fighting kamikazes had produced no positive results, and therefore just about everyone was willing to listen to Halsey's theories. His main theory was that the best defense was an effective offense. With the capture of Naha and other areas, the Americans controlled much of the land of Okinawa, and they could bring in hundreds of army and marine fighter planes. These fighters could replace the carrier planes that in May were still combatting the suicide planes—very successfully, in terms of numbers of Japanese planes destroyed, but not very effectively in terms of the Japanese success in damaging and sinking American ships. The kamikaze, in Admiral Nimitz's words, was the most effective weapon ever devised by the Japanese navy. "We are a high speed stationary target for the Japanese air force," Nimitz once remarked ruefully.

Nimitz had even approached the Joint Chiefs of Staff and persuaded them to order General Curtis LeMay, chief of the 20th Bomber Command in the Marianas, to suspend his attempt to win the war by burning up all Japan with incendiaries, and to concentrate on bombing Japanese aircraft factories. The campaign was not very effective, though. The planes kept coming off the assembly lines.

Halsey's idea was to bring the carrier fleet close along the Japanese shore, and day after day to strike the Japanese airfields on Kyushu and Honshu islands. Thus the kamikaze planes would be prevented from ever leaving the ground.

At the end of April, Admiral Halsey had flown to Guam to visit Admiral Nimitz, who had moved up to that island to establish the forward base of the U.S. Pacific Fleet. He explained his plan: The American fleet did not have to continue to be a high speed stationary target for the Japanese. There it was decided that Admiral Halsey would take over the fleet again, Admiral Spruance would go back to Guam to plan for future operations, and the fleet would go out to get the kamikazes at their source.

From Guam, Admiral Halsey flew to Okinawa and conferred with Admiral Spruance. When Spruance explained that the only way to deal with the kamikazes was to shoot them down over the sea, Halsey only grunted. There was no point in trying to educate Spruance at this late date. He listened to Spruance's litany of failure and then went back to Pearl Harbor to prepare for sea.

———

On May 18, Admiral Halsey boarded the flagship *Missouri* to sail for Okinawa and the new sort of battle he had in mind. He had no regard for the "static" defense employed by Admiral Spruance, and he intended to change that immediately. He was going out to "get 'em where they was," and that meant to attack the Japanese planes in the Japanese homeland.

The fleet had been given something of a respite in the past two weeks, because the spring rains had been dumping enormous quantities of water on Okinawa, and the flying was almost impossible. The seventh mass attack of the kikusui squadrons was largely ineffective because of the weather. Time and again the planes took off and then returned to base without attacking. The Americans had the idea that the Japanese were not pursuing the tactic very vigorously, but they were wrong.

On May 26 Admiral Halsey arrived off Okinawa and conferred with Admiral Spruance. He met with the other commanders in the area, and then he announced his decision. He would not stick with the static defense plans of Admiral Spruance. He would blanket all the local airfields or anything anywhere near that anyone wanted, and then he would go out and strike the Japanese at home. On May 27, the American fleet off Okinawa stopped being the Fifth Fleet and became the Third Fleet. The change seemed to be largely on paper: same ships, same officers, same pilots, but the attitude, when Halsey took command, was not the same. The morale, which had been sagging, suddenly took a change for the better. Halsey had done it before. Halsey would do it again. Now the fleet would show the Japanese a thing or two.

Admiral Halsey then sent Admiral Sherman's task group off to Leyte for a rest after having taken much punishment off Okinawa. The British Pacific Fleet, having operated off Okinawa too for a month, was also sent back to Australia for a rest.

Admiral John McCain replaced Admiral Mitscher as commander of the task force. A marine air group was ordered up by Admiral Nimitz to go to Okinawa and protect the supply ships there from the kamikazes. On the morning of June 2, the fleet was at sea, and Admiral Radford's task group sent its planes to hit the airfields of Kyushu. The operation was successful. The pilots destroyed many aircraft on the ground at Kanoya and other airfields.

On June 3 the carrier planes hit Kyushu again. This time they shot down a few planes in the air as well. The weather changed, and Halsey ran into another typhoon. Trying to avoid it, he moved directly into the eye of the typhoon because of bad information from Pearl Harbor. Again, nature did to the carrier fleet what the Japanese could no longer do: Three destroyers were sunk, and 29 other ships damaged, including several carriers; 150 planes were lost, and nearly 800 men died. From the Japanese point of view (and they were not really aware of the damage), it was another kamikaze, a Divine Wind, attacking Japan's enemies.

After his first typhoon, Admiral Halsey had recommended several changes in the weather reporting system, including constant monitoring of weather by special planes and giving weather messages highest priority. None of these changes had been made; Pearl Harbor had been getting very sloppy now that Nimitz was in Guam. Several of the ambitious young admirals cried for Halsey's head, saying that he had erred grievously in his assessment of the weather, but that was to be expected. Admirals King and Nimitz paid no attention. The Third Fleet hit Japan all week long in that first part of June. Then they moved back to the Philippines for a rest. On June 17 they began their shore leave.

———

On June 30 the fleet was ready to go again. The damage from the typhoon to some ships had been repaired, and other ships had replaced those that had had to be sent home for major repair. With 13 carriers and eight battleships and all the support ships he needed, Halsey set sail once more for Japan, striking Honshu Island on July 10. On July 11 and 12 they fueled and on July 13 the weather prevented operations, but on July 14 they hit northeastern Honshu. They bombed and strafed anything and everything, including 14 locomotives, but they encountered only one plane in the air, a two-engined bomber. The reason, as Admiral Halsey had deduced, was that the Japanese were saving their air power for the day that the Allies invaded Japan, which now everyone knew could not be too far away.

Halsey's planes continued to strike the airfields and other targets. On July 16 the Third Fleet fueled, and on this day the British Pacific Fleet returned to join up for duty. That night the Allied fleet moved southwest to prepare for dawn strikes on Tokyo. For a week the ships moved around the area, striking when the weather allowed them to, refueling almost within sight of what remained of the Japanese fleet, and striking again. One of Halsey's main targets was the remnants of the fleet, wherever he could find them. The battleships bombarded land targets. Altogether it was an impressive display of Allied force on the very shore of Japan. The results were not as great as might have been hoped, however, because the Japanese were dug in, most of their industries protected, and the airfields were barren of planes, which were either stored off in the woods away from the fields or underground.

Back around Okinawa, although the number of kamikazes had decreased greatly, the planes of the marine air wing still had to be alert. They continued to shoot down suicide pilots day after day.

The strikes by the carriers did bring forth some air opposition, but Halsey's methods of maintaining a much larger combat air patrol and keeping rigid control of the aircraft in the air kept the Japanese from any successes in hitting the ships. In fact, for a solid year when the fleet was under Halsey's control, only one ship was lost to enemy attack. Halsey had discovered the method of dealing with the kamikazes.

The carriers continued to work along the Japanese coast in July. At the end of July the kamikazes began again with renewed fury and sank or damaged more ships off Okinawa. The U.S. fleet returned to the Okinawa area. Another typhoon came along; the fleet evaded it, but operations had to be suspended early in August. Then came August 5 when the atomic bomb was dropped on Hiroshima. It changed the war, but it did not radically change Admiral Halsey's method of operations. He continued, with Admiral Rawlings of the British Pacific Fleet, to strike Hokkaido and Honshu airfields. The pickings were very slim. The planes concentrated on airfields and on the remnants of the

Japanese fleet that they found in this or that harbor. On August 9 American and British planes destroyed or damaged about 400 Japanese aircraft on nine airfields.

During the second week of August, the Japanese were considering the question of surrender. The generals were against it, and just about everyone else was for it. Admiral Halsey was doing everything he could to persuade the generals that the jig was up, that surrender was the only course. The emperor was listening; he told the Supreme War Council that there would be no surcease of American strikes against the Japanese until they surrendered. For emphasis, on August 10 the Allied planes staged more great raids on airfields, using a new technique: flying at treetop level to spot the camouflaged aircraft. That day they destroyed about 175 planes on the ground, losing 15 American planes and six British planes because of the low-level approach into heavy antiaircraft fire. The British were becoming experts at shooting up trains, too.

On August 12, Admiral Halsey was warned by Admiral King that he probably would have to "occupy" Japan and to get a landing force ready.

On August 13 the Third Fleet was back in action, striking Japanese targets from Tokyo north to Sendai. American and British fighter planes destroyed 250 planes on the ground and damaged 150.

On August 14 the fleet fueled. Halsey had been 40 days at sea now without a hitch. He was ready to hit more airfields, more rail lines, more ports, more industrial plants in the Tokyo area.

On the morning of August 15, even as the emperor called for surrender of all Japanese forces, Admiral Halsey sent off an air strike to hit Japan again. The planes left the decks of the carriers at 5:00 A.M., but at 6:30 orders were received from Admiral Nimitz to suspend operations. The war was over.

The pilots of the *Yorktown* were already over Japan, fighting Japanese defenders. Four *Yorktown* pilots and a number from other carriers were lost that morning after the war had been called off.

———

And so the carrier war against Japan came to an end. In a few weeks, Admiral Halsey, who had once boasted that he would ride through the streets of Tokyo on Emperor Hirohito's white horse, did in fact ride into Yokosuka Naval Base aboard a white horse, grinning very broadly. Halsey had brought several new dimensions to carrier warfare, and more than any other he had shown how to defeat the suicide attack by launching a whirlwind attack and defense of his own. His contribution to naval warfare was greater than that of any other in the Pacific War: the aggressive campaign of the early months, the turnaround of what seemed to be a losing battle for Guadalcanal, the mopping up of the Solomons, the destruction of the Japanese fleet at Leyte, and the basic solution to the kamikaze problem.

The Korean War

During the five years after the end of World War II, many changes came to aeronautics, the most important of which was the development of jet aircraft and helicopters. The development was slowed considerably by popular demand. As was usual in the United States, peace brought reaction against war, and Secretary of Defense Louis Johnson presided over the dismemberment of the United States Navy. Britain was in the throes of a social revolution and a new poverty brought on by the costs of a long war—and at the end of it the ending of imperial privilege and constriction of her industries.

Although the technology of carrier warfare received many shots in the arm, the practice remained highly constrained. By June 1950, the United States Navy had only 270 combatant ships in commission, among them 15 carriers in service and another four under modification in shipyards.

The U.S. Navy had only one carrier in the western Pacific, the 27,000-ton ship *Valley Forge*. She was just north of Hongkong on that day in June 1950, when the North Koreans marched into South Korea and vowed to liberate the whole Korean peninsula in the name of the North Korean People's Republic. The *Valley Forge* immediately set course for the Philippines. She carried 30 F9F-2B fighters, 28 F4U-4B Corsairs, and 14 AD-4 Skyraiders. This mixture of propeller and jet planes was brought about because of the small payload (1,000 pounds of bombs) of the F9F-2 and its limited endurance in these early days of jets.

The *Valley Forge* went to Subic Bay and picked up ammunition and supplies. On June 27 she steamed north and stopped off in Okinawa to wait developments.

Meanwhile a British carrier, *Triumph*, was in the area. They met at Buckner Bay and formed Task Force 77 with the two carriers and several Allied cruisers and destroyers.

On July 1 the combined carrier force steamed northward again into the Yellow Sea. The *Triumph* flew off Fireflies and Seafires to attack North Korean targets at Haeju, and the *Valley Forge* sent a strike against Pyongyang, the North Korean capital. They hit the airfield, shooting down two Yak fighters and destroying nine planes on the ground. They burned a great deal of fuel, demolished three hangars, and cratered the runways. That same afternoon the two carriers sent strikes against rail facilities. All planes returned, but one Skyraider was hit by antiaircraft fire. When it landed, very hot, it bounced over the barrier and into one Skyraider and two corsairs, which were destroyed; six other planes were damaged.

―――――――

Task Force 77 went into action again in the Korea Strait, covering the American landing of forces at Pohan, north of Pusan. Thereafter for several days the carriers hit targets in North Korea. At the North Korean port of Wonsan, the planes destroyed a petroleum refinery.

―――――――

On July 31 the *Valley Forge* was back in Okinawa, and here she was joined by the American carrier *Philippine Sea*. The British *Triumph* was detached and went to join a blockade force to stop the operation of North Korean ships in coastal waters. Also the American carrier *Boxer* was getting ready for sea in San Francisco. The *Sicily* was in Hawaiian waters. So was the *Badoeng Strait*. And within a month all five American carriers in the Pacific were committed to the Korean war.

These were the desperate days of the Pusan Perimeter, when the Americans were very nearly forced out of Korea altogether. The carrier planes flew mission after mission in close support of troops, sometimes bombing targets in the area of the North Korean lines. So, by August, six Allied carriers—five American and one British—were involved in the Korean war. The *Philippine Sea* and the *Valley Forge* were the big carriers, each with about 80 planes. The *Philippine Sea* planes concentrated on strategic targets, bridges, and rail lines. The *Valley Forge* flew close support missions. And for the month of August most of the carriers were thus used, in close support, as the ground forces fought literally for their lives and to maintain their toehold in South Korea. In August the carriers were on the east side of Korea. By September, most of them had moved to the west side into the Yellow Sea.

On September 4, the American carrier pilots had their first fights with Soviet aircraft. Task Force 77 was steaming off the Korean coast 100 miles from Red China and just about that far from the Soviet naval and airbases at Port Arthur on the Liaotung Peninsula. They were, in effect, only about 10 minutes of flying time from the Soviet bases. At about 1:30 P.M. on September 4, a destroyer in Task Force 77 reported unidentified aircraft approaching from the direction of Port Arthur. Moments later the *Valley Forge* picked up a contact at about 60 miles out. Two divisions of Corsair F4U fighters were airborne on combat air patrol. They were ordered to meet the approaching aircraft.

One plane was coming in, and 30 miles from the American ships the American planes intercepted. It was a bomber bearing the red star of the Soviet air forces. When the bomber pilot saw the gull-winged American fighters, he took evasive action and headed east toward Korea. The fighters closed in, and the bomber opened fire on them. The American fighter pilots checked with their carrier. They were told to return the fire. One fighter fired and missed. The second American fighter fired and caught the bomber with shells from its four cannon. The Soviet bomber went down in flames. More planes were launched by the carriers, and a destroyer steamed to the spot where the plane had gone into the water. The destroyer recovered the body of a Soviet flier.

———————

The big operation of the carriers was a part of the Inchon landing of General MacArthur's forces in Korea. Task Force 77 now had three fast carriers: *Philippine Sea, Valley Forge*, and *Boxer*. And the *Sicily* and the *Badoeng Strait*, escort carriers, were a part of the invasion force that would land the troops ashore at Inchon.

HMS *Triumph* first created a diversion on the other side of Korea, and then raced around to join in the landing operation. For two days planes from the *Valley Forge* and the *Philippine Sea* softened up the Seoul-Inchon area with bombing and strafing attacks. Then on the morning of September 15 all the carriers flew air support as the troops landed at Inchon.

On September 17 the Americans captured Inchon and Kimpo Airfield. Also on that day two Yaks, Soviet-built fighters, attacked a British cruiser and an American cruiser anchored offshore at Inchon. One bomb dropped on the American ship and bounced off. The Yaks then strafed the British cruiser and killed one man, but the British cruiser's guns destroyed one of the Yaks. Soon the British carrier *Theseus* also joined up with Task Force 77; as did the American *Leyte*, which had come around from the Mediterranean. She was also a 27,000-ton fleet carrier. So by late September the carrier force was formidable: Task Force 77 had about 350 aircraft, and the escort carrier group of Task Group 96.8 had 50 more planes.

When the Americans and South Koreans landed at Wonsan on the east coast, they had to be supplied by air because the waters were mined and ships could not at first come in. The carrier planes did the supply. And for 12 days they supported the marine fighter squadron that had landed at the Wonsan airfield.

By October 22 it seemed that the battle of Korea was about to end, and the carriers began to depart for Japanese waters. Only two American escort carriers were left off the Korean coast. In late October the war heated up again. The Chinese communists entered, and a number of Soviet-built aircraft came into the war. Task Force 77 came out of the waters of Japan to fight again. On October 29 the carriers *Leyte* and *Valley Forge* were at sea, heading again for Korea.

The fighting in the air was very complicated, made more so by the interdiction against crossing the Yalu River into Chinese Manchurian territory. Task Force 77 was given the job of knocking down bridges at Sinuiju, because the B-29s were too big to operate against them. The carrier planes knocked down the highway bridge and damaged the railroad bridge, but the latter withstood their attacks. Anyhow, soon enough the river had frozen over and the communists were moving directly across the ice.

For the next few weeks much of the effort of the carrier planes was devoted to the Yalu bridges. On November 9, Lieutenant Commander W. T. Amen, flying an F9F, shot down a MiG, then believed to be the hottest jet in combat. On November 18, F9Fs from the *Valley Forge* and the *Leyte* shot down two more MiGs.

Late in November, the Chinese launched their first big attack, catching the Americans by surprise. The fast carrier *Valley Forge* had left the area for the west coast, and the escorts had also departed; the *Leyte* and the *Philippine Sea* were the only carriers left in the area. Soon the *Sicily*, the *Badoeng Strait*, and the *Theseus* were all moving back into combat. And now in came the light carrier *Bataan* and the escort carrier *Bairoko*, bringing in the new swept-wing F-86a, an American fighter believed to be the equal of the MiG15. It had a speed of 675 miles an hour.

Now more carriers began to come. The *Essex*-class *Princeton* had been reactivated, and she reached Korea on December 5. So eight American carriers and a British light carrier were coming into Korean waters in December 1950.

The retreat from the Yalu became almost a rout: It was the worst defeat the United States had suffered since the fall of Corregidor in the Pacific War. The carriers covered the retreat, and afterward Task Force 77 was on the line. At all times two fleet carriers were to be kept in action and a third replenishing in Japan. Off the west coast of Japan, the *Bataan* and the *Theseus* alternated on duty.

The carrier force was augmented constantly: by June 1953, 39 carriers of various kinds and sizes would be activated by the U.S Fleet, and the keel for the new supercarrier *Forrestal* was laid in July 1952. She would displace 59,000 tons and have an overall length of 1,039 feet and a width of 252 feet, and would make 35 knots. Another large carrier, the *Saratoga*, had also been authorized. The Congress had indicated that it would build one large carrier a year for five years.

Other changes came to the carrier force. The S2F Tracker became the antisubmarine plane. Helicopters were brought in for operations against submarines and for land operations as well. The first helicopter carrier was the *Siboney*, whose helicopters were HUP-2, 31.5 feet long. The next helicopter to join the fleet was the 49-foot HSS-1 with a crew of four. Helicopters were found to be part of the answer to minesweeping because they could spot and hover over the mines so that they could be destroyed by minesweepers. So several LSTs were converted to become minesweeper tenders and helicopter bases.

In the summer of 1951 the modernized *Essex* carrier had come to Korea for operations. Also in the western Pacific were the *Bon Homme Richard*, the *Boxer*, and the *Princeton*. They were involved in Operation Strangle, which was an effort to sever the communist supply lines across Korea. Operation Strangle lasted from June through September, but it was not outstandingly successful. The carriers also supplied fighter support for B-29 missions.

In October the carriers were flying railroad strikes and hitting bridges. They flew night strikes as well as day raids. The *Essex* was given one special mission. Allied guerillas had reported a meeting of high-ranking Chinese and Korean communist leaders to take place at Kapsan, in the mountain area of North Korea. The *Essex* was ordered to break it up. She flew off eight Skyraiders, each carrying two 1,000-pound bombs and a napalm bomb, as well as 20-millimeter cannon ammunition. The planes were launched from 100 miles offshore. They flew in low and then up the valleys to avoid the enemy radar. At 9:13 A.M. on the morning of the communist meeting, the bombers were overhead and bombing. All bombs fell within the target area. The report came back: The strike had killed 509 high-ranking communists in that meeting place.

The eight navy pilots who returned to the *Essex* were called "the butchers of Kapsan" by Radio Pyongyang, and the communists put a price on their heads.

———

The command of the Seventh Fleet changed hands several times in these years. And in 1951, Vice Admiral Jocko Clark, who had come up through the command ranks in World War II as one of the young Turks of naval aviation, became commander of the Seventh Fleet.

In June 1952 the fast carriers launched a major strike against the Suiho Dam, whose hydroelectric system was a major source of power for North Korea and Manchuria. On June 23 the carriers *Boxer*, *Philippine Sea*, and *Princeton* launched planes for the strike. Air Force planes followed up. And other planes hit other power stations. When it was all done, after three days of strikes, 11 power plants had been knocked out.

———

This was a different sort of war from anything the Americans and British had fought before. The problem was primarily one of politics. The Allies never did call it a war but a "police action" of the United Nations. And because of that it was decided that atomic weapons would not be used, lest they force the Soviets into the war and make of it a global atomic war.

Therefore a good deal of attention was paid to methods of saving lives and yet meeting the needs of battle. One development was a sort of "push button" warfare. F6F-5 Hellcats of World War II age were fitted with guidance systems and loaded with high explosives, thus becoming flying bombs. They were catapulted off the carriers with engines running and guided by remote control to bridges and other targets, and then crashed into the targets. Between August 28 and September 2, 1952, six of these guided missiles were used with very good success.

———

During the last year of the war, the carrier force undertook a number of special missions. One was the destruction of the oil refinery at Aoji, near Manhua. On October 8 a joint strike was made with the air force against Kowon, a railroad junction ringed by antiaircraft batteries that had been giving the navy planes a lot of trouble. The B-29s hit first, and then 89 carrier planes came in to strafe, bomb, and knock out the antiaircraft installations.

On November 18, 1952, the Americans and the Soviets mixed it up in a serious aerial combat. Four F9F-5 Panther planes were on patrol over Task Force 77, about 100 miles east of the Soviet base at Vladivostok. The task force was supporting a fleet bombardment of the northeast Korean coast.

Then a group of "bogies" (unknown aircraft) was reported north of the task force. One of the American planes was having trouble with its fuel pump, and the pilot's wingman stuck with him while the other two American planes went off to investigate.

They discovered that seven aircraft had broken off from the Soviet group and were coming in. They were ordered to close with the Soviet planes, identified as MiG-15s. The two planes moved in and were soon followed by the wingman of the plane with the bad fuel pump. They fought a brief battle with the communist planes, shooting down two of them and damaging a third. All the American planes made it back to their carrier, the *Oriskany*, although one of them had been hit and damaged by the Soviet planes.

The judgment then was that although the Soviet MiG-15 was a better plane than the American fighter, the American fliers were better fliers than the Soviets.

For an hour after the battle, Task Force 77 screens showed Soviet planes to the north, some of them coming to within 40 miles of the American force, but there were no more confrontations that day.

The carriers had all sorts of missions. One of the power plants of the Chosin Reservoir had always been a hard target to hit because of antiaircraft batteries. On May 3, 1953, the *Valley Forge* launched three AD4-N Skyraiders, each carrying two 1,000-pound bombs. They moved in, dropped flares, then bombed and destroyed the installations.

During the final months of the Korean war, the communist planes flew many night missions over the Allied lines, using propeller-driven craft. American jets were too fast to take care of these slow planes. So the navy came to the rescue, employing many of the F4U-5N Corsairs, which went ashore to an airfield near Seoul and then began operations. On the night of June 29, 1953, Lieutenant Guy P. Bordelon from the *Princeton* shot down two enemy planes, and the next night he shot down two more. The third night he got a fifth plane. This made Bordelon an ace—in fact the only Navy Ace of the Korean war.

So the Korean war came to an end. It was not a war marked by many battles between carriers and fleet, as had been the Pacific War. There were none of these. It was quite a different matter, involving a great deal of troop support, a great deal of strategic bombing to interdict supplies and to damage installations, and it was not very romantic in the old sense of the word. And yet the tactics were very much like those of the Pacific War days, even though jets were used in many areas and for many missions.

As with the Pacific War, in the beginning the enemy had the best aircraft. The MiG-15 was the world's best fighter plane of its day, and this fact created many problems for the American naval fliers.

Importantly, the Korean war emphasized the continued need for carriers and for naval strength. Korea was a sea war—the materials were delivered to Japan and to Korea by sea—and from the beginning the aircraft of the carrier provided the most effective air cover. In fact, in the beginning the American planes operating from Japan could not stay over the target in Korea for more than 15 to 20 minutes. The carriers' fighters had to do the job. Later on things changed, but the more they changed the more evident it became that carrier operations were essential to the success of the American and British forces in Korea.

During the Korean war, 17 American carriers operated at various times, flying a total of more than 250,000 missions. The British and Australian carriers in the war flew another 30,000 missions. Carriers contributed a third of all the air operations in Korea, which included the B-29 missions. Although before the Korean war there was a good deal of debate about the need for naval forces, afterward the debate no longer raged. The carrier had a new lease on life.

———————

And in Korea a new element was added to the carrier war: the helicopter.

In December 1950, when the Americans were struggling to escape from the apparent entrapment of the forces up around the Chang-jin Reservoir, the Chief of Naval Operations set up a new operation. A dozen pilots and eight helicopters were ordered to move to the West Coast. There they boarded the *Valley Forge* and were shipped to Korea. They operated from the decks of the *Valley Forge* and of the converted *LST-799*. At Wonsan the helicopters spotted the mines and helped destroy them. They ran missions to rescue downed airmen behind the lines and many other secret missions, delivering and picking up American and ROK agents behind the enemy lines. In the carrier war of Korea, the carriers developed a new mission and a new importance.

After Korea the carriers changed in many ways, but after Korea also it was apparent that as long as there was a naval force—and there always had to be one—the highly vulnerable, highly volatile, and highly effective aircraft carrier would remain.

20

Old World vs. New World

The eyes of the world had scarcely left the battlefields of Korea when they were turned toward another area of Asia, the old French colony of Indochina, now tortured by a revolution that had begun in 1945 when the Annamite people of the north and central sections of the country decided they must have independence.

The French resisted this attempt to subvert their colonial system. By the fall of 1945 a civil war had begun, with the Vietminh political movement pitting itself against the French colonial government. In 1946 the French made an attempt to reoccupy Haiphong and Hanoi and take over the government that had been "usurped" by Ho Chi Minh. The old French carrier *Bearn* was used to transport French troops of the Foreign Legion to Haiphong in this initial move. For the next two years, the French drove the Vietnamese back out of the cities. Part of the war was waged against Ho Chi Minh by the two French carriers *Arromanches* and *Dixmude*. The *Dixmude* was flying support missions for French troops in the spring of 1947 along the central coast of Anam, for this area lay beyond the range of land-based aircraft at Hanoi in the north and Saigon in the south. The Annamites occupied the territory in between. The *Dixmude*'s dive bombers supported various French landings along the coast of Indochina.

The *Dixmude* returned to France in May 1947 to pick up more planes and for maintenance. She returned to Saigon in October to continue operations. Her first task was in Operation Lea, a parachute assault on the Vietminh headquarters in the Tonkin delta north of

242

Hanoi. In three weeks the *Dixmude*'s pilots flew more than 200 missions and dropped 65 tons of bombs.

The *Dixmude* continued operations in support of the French army until 1948, when she returned to France and her place was taken by the carrier *Arromanches*. The *Arromanches* was more modern; she could make 25 knots, and carried SBD dive bombers bought as surplus from the Americans and Seafire fighters bought from the British.

The *Arromanches* was 695 feet long and weighed in at 13,000 tons. She was the largest ship ever to navigate the Saigon River. She spent a bit of time in Saigon and then operated off the French Indochina coast until January 1949, mostly doing troop support missions.

Late in the summer of 1950, the French made a deal with the Americans for new carrier planes, and the *Dixmude* went to the United States to take aboard F6F Hellcat fighters and Sb2C Helldiver dive bombers. She then went to Saigon, arriving on October 28. The two carriers operated again when the *Arromanches* went back to Indochina in the fall of 1951. Then along came the light carrier *LaFayette*, which in World War II had been the American *Langley*. She was a fast light carrier, capable of making 32 knots.

Despite carrier operations, never very extensive, the French were not doing well in Indochina. In 1949 the communist forces had begun a counteroffensive, and in 1950 Chinese-trained Vietminh troops gave the battle a new life.

The forces of Ho Chi Minh moved toward Laos and Thailand, and the French made a big parachute drop at Dienbienphu, a valley town that lay astride the route into Laos. On November 20, 1953, thousands of French troops dropped from the sky to occupy this place and make it an advanced base for operations against the Vietminh.

The war soon took a different turn, however. The French underestimated everything about the revolution in Indochina: first that it was real, second that it was local, and third that it could sustain itself, with or without help from Red China. Dienbienphu, instead of a forward base, became a forward trap for the French.

All this while the planes from the *Arromanches* flew support missions into the heat of the Russian-made antiaircraft guns with which the Vietminh troops surrounded the valley of Dienbienphu. This flak was regarded as heavier than that in Germany in World War II: It destroyed 47 planes over the valley and damaged another 167 planes.

The American navy began its involvement in Indochina on the side of the French. On April 26, 1953, the American carrier *Saipan* arrived at Danang, and marine pilots flew ashore 24 F4U-6 planes for the French navy. And then the United States was importuned to stick its fingers into the Vietnam revolution. The French wanted the U.S. Navy to make a big strike against the Vietminh in support of Dienbienphu. The Americans refused, and Dienbienphu fell to the Vietminh on May 7, 1954.

The fall of Dienbienphu persuaded the American military that it had to give more aid to the French. Why? It was a part of the miasma of American misunderstanding of revolutions in Asia. On July 21, 1954, at Geneva, the Vietminh revolutionaries won part of what they wanted, control of about half of the old Indochina colony.

By this time the American navy had a feeling that American intervention in Indochina was going to become a reality, and three strike carriers of Task Force 77 were maintained on constant watch in the western Pacific.

The Americans continued to supply the French. The old carrier *Belleau Wood* from World War II was turned over to the French in 1953 and became the *Bois Belleau*. And the French laid a new keel for a 22,000-ton carrier to be called the *Clemenceau*.

At that time the French had a three-carrier force, the *Arromanches*, the *Bois Belleau*, and the *LaFayette*. For the next months they conducted the same old grind, mostly supporting French infantry operations in the Indochina war.

The British also had their carrier wars during this postwar period. On the evening of July 26, 1956, President Gamal Abdel Nasser of Egypt declared his intention of taking over the Suez Canal, much to the annoyance of the British and French, who decided they would not stand for it. The British decided that they would employ force, and particularly their carrier force, to teach Nasser and Egypt a good lesson.

The British light carrier *Bulwark* embarked an air group and sailed for the Mediterranean on August 6. Her sister ship, the *Albion*, was rushed through a refit. Vice Admiral M. L. Power was given command of the Allied carrier force for the forthcoming operation against Egypt. Ports and facilities in Malta and Cyprus were rehabilitated. Plans were made for 45,000 British troops and 34,000 French troops to go into action, many of them by parachute. The British carriers *Theseus* and *Ocean* were brought into the picture, but these two carriers were now helicopter carriers. The U.S. Marine Corps had been studying the feasibility of landing troops on assault missions by helicopter, and the British had adopted the idea.

On October 29 the operation began with an Israeli airdrop into the Sinai Peninsula. The resulting independent Israeli fight against the Egyptians created an excuse for the British and French to intervene in behalf of the Canal Zone. On October 30, the British and French demanded that the Israelis and Egyptians stop military activities around the canal. The Egyptians refused. Bombing of the Canal Zone began on October 31. Five Allied aircraft carriers went after the Egyptian positions: the *Eagle, Albion, Bulwark, Arromanches*, and *LaFayette*. They carried both strike planes and helicopters.

Bombing raids from the carriers continued through the night of October 31 and the morning of November 1. They sank Egyptian motor torpedo boats and other small craft, and they hit the Delta airfields. Antiaircraft fire damaged some of the aircraft.

On November 3 the helicopter carriers *Theseus* and *Ocean* left Malta. The landing began on November 6, and it was not without its moments of excitement. The first Whirlwind helicopter crammed with British troops lifted off and moved into the landing zone, supported by air missions flown by planes from the carriers. The landing zone was covered with smoke. The pilot sought a clear area. He came down in a sports stadium, and the British marines jumped out to find that they were completely surrounded by Egyptian soldiers who had just lately occupied the stadium. Amidst a lot of gunfire, the troops got back in the helicopter and it took off, holed by many bullets and carrying a wounded pilot. They made a safe landing near the western breakwater of Port Said.

Ultimately the Suez campaign came a cropper, largely because of strenuous opposition within the United Nations and from the United States. But what the carriers had proved in this campaign was that carriers still could provide all the close support needed for fast military operations, and that now helicopter carriers added a new dimension to military operations.

———

In the 1950s the United States was building supercarriers. The *Forrestal* was commissioned in October 1955, and others were coming along. New jets, the F7U Cutlass, the F9F Cougar, the 1FJ-2 Fury, all brought technological changes to carrier warfare. Air-to-air missiles replaced machine guns and cannon. The F4D Demon fighter came along, and the F8U Crusade.

On April 14, 1956, the supercarrier *Saratoga* joined the fleet. The United States began flexing the muscles of its carrier fleet, too, in the late 1950s when all sorts of troubles developed in the Middle East.

On July 14, 1957, Arab nationalists seized the government of Iraq, killing the pro-Western king and prime minister. This move frightened the president of Lebanon, and he asked for American troops to come and preserve order. On October 14 Operation Blue Bat began. The carriers *Saratoga, Essex*, and *Wasp* headed toward Lebanon. On July 15 American marines landed outside Beirut, and the local people came flocking up to sell souvenirs and ices. Fighter planes from the *Essex* zoomed overhead. The *Essex* maintained a constant patrol over the beaches for five days. And soon the *Forrestal*, the *Randolph*, and the *Wasp* all appeared off the Lebanese coast. The carriers came and went. The marines stayed on until October 1958 before they were withdrawn.

———

More and more carriers came along, to meet the changing design standards brought by changing aircraft. The new *Enterprise* became the largest ship, with 74,000-ton displacement and a length of 1,123 feet. She was "nuke," powered by eight nuclear reactors. The planes changed and became ever more electronic, ever more complex. The first U.S. Navy fighter to have no guns at all was the F4H Phantom. Instead, it carried six Sparrow radar homing missiles or four Sparrows and four Sidewinder missiles.

Following the Geneva agreement of 1954, there came a hiatus in military activity in the Indochina area, but it did not last long. The Americans made the vital error of stepping in as "military advisors" to the South Vietnam government, an action that drew them inevitably into the war. By the end of the 1950s, the North Vietnam government was back on its road of revolution, bent on unifying the whole area under the Vietnamese banner. In 1964 American intervention became obvious; the *Kitty Hawk* attack carrier was flying reconnaissance missions off the coast, and the Americans were taking casualties. On June 6 ground fire downed Lieutenant Charles E. Klusmann's jet. He parachuted to safety, was captured by the North Vietnamese, and escaped three months later.

The Tonkin Bay incident occurred in August, giving the American President Lyndon Johnson the excuse he wanted to step up the intervention. The attack carrier *Constellation* was ordered to the Vietnam coast to join the *Ticonderoga* in patrolling. It was not long before the brushfire war in Vietnam became the most onerous war the Americans had ever undertaken.

21

Vietnam and Recent Brush Fires

The Americans were drawn into the Vietnam civil war without any real concept of what was happening. The politicians of the United States had become so bemused by the threat of "international communism" that they failed to recognize the legitimacy of the concept that they themselves had invented: the right of any people to self-determination. And so the Americans took over for the French to try to maintain the status quo in Asia, and they tried, and tried, and tried.

For the next 10 years after 1963 the Americans poured billions of dollars, millions of hours of manpower, and thousands of lives into this effort, and they failed miserably. It was not for lack of effort or for lack of the most modern weapons of warfare, including ever-more-complex aircraft carriers. Even before the Gulf of Tonkin confrontation, the American carriers had been engaged off Indochina. Then with the Gulf of Tonkin declaration, following the provocative journey into North Vietnam waters by two American ships, the carriers began full-time effort. The *Constellation* and *Ticonderoga* began hitting targets in Vietnam. The carriers *Ranger* and *Kearsarge* came along very quickly. By February 1965 the carriers *Coral Sea, Ranger*, and *Hancock* were in action, striking targets in North Vietnam and in the battle area of South Vietnam. At this time there were about 24,000 American troops in Vietnam.

The troop strength kept going up, up, and up, and so did the carrier activity, as the carrier-based aircraft continued striking North Vietnam bases. By the spring of 1965, Task Force 77 (U.S. Seventh Fleet) was sending strikes over North Vietnam almost daily. Some planes were lost but not very many in terms of the effort. There was virtually no air opposition, although it was advertised that Communist MiGs were in North Vietnam bases. Once in a while a few MiGs were encountered, as on April 9, 1965, when a half dozen Chinese MiGs challenged the American aircraft. The MiGs came off very much second best; one MiG was crashed that day.

In the confrontations that was how it went; one, two, three planes shot down, sudden disengagement, and then quiet.

Day after day the carriers operated against bridges, roads, and rails. In May 1965, the carriers *Bon Homme Richard* and *Oriskany* entered the war, too. Sometimes there were losses, as at the beginning of June when American carriers lost five planes and 11 crewmen in two days. Of course, these losses were nothing like those of World War II. (For example, in the Battle of the Philippine Sea, the United States lost 150 planes and airmen in one day.) But the Americans were not now used to losses. This was not the sort of war where plane encountered plane, where carrier was pitted against carrier. The Americans now counted their losses and their "kills" in ones and twos, not in 20s and 50s.

The air war escalated, as did the war on the ground. It became ever more complex, with use of air-to-ground missiles and ground-to-air missiles against the carrier planes. Downed pilots were given a feeling of security by the helicopter rescue forces of their carriers. By August 1965 the carriers were in action, hauling ground troops by helicopter as a part of Operation Starlite at Chu Lai, about 50 miles south of Danang.

Soon helicopter carriers were an integral part of the American military system in Southeast Asia.

The carriers began coming and going, the first to come back having been worn down and sent back for rest and replacement. The *Enterprise* came out to take its part in the war.

On December 2, 1965, the "Big E" prepared for air strikes against the Vietcong near Bien Hua. Its planes attacked enemy positions along the entire 450-mile length of Vietnam, dropping 167 tons of bombs and rockets.

On December 16, *Enterprise* planes were attacking enemy gun emplacements. On December 22, planes of the *Enterprise*, the *Kitty Hawk*, and the *Ticonderoga* attacked the Yong Bi power plant, which produced two-thirds of Hanoi's power.

Then a hiatus was declared in the bombing of North Vietnam, with the object of persuading the North Vietnamese to negotiate peace.

On January 8, 1966, the "Big E" sent 116 sorties against Vietcong targets. She operated for a week then with the *Ticonderoga* and the *Hancock* before going back to Subic Bay for a rest.

So it went, in and out of combat. In March the *Enterprise* was back on the Vietnam station.

On that day Lieutenant Greenwood of Fighter Squadron VF-92 was making a low-level run on a bridge in North Vietnam when his jet was hit by antiaircraft fire and burst into flames. He climbed and turned north toward the Gulf of Tonkin. He had hoped to reach water and bail out, but he could not see down through the cloud cover. Finally the condition of the aircraft became such that he had to eject. When he came down through the cloud cover in his parachute, he found himself landing in the water just a few yards off the enemy shore. He saw men with guns getting into sampans and junks to come and get him. But help was already on the way. As soon as Greenwood's plane had been hit, the rescue forces were in action. They came in and found him in the gloom of late afternoon. One rescue plane approached but was driven off by heavy ground fire. Greenwood lighted flares. As he lighted his last flare, a helicopter saw him and came in to pick him up. By this time the nearest enemy boat was only 130 yards away from the downed pilot. Men were firing on Greenwood and on the helicopter. The waist gunner began firing his 50-caliber gun, and the pilot fired his tommy gun. Together they held the Vietcong off long enough to hoist Lieutenant Greenwood into the helicopter for an uneventful ride back to the carrier.

———

Defense Secretary MacNamara proposed to build more supercarriers to prosecute the Vietnam War. The costs escalated and escalated again. A new 15 carrier force was proposed, with four nuclear-powered ships. As noted, just before Christmas 1965, a long pause occurred in the bombing of North Vietnam. It lasted for 137 days. But by April the air war was going stronger than ever, and MiGs were coming up to challenge American planes more and more often. Again, the aerial encounters were numbered in ones and twos. Nothing significant by the old World War II standards. Indeed, in the fall of 1966 the carriers *Oriskany* and *Forrestal* suffered disasters, but both were self-created, not the product of enemy action. Hundreds of men were killed and many planes destroyed by accidental fires.

———

All through the Vietnam War the carriers continued to fight, to strike targets in North Vietnam, and to indicate great successes. But the fact was that the enemy managed to repair the damages, and because of the nature of the war, where territorial control was declared not to be the major issue, there was no real way of measuring success. Indeed, there was no real success for the Americans, not because the carriers were ineffective, but because air power alone cannot win wars. The war settled down to a slogging match that finally ended in the worst moral defeat the United States had ever known.

After Vietnam, American carriers continued to proliferate. As the Soviet Union developed its own air fleet with supercarriers and super-carrier task forces, the Americans were constrained to follow the same approach. And there were other problems. For example, in the spring of 1980, a plan was made to rescue by use of helicopters the American hostages held in the U.S. Embassy in Tehran. The helicopters, to be flown by marine and army specialists, were to take off from an American carrier. Eight helicopters took off from the *Nimitz* and the *Coral Sea*. One of the helicopters developed trouble on the way to the desert, and then another failed, and the total number was reduced to six before they got fairly started on the mission. The six helicopters landed at the base they had chosen, called Desert One, but two of them arrived 85 minutes late for the mission. Several of them had already developed mechanical difficulties. And when they were down to five helicopters, it became impossible to carry out the mission of rescuing the hostages, so the whole mess was aborted. It had been one of the signal failures of American air arms in the history of American air operations.

———

Meanwhile the British had given up the heavy fleet of aircraft carriers as too expensive for their pockets and not in line with their defense requirements. In 1980 they commissioned the first *Invincible*-class CVS carrier. In April 1982, the British got into conflict with the Argentine government over the future of the Falkland Islands. The Argentines, deciding that Britain had become a paper tiger, invaded the Falklands, and the *Invincible* went into action along with the *Hermes*, a similar carrier.

Argentine marines first invaded the Falklands. At that time the *Invincible* was exercising her very short takeoff aircraft off Norway. So the *Invincible* and the *Hermes* were sent to the south Atlantic, loaded with Sea Harrier planes and helicopters.

They would go into action against the Argentine carrier *25 de Mayo*, originally a British post-World War II carrier, sold to Buenos Aires in friendlier times. She was armed with A-4 Skyhawk planes. In May 1982, the *25 de Mayo* launched some of her Skyhawks against the British frigate *Ardent*, and sank her with a single missile. It was the greatest shock of the sea war in the Falklands. Thereafter, however, the Argentine carrier did not distinguish herself, and the British carriers more or less had the air above the area to themselves.

The carriers *Hermes* and *Invincible* distinguished themselves time and again in the actions in the south. The war against Argentina was won, and the Falklands again became a peaceful grazing land for a handful of sheep.

After that, American carrier operations were conducted with greater consideration for security and the possibilities of success. They constantly became more complex, as demands quite out of the ordinary were made on the carriers and their pilots for specific missions.

In the quarrels with Colonel Qaddafi of Libya, carriers operated in the Gulf of Sidra off the Libyan coast, which the colonel declared to be Libyan water. There were several confrontations. Two Libyan planes were destroyed. Much noise was made in the UN and elsewhere. The carriers played a major role in American policy, including the 1986 bombing of Tripoli to underscore warnings to Qaddafi about sponsoring terrorist activity in the Middle East. This bombing was something new in carrier operations, a sensitive pinpoint operation where even Colonel Qaddafi's own house and compound had been identified as targets.

What the Gulf of Sidra operation proved is that the modern aircraft carrier is remarkable in many ways. The flexibility of the carrier is enormous; carriers can be 1,200 feet long or 500 feet long. There is a place for them all in modern warfare. Carrier and manned aircraft are obviously necessary for the sort of limited military operations that have replaced "war" in the last part of the twentieth century. The earth's area is still three-quarters water, and Allies come and go, whereas military requirements live on. As long as there are those requirements, there will always be a place for the aircraft carrier.

As the bibliography indicates, this book was largely derived from my own works on various wars, and the original sources for the material are indicated in the previous works. Where it seems appropriate, I have referred back to the original sources.

Introduction

The material for the Introduction comes largely from Roskill's *The War at Sea* and from studies of German and British records for several books I have written on the U-boats and the battle against them. The material about Japanese developments comes from studies made for my biography of Admiral Yamamoto and from several biographies in Japanese. I also used several volumes of the Japanese official *History of World War II* in this regard, and the files of the U-Boot Archiv Moltenort, in Westerland, Germany, and the Deutsch Marine Bund in Wilhelmshaven.

Chapter 1

The story of the *Athenia* is from Roskill and from my own *The U-Boat Wars*. The tale of the *Ark Royal* is from that ship's history. The material about the *Courageous* and the *Hermes* is from Roskill. The story of the sinking of the *Courageous* is from Roskill and *The U-Boat Wars*, and from the Naval Intelligence reports of the sinking, in the files of the British Public Records office at Kew. I also used Winston Churchill's *The Gathering Storm*.

Chapter 2

The story of the German and British efforts in Norway comes from Churchill and from studies of U-boat and carrier operations in the British Public Records Office. I also used Admiral Doenitz's *Memoirs* and the Office of Public Records British naval archives in Kew.

The story of Force H is from the British naval records and from Roskill. The story of the attack on Taranto is from Roskill and from Lamb's *War in a String Bag*.

Chapter 3

The story of the *Ark Royal* is from the ship's official history, the Naval records at Kew, and from *Ark Royal*, a pamphlet detailing the life of the carrier. I also used materials from the German archives that had been acquired for my book *The U-Boat Wars*, also from my book *HMS Hood*, and from an unpublished manuscript *HMS Repulse*. From these latter sources, I put together the story of the sinking of the *Bismarck*. The sinking of the *Ark Royal* comes largely from the offical inquiry into that affair in the files of the British Public Records Office.

Chapter 4

The chapter on Admiral Yamamoto's Pearl Harbor strike comes from material gathered for my biography of the admiral. I also used Gordon Prange's *At Dawn We Slept*, the best single-volume history of the attack on Pearl Harbor. Admiral Matome Ugaki's secret war diaries were also very helpful.

Chapter 5

Much of the material for this chapter comes from my own research for *The Lonely Ships*, the story of the life and death of the U.S. Asiatic Fleet, published by David McKay Co. I also used materials relative to the submarine forces collected from the Submarine Museum at Pearl Harbor.

Chapter 6

The material about the American carrier task forces comes from U.S. Naval sources I consulted at the Washington Navy Yard. The story of the *Hermes* comes from research materials in the Public Records office of the British government, and particularly the action reports and investigation reports on the sinking of the *Hermes*.

Chapter 7

The material about the U.S. Navy activities and the Doolittle raid comes from conversations with General Doolittle and research for my *Nimitz and His Admirals*. The story of the Japanese side is from the volumes of the Japanese War history. The story of the Japanese misadventures that led to the Battle of the Coral Sea is from my own *Blue Skies and Blood* and from interviews with Admiral Aubrey W. Fitch.

Chapter 8

The material about the Japanese approach to Midway is from my own book on Admiral Yamamoto. The material on the Americans is largely from my own *Nimitz and His Admirals* and from the *War Diary* of the U.S. Pacific Fleet at Pearl Harbor.

Chapter 9

The story of the Battle of the Mediterranean is from Churchill, from Roskill, and from my own submarine researches in Germany and at the Office of Public Records in Kew. The material about the jeep carriers comes from research for *The Men of the Gambier Bay*.

Chapter 10

The material for this chapter comes largely from research done for my books, *Guadalcanal* and *The Glory of the Solomons*. The Japanese side comes from Yamamoto and the Boei Shinshshitsu War history series put out by the Japanese government.

Chapter 11

The growth of the American carrier fleet was depicted in detail in my books, *How They Won the War in the Pacific* and *Nimitz and His Admirals*. The story of the raid on Rabaul is from my *The Glory of the Solomons*.

The descriptions of the operations of the carrier fleet come from my books, *Storm Over the Gilberts, To the Marianas, The Battle of Leyte Gulf*, and *McCampbell's Heroes*.

Chapter 12

Much of this material comes from my *To the Marianas*. The gradual collapse of the Japanese naval air force is detailed in the Japanese war history series. The story of the Battle of the Philippine Sea comes from *McCampbell's Heroes* and *To the Marianas*.

Chapter 13

The story of the Battle of the Philippines is from *McCampbell's Heroes* and the materials used for *The Battle of Leyte Gulf* and *The Death of the Princeton*. The Japanese side is from the Boei series and from Japan's War.

Chapter 14

The story of the Battle of Formosa and the continuation of the Leyte operation is from the various sources cited, *The Battle of Leyte Gulf, McCampbell's Heroes*, the British war records, and the records of the American fleet in the these battles. The Japanese side is from the history of Japanese naval operations in the Philippines.

Chapter 15

This study of the Battle of Surigao Strait and the other naval operations in the Philippines is from research done for several previous books, particularly *MacArthur's Navy, The Battle of Leyte Gulf*, and *McCampbell's Heroes*.

The research materials include interviews with Admiral Kinkaid, Admiral Barbey, David McCampbell, various officers of Halsey staff, and many others. For the Japanese side I used Admiral Ugaki's diary, the Boei history, and interviews with various Japanese participants.

Chapter 16

The story of the Battle of San Bernardino Strait comes from the same basic sources as Chapter 15, plus the research for *The Men of the Gambier Bay*. That escort carrier was the only carrier sunk by surface ship action in the Pacific War.

Chapter 17

This chapter also depended on the materials listed in Chapters 15 and 16 and the oral histories of several admirals and other officers who participated in the battle.

Chapter 18

This chapter about the new American carrier strategy and the effect of the kamikazes comes from sources already mentioned, and a number of books on the kamikazes. Several studies of the kamikazes were made by naval personnel during and after the war. No one ever found a really effective antidote for them except to be lucky and skillful enough to blast them out of the sky before they could strike. The material about the British fleet in the Pacific comes from the files of the Royal Navy in the Public Records Office at Kew. Admiral Ugaki's story comes from his diary.

Chapter 19

The material about the Korean war comes from my three-volume history of the Korean war and from the U.S. Navy's files and their own studies of U.S. Naval Operations in the Korean war. The British material comes from the Public Records Office at Kew.

Chapter 20

The study of the use of carriers in the Vietnam War comes from the U.S. Naval records and from Admiral Hooper's book,

Chapter 21

The story of the last days of Vietnam and various "brush fires" includes the engagements in the Falkland Islands, which the British have dignified with the name of "war," although it was scarcely that and the issue was never really in doubt, except perhaps in the British psyche. My British friends will not appreciate it much, but in terms of the application of aircraft carriers to military problems it was very small stuff indeed. Poolman's *Escort Carrier* was valuable here. But more important were the files of the *New York Times*.

BIBLIOGRAPHY

Agawa, Hiroyuki. *The Reluctant Admiral*. Tokyo: Kodansha, 1980.

Churchill, Winston. *The Second World War*. Vols. 1–6. Boston: Houghton Mifflin, 1948–1953.

Clark, J. J. with Clark Reynolds. *Carrier Admiral*.

Doenitz, Karl. *Memoirs: 10 Years and 20 Days*. Translated by R. H. Stevens and David Woodward. 1959. Reprint. Westport, Conn.: Greenwood, 1976.

Dyer, George Carroll. *The Amphibians Came to Conquer*. Washington, DC: U.S. Navy, 1975.

Forrestel, Emmet P., *Admiral Raymond A. Spruance*. Washington, DC: U.S. Government Printing Office, 1966.

Halliday, Jon. *Korea, the Unknown War*. New York: Pantheon Books, 1988.

Halsey, W. F. *Admiral Halsey's Story*. New York: Da Capo Press, 1976.

Hooper, Edwin Bickford, Dean Allard, et al. *The United States Navy and the Vietnam Conflict*. Washington, DC: Naval History Division, Department of the Navy, U.S. Government Printing Office, 1976.

Hoyt, Edwin P. *The Battle of Leyte Gulf*. New York: David McKay, 1973.

———. *The Bloody Road to Panmunjon*. New York: Stein and Day, 1985.

———. *Blue Skies and Blood*. New York: Paul Eriksson, 1965.

———. *Closing the Circle*. New York: Van Nostrand, Reinhold, 1982.

———. *The Death of the Princeton*. New York: Lancer Books, 1972.

———. *The Glorious Flattops*. Boston: Atlantic, Little, Brown, 1965.

————. *The Glory of the Solomons*. New York: Stein and Day, 1978.

————. *Guadalcanal*. New York: Stein and Day, 1977.

————. *Heroes of the Air*. New York: Doubleday, 1960.

————. *HMS Hood*. London: Arthur Barker, 1978.

————. *How They Won the War in the Pacific*. New York: Weybright and Talley, 1970.

————. *Japan's War*. McGraw-Hill, 1984.

————. *The Kamikazes*. New York: Arbor House, 1983.

————. *The Lonely Ships*. New York: David McKay, 1974.

————. *MacArthur's Navy*. To be published by Crown.

————. *McCampbell's Heroes*. New York: Van Nostrand Reinhold, 1983.

————. *The Men of the Gambier Bay*. Middlebury, Vt.: P.S. Eriksson, 1979.

————. *Nimitz and His Admirals*. New York: Weybright and Talley, 1970.

————. *On to the Yalu*. New York: Stein and Day, 1984.

————. *The Pusan Perimeter*. New York: Stein and Day, 1984.

————. *Storm Over the Gilberts*. New York: Van Nostrand, Reinhold, 1978.

————. *To the Marianas*. New York: Van Nostrand, Reinhold, 1981.

————. *The U-Boat Wars*. New York: Arbor House, 1984.

————. *Yamamoto*. To be published by McGraw-Hill in 1990.

Lamb, Charles. *War in a Stringbag*. London: Cassell and Collier, Macmillan, 1977.

Morison, Samuel Eliot. *History of United States Naval Operations in World War II*. 13 vols. Boston: Little, Brown, 1951–1960.

Poolman, Kenneth. *Escort Carrier*. London: Leo Cooper, 1988.

Prange, Gordon. *At Dawn We Slept*. New York: McGraw-Hill, 1981.

Reynolds, Clark G. *The Fast Carriers: The Forging of an Air Navy*. 1968. Reprint. Melbourne, Fla.: Krieger, 1978.

Roskill, Stephen Wentworth. *The War at Sea 1939–45*. London: H.M. Stationery Office, 1976.

261